Shakespeare-Middleton Collaborations

also by Mark Dominik

William Shakespeare and The Birth of Merlin

Shakespeare-Middleton Collaborations

Mark Dominik

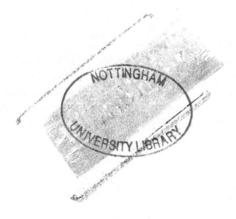

Alioth Press
Beaverton, Oregon

1000334652

Library of Congress Cataloging-in-Publication Data

Dominik, Mark
   Shakespeare-Middleton collaborations / by Mark Dominik.
      p.   cm.
   Bibliography: p.
   Includes index.
   ISBN 0-945088-01-9 : $22.50
      1. Shakespeare, William, 1564-1616—Authorship—Collaboration.
   2. Middleton, Thomas, d. 1627—Authorship—Collaboration.
   3. Shakespeare, William, 1564-1616—Spurious and doubtful works.
   4. Shakespeare, William, 1564-1616. Timon of Athens.   I. Title.
   PR2958.M53D66 1988
   822.3'3—dc19   87-37358
                                                                    CIP

First Printing, 1988

Published by Alioth Press
Box 1554
Beaverton, OR 97075-1554

Designed by Susan Applegate of Publishers Book Works, Inc.

Note

The texts of *A Yorkshire Tragedy* and *The Puritan* quoted in this book and reproduced in full as appendices are from *The Shakespeare Apocrypha*, edited by C. F. Tucker Brooke (London, Oxford University Press, 1908).

All citations of, and quotations from, the works of Shakespeare refer to *The Riverside Shakespeare*, G. Blakemore Evans, textual editor (Boston, Houghton Mifflin, 1974).

Contents

Introduction

THIS BOOK STUDIES the authorship of two of the plays in the Shakespeare Apocrypha, *A Yorkshire Tragedy* and *The Puritan*, and is meant to follow the precedent set by my earlier study in the Apocrypha, *William Shakespeare and The Birth of Merlin*. This book uses the same approach and general methodology to make the same argument—that Shakespeare contributed to the authorship of the plays under consideration. If there appear to be points in this study where underlying methodological questions are left unaddressed, I refer the reader to my study of *The Birth of Merlin*, where such basic concerns are dealt with more fully. But the fundamental argument of that earlier study can be reiterated usefully here: the standard of evidence and of judgment that I apply to the plays in this survey is the standard defined for us by the Shakespeare canon—the standard by which Shakespeare's title to his own works is upheld, the standard that has led to the acceptance of *Pericles*, *The Two Noble Kinsmen*, and *Sir Thomas More* as valid additions (in their various ways) to the thirty-six plays of the First Folio. It is my contention that when this pre-existent standard of evidence and reasoning is applied to the plays under examination, plausible cases can be made for them as partial products of Shakespeare's pen. We can also cite successful attribution studies for other authors as precedents—in the context of the plays in this volume, the identification of Thomas Middleton's hand in *The Puritan* is the obvious example. The same standard of evidence that leads us to recognize that play as Middletonian in authorship leads us to realize that that play is partially Shakespearean as well. As in the case of my study of *Merlin*, I rely most strongly on stylistic evidence for the demonstration of Shakespeare's hand in these plays. I will, however, also argue that the stylistic evidence of Shakespeare's contributions is supported and confirmed by textual and by external evidence—so that, in each case, the totality of the evidence favors the hypothesis of Shakespeare's authorial involvement in both *A Yorkshire Tragedy* and *The Puritan*.

I am sure that the subject of this study will appear suspect, in many people's minds, from the outset; as with *The Birth of Merlin*, I think many people will assume that any Shakespearean contribution to these plays, so long connected with the Shakespeare canon through their inclusion in the Apocrypha, would have been identified long ago. Yet the reader should understand that something like this has indeed occurred; I am far from being the first person to recognize the Shakespearean nature of the fourth scene in *A Yorkshire Tragedy*, and a substantial minority of respected commentators on Shakespeare have held the opinion that this scene is his work. As far as I have been able to determine, no one else has perceived the specific Shakespearean features in the Pye-boord subplot of *The Puritan*, or has realized that these plays could be taken, together with *Timon of Athens*, to reveal a period of sustained Shakespeare-Middleton collaboration in the years 1605-8. For these views, I can only plead for an open-minded and objective evaluation of the evidence. But if this enterprise strikes the reader as inherently eccentric and fantastic, there is little I can say in response—for I believe that there are still other plays, both within and beyond the confines of the Shakespeare Apocrypha, that possess unrecognized

Shakespearean contributions. I would like to suggest a few considerations to the reader, which I believe can help to correct some misconceptions in the consensus view of Shakespeare and his works, and enhance our understanding of the poet in the context of his historical era.

About collaboration: many Elizabethan dramatists, we know, collaborated widely with their contemporaries; others (Jonson, Chapman, and Marston being good examples) tended to eschew collaboration, preferring solo composition. Perhaps the primary factor that determined whether an author collaborated extensively or not (apart from the incalculable degree of each playwright's personal independence) is the frequency with which the author wrote for the popular companies. I do not adhere to, and do not mean to suggest, a rigid distinction between "popular" and "coterie" companies, and I certainly recognize that there were some writers, like Jonson and Middleton, who wrote for both; the qualifications that later scholars have made in Alfred Harbage's original dichotomy between popular and coterie companies are well known, and well taken. It does seem indisputably clear, however, that for the authors who wrote most frequently for the popular companies, collaboration was the standard method. Of the more than fifty plays in the Beaumont-Fletcher canon, only thirteen are solo works by Fletcher, and only one is wholly the work of Beaumont.[1] Of the seventy to eighty plays, masques, and civic entertainments (or more) that Dekker produced during his career, forty to fifty were collaborations.[2] Heywood's claim to have had "a hand, or at least a main finger" in the authorship of some 220 plays is well known and widely quoted—eloquent testimony to a playwrighting career dominated by collaboration.[3] This is only sensible, given what we know about the operation of the popular companies: the evidence of Henslowe's Diary has been used to show that the main popular companies, the Admiral's Men and the Lord Chamberlain's, needed a new play at least once every two weeks, so that the pressure on their regular dramatists to produce must have been intense.[4] We could cite other examples of frequent collaboration among the "popular" dramatists—the case of Rowley, discussed in my study of *Merlin*, fits the pattern very well—but the truth of this general pattern is, I think, beyond dispute.

The one great exception to this tendency, at least in the traditional view, is Shakespeare: though he spent all of his mature playwrighting career as the house dramatist of the most popular of the popular companies, he seems hardly ever to have collaborated with his contemporaries. But this apparent anomaly is less a reflection of the reality of Shakespeare's career than it is a distortion in our understanding of it. If we put aside our preconceptions and look with open eyes, we can see clear evidence that Shakespeare did indeed collaborate with a variety of co-writers. It remains true that Shakespeare was something of a special case: he was a sharer in his company, and thus was insulated from some of the financial pressures endured by less fortunate playwrights—I am certainly not asserting that Shakespeare collaborated as often as Dekker or Heywood or Fletcher. And please don't misunderstand me, reader: I am not suggesting that we should assume *a priori* that Shakespeare would have collaborated, and then charge off into the underbrush of Elizabethan drama in search of the missing works—for this has not been my approach. Neither do I believe that Shakespeare must have collaborated only to supply his own company with plays; his motives may have varied greatly from case to case. (*A Yorkshire Tragedy* was in fact acted by the King's Men, while *The Puritan* was performed by the Children of Paul's, one of the "coterie" companies for which Middleton wrote regularly in the first decade of the 1600s. Such a division does not strike me as in any way surprising.) The point I am making is a basic one—simply that when we find evidence of Shakespeare's hand in non-canonical plays, we can recognize that Shakespeare was less of an anomaly in Elizabethan drama than the consensus view makes him appear to have been.

The plays that reveal evidence of Shakespearean collaboration are sometimes written in modes and styles atypical of Shakespeare's solo works—the domestic tragedy of *A Yorkshire Tragedy*, the city comedy of *The Puritan*—which help to explain how their Shakespearean aspects have escaped general recognition and acceptance. Yet these divergences are more than adequately accounted for by the fact that these plays are collaborations and not solo works. Indeed, the recognition of Shakespeare's hand in such divergent plays reveals him as an even more interesting writer than we've previously been able to perceive him as being—if the reader can conceive of such a thing.

About the First Folio: the thirty-six plays of the original collection of Shakespeare's works have been supplemented in only the most cautious ways by modern scholars and editors. The most thorough modern editions add only *Pericles*, *The Two Noble Kinsmen*, and the portions of *Sir Thomas More* that are accepted as Shakespeare's by scholarly consensus. If this were truly the full extent of Shakespeare's dramatic output, then it would seem that John Heminges and Henry Condell came close to issuing a complete collection of Shakespeare's plays when they published the First Folio. But, how credible is this idea? We need to remember that the concept of collecting the works of a contemporary playwright in a single volume was something very new in 1623; it had been done only once before, when Ben Jonson published (to considerable ridicule) his folio collection of 1616. That edition, though it was produced under the guiding hand of the author, was not a complete collection of Jonson's works to that date; it omitted collaborations, like *Eastward Ho*, and early works like *The Case Is Altered*; it was obviously designed as a volume of "selected works," not "complete works."[5] An even more apposite example is the first Beaumont-Fletcher folio of 1647: both the Shakespeare First Folio and the Beaumont-Fletcher folio were published by other men after the dramatists' deaths. The first Beaumont-Fletcher folio contains thirty-five plays by Fletcher and his various collaborators and by Fletcher alone—along with one apparent misattribution, the play *The Laws of Candy*, which has been judged to be a solo work by John Ford on the basis of the play's internal evidence. This 1647 collection, however, was not complete by any means, so that the second Beaumont-Fletcher folio of 1679 was expanded to contain fifty-three plays, without any more apparent misattributions. The parallel with the Shakespeare folios is worth drawing: both of the plays discussed here were among the seven added to the Third Folio of 1663-4.[6] Of those seven plays, only one, *Pericles*, has been accepted into the Shakespeare canon; the others are dismissed as spurious attributions, with accompanying harsh judgments on the motives and character of Philip Chetwind, the Third Folio's publisher. Yet the example of the two Beaumont-Fletcher collections shows us that there is nothing inherently suspicious in the idea that the first version of such a collection may be incomplete and may require emendation. I do not assert that all the plays attributed to Shakespeare during the seventeenth century are actually his work—there is a minor misattribution problem in the Shakespeare canon, just as there is in the Beaumont-Fletcher canon, but the problem is not as extreme as scholarly opinion supposes.

When we think about the achievement of Heminges and Condell in putting together the First Folio, we have to struggle hard against the anachronistic elements in our viewpoint. It is highly unlikely that Heminges and Condell could have succeeded in, or could even have attempted, the task of producing an edition of the complete dramatic works of their author; to have done so they would have had to think and act like moderns, rather than like the Elizabethans they were. Judging them in the context of their own era, we can give them credit for a remarkable achievement: they came close to publishing all of Shakespeare's mature solo works in one volume; they did a better job for Shakespeare than Humphrey Moseley and Humphrey Robinson did for Fletcher and company in 1647, with less precedent to guide them. It does not detract from their accomplishment for us to realize that there are minor works by Shakespeare that are not, and were not meant to be, included in the First Folio.

About the external evidence: I have come to believe that the Shakespearean title-page attributions in Elizabethan quartos are proportionately as reliable as such attributions generally are for the dramatists of the era—not perfect, but quite sound overall. (Please note that I am speaking specifically of title-page attributions; other forms of external evidence, such as the play lists printed by Edward Archer and others after 1656, are much more problematical.) I think it has to be said that traditional scholarship has done a poor job in dealing with the record of attributions to Shakespeare. When faced with an attribution that demands a certain degree of perspicacity or subtlety to perceive its validity—*The Birth of Merlin* being an excellent example—too many commentators have simply retreated into irrelevant *ad hominem* accusations of dishonesty and greed against the recorders of the evidence. (Is there another area of historical inquiry in which documentary evidence is handled in such a cavalier fashion?) Happily, this tendency is less prevalent now than it was in the last century, but modern scholars have been lamentably slow to correct the excesses of their predecessors (perhaps the scholars of the coming century will do better). I would like to suggest a basic rule or guideline for dealing with external evidence of authorship: all speculations about the personal motivations of the recorders of the evidence fall into the category of conjecture, and conjecture cannot replace, or displace, evidence. Since the evidenciary record is not perfect or flawless, it is of course legitimate to question the accuracy of any individual attribution. The appropriate response to such questioning, however, is not to lapse into fruitless and groundless speculation about people's motivations, but rather to look for other evidence for confirmation or contradiction. In the cases of the plays considered in this study, the internal evidence provides confirmation of the external evidence rather than contradiction.

It is a qualified confirmation, true, in that neither of the plays is wholly the work of Shakespeare. But it is a form of confirmation nonetheless.

There is relatively little reason to think that the stationers of the seventeenth century would have made deliberately false attributions to Shakespeare in order to increase the sales of their books. Here again we have a reflection of our own anachronistic thinking: we overestimate the interest in Shakespeare among his contemporaries and immediate successors, because our own interest in his works is so intense, and thus we exaggerate the possibility of fraudulent attributions. Shakespeare is for us the ultimate in English literature; any work that claims to be Shakespearean but which falls short of our expectations of "greatness" is therefore suspect, and unworthy of being associated with the Immortal Bard. (The recent reception given to the poem "Shall I die?," a work that reveals itself to be clearly Shakespearean on close inspection, shows that these tendencies are still alive and well.) But bardolatry and anachronism are poor foundations from which to further our comprehension and appreciation of Shakespeare's achievement. Cognitively, we all know this, but on an emotional level these retrograde mental habits still exert their influence on our perceptions.

Finally, about imitation: bardolatry and anachronism leave deep taints in our thinking on the question of imitation of Shakespeare by other writers. Let us make a key distinction here: Shakespeare's works certainly had an influence on his contemporaries and successors, as any popular plays would, and this influence is not hard to perceive—the memorable line that is quoted or paraphrased (or parodied), the memorable situation that is reproduced; plays from the era that are known to be the works of other men regularly feature such elements (the obvious debt to *Hamlet* in Middleton's *The Revenger's Tragedy* is one good example; there are many others). But in plays like *Merlin* and the two in this volume, we find a very different phenomenon: plays that show very specific, subtle, detailed, and intricate commonalities with Shakespeare's acknowledged works—the kind of commonalities the acknowledged works share with each other as valid evidence of their common authorship. If these works were produced by imitators of Shakespeare, it is difficult to see how they could have been produced without deliberate effort, conscious mimicry—which is much less likely to have happened than many commentators think.

Some scholars now realize that bardolatry has exaggerated the degree of admiration that Shakespeare's contemporaries felt for his work, and that the idea that Shakespeare was "rated at something like his true value by most persons of taste and judgment" in his own time is one of our anachronistic delusions.[7] We can see now that some of the contemporary allusions to Shakespeare's works that earlier generations naively accepted as expressions of approval (the references in the *Parnassus* plays, for instance) are actually ironic or equivocal in tone. Shakespeare clearly was not universally admired in his own day; the positive notices so often quoted by scholars and critics (Gabriel Harvey's praise of *Hamlet*, for instance) need to be balanced against the less complementary allusions for a truer picture to emerge (in his Notice to the Reader in the 1612 quarto of *The White Devil*, Webster ranked Shakespeare with Dekker and Heywood and well below writers like Chapman and Jonson). Throughout the seventeenth century, the plays of Fletcher and his collaborators were as popular and as highly regarded, in many cases, as Shakespeare's, and some intelligent and perceptive readers (Dryden, for one) judged Fletcher's achievement superior to that of Shakespeare.[8] Recall too some of the derogatory remarks Pepys makes in his diaries about Shakespeare's plays. It is important for us to realize that Shakespeare's coin was far from winning universal acceptance, in his own era, as the gold standard of the literary realm—and once we accept this fact, we can see that attempts to counterfeit his currency would have been much less likely than we often suppose. (If Francis Kirkman, in 1662, had wanted to fix *The Birth of Merlin* with a false attribution to increase his sales, it would have made more sense to assign that play to Beaumont and Fletcher than to Shakespeare and Rowley.)

When, therefore, we find plays like *A Yorkshire Tragedy* and *The Puritan*, which show specific, subtle, detailed, and intricate commonalities with Shakespeare's acknowledged works, it is inherently more sensible to assign the material in question to Shakespeare rather than to some hypothetical imitator. Even if someone in the 1605-8 period had wanted to produce a close imitation of Shakespeare (an unlikely thing in itself), it is hard to understand how such an imitator could replicate nuances from Shakespearean works that were not yet in print, and in some cases not yet written. Consider an elementary fact: we know for certain that Shakespeare was writing in a Shakespearean style in 1605-8; we don't *know* that anyone else was. And isn't the idea of two Shakespearean stylists operating at that time fundamentally less plausible than the idea of one? If we weigh a doubt against a certainty, the verdict should fall on the side of certainty. There are other factors that could be brought into the discussion—the Conclusion to my study of *The Birth of Merlin* deals with the alternatives of influence and imitation in greater detail, but I think that the essential point of my argument is clear.

There is one strategy that I would like to suggest for handling this type of question; it is one that I have been exploiting in this Introduction. In many respects, Shakespeare's canon can be usefully compared with that of Fletcher and his collaborators; the two are similar historical and literary phenomena. If we wish to test any hypothesis about Shakespeare and his work, we could do worse than apply the same idea to the Beaumont-Fletcher canon to see how much sense it makes. I don't propose this as an infallible test—but I do think that it has significant potential for helping to clear away some of the obfuscations of bardolatry and anachronism that still encumber us. During most of the seventeenth century, for instance, unscrupulous publishers would have had as much reason (or more) for making false attributions to Beaumont and Fletcher as to Shakespeare—but by and large such things did not occur; imitators would have been as strongly motivated (or more so) to produce close imitations of the Beaumont-Fletcher plays as they would of Shakespeare's—yet once again the thing did not occur. Surely, this discrepancy in rational expectation can lead us to question the degree to which these hypotheses are valid in the case of Shakespeare when they aren't for Beaumont and Fletcher. (I can feel the urge in many readers to protest that Beaumont and Fletcher simply weren't Shakespeare, and that the comparison is misleading and unsound. But once again this involves the imposition of modern evaluations and modern standards of judgment, or misjudgment, on a previous historical era in an anachronistic manner.)

The Beaumont-Fletcher canon is further useful in that it presents us (as the Middleton canon does) with a range of attribution problems that have been addressed with an impressive measure of success. Cyrus Hoy is justly admired for his study of the textual evidence in that canon—but it is worth remembering that his study largely only confirmed the divisions of authorship among the collaborators involved (Fletcher, Beaumont, Massinger, Field, etc.) deduced by earlier commentators.[9] If we apply to the plays in this volume the same standard of evidence that has been applied successfully to the canon of Fletcher and his collaborators, we are led, I believe, to accept Shakespeare's contributions as literary-historical realities. Should Shakespeare be held to a higher standard of proof than the one we apply to his colleagues? I have to think that the correct answer to that question is: No, he shouldn't be. If we are talking about historical evidence, there can be no justification for a double standard, one for Shakespeare and one for everyone else. If the external evidence assigned these plays to another dramatist, and the internal evidence was as strongly affirmative for that other writer as it is for Shakespeare, then I have to think that that author's presence in these plays would be accepted as a matter of course.

The caveats I made in connection with my study of *The Birth of Merlin* are equally applicable here: I certainly do not claim to have "proven" that the plays considered in this volume are partially Shakespearean; this study, like its predecessor, is meant to be introductory and not definitive—it is designed to begin a discussion, not to end one. My hope is to be able to re-focus attention on these plays in a productive way. I do think it is fair to say that the evidence recorded in this study shows the hypothesis of partial Shakespearean authorship of *The Puritan* and *A Yorkshire Tragedy* to be a reasonable one, worthy of serious consideration. I hope that readers, both academic and general, will be prepared to extend such consideration to its arguments—after all, Reader, you have nothing to lose but a few hours of your time, and potentially something worthwhile to gain.

Timon of Athens

A SHORT REVIEW of the evidence of Middleton's hand in *Timon of Athens* will provide a good introduction to the main business of this study. *Timon*, perhaps Shakespeare's final tragedy, and certainly one of his most problematical plays, has inspired scholars, critics, and commentators to propose various explanations for its "unsatisfactory state," as Samuel Schoenbaum describes it. "It has been suggested that *Timon*, as it has come down to us, is (1) an incomplete version of a play started by Shakespeare and then abandoned; (2) an adaptation by Shakespeare of an earlier work, now lost, by a different playwright; or (3) a revision of a Shakespearean play by some other dramatist. A number of possible collaborators—Heywood, Tourneur, Wilkins, Chapman, and Field—have been proposed, but the most elaborate case has been made for Middleton."[1] That case was stated originally by William Wells and H. Dugdale Sykes in works published in the 1920s; both Wells and Sykes relied on stylistic evidence—parallel passages between *Timon* and Middleton's undoubted works—to illustrate the Middletonian aspects of the Shakespearean play. "Some of the parallels are indeed striking," as Schoenbaum notes in his discussion of the play, but this type of evidence is not regarded very highly by many scholars. And since the works of Wells and Sykes are generally (and, on some points, deservedly) held in low repute,[2] the case for a connection between Middleton and *Timon* has not received wide acceptance. But David Lake, in his survey of authorship problems in the Middleton canon, was able to throw new light on the question by analyzing the play's textual evidence, which gives significant support to the hypothesis of Middleton's presence in the play.[3] On the basis of his textual analysis, Lake tends to favor the view that *Timon* is an early work by Middleton heavily revised by Shakespeare.

In the context of the case for Middleton's presence in the play, the most interesting scene in *Timon* is I,ii, because in this scene it appears as though Shakespeare left Middleton's original version largely untouched, so that the Middletonian features "shine through" quite clearly. Lake singles out Apemantus' speech in I,ii,38-52, which shifts from prose to blank verse to rhymed verse, then back to prose and back to rhymed verse again, as one such feature: such rapid changes of form in a single speech are wholly atypical of Shakespeare, but common in Middleton's early style. Let's quote the relevant passage in full:

> I scorn thy meat, 'twould choke me; for I should ne'er flatter thee. O you gods! what a number of men eats Timon, and he sees 'em not! It grieves me to see so many dip their meat in one man's blood, and all the madness is, he cheers them up too.

> I wonder men dare trust themselves with men.
> Methinks they should invite them without knives;
> Good for their meat, and safer for their lives.

> There's much example for't: the fellow that sits next him, now parts bread with him, pledges the breath of him in a divided draught, is the readiest man to kill him; 't'as been proved. If I were a huge man, I should fear to drink at meals,

> Lest they should spy my windpipe's dangerous notes:
> Great men should drink with harness on their throats.

In addition to the shifts in form in this passage, and the textual features that are more usual for Middleton than Shakespeare ("'em," "'t'as"), we can observe, from a stylistic viewpoint, that this passage simply does not read much like Shakespeare, in contrast to other portions of the play that do show Shakespeare's characteristic traits of style. Consider, for instance, the frequency of word pairs in a short section of the play's first scene (I,i, 52-8):

> You see how all conditions, how all minds,
> As well of glib *and* slipp'ry creatures as
> Of grave *and* austere quality, tender down
> Their services to Lord Timon. His large fortune,
> Upon his good *and* gracious nature hanging,
> Subdues *and* properties to his love *and* tendance
> All sorts of hearts;

This, we know, is how Shakespeare often writes; and it illuminates the larger contrast that exists between the generally non-Shakespearean and Middletonian scene I,ii and the Shakespearean scenes that surround it, scenes that abound in the normal features (the word pairs and triplets, the rich vocabulary, etc.) of Shakespeare's style. (Also, there is the variation in names in the Folio text of *Timon*, the only source for this play: in I,ii "Apemantus" is spelled "Apermantus," and the Steward is identified as "Flavius," features that occur nowhere else in the text. Lake quotes Charlton Hinman's opinion that these differences "inevitably suggest different hands.")

While I,ii of *Timon* gives us the play's most blatant departure from the style of Shakespeare toward the style of Middleton, there are other passages in the play that support the same conclusion; the lines in III,v,40-59, which combine a Middletonian roughness of versification and intermixture of rhyme and blank verse with an absence of specifically Shakespearean characteristics, form one good example. And then there are, scattered through the play, the Middletonian parallels detected by Wells and Sykes; let's cite just a few of them, to get a taste of their argument. For "He's opposite to humanity" (*Timon*, I,i,273), compare "you are so opposite / To love and kindness" in Middleton's *The Phoenix*, I,ii,79-80; for "O, what a precious comfort 'tis" (I,ii,103-4), compare "What a precious joy and comfort's this" in *The Phoenix*, I,vi,81, with another "precious comfort" in *A Trick to Catch the Old One*, II,i,213; for "you are very respectively welcome, sir" (III,i,8), compare "Gentlemen, you are all most respectively welcome" in *Your Five Gallants*, II,i,82-3; for "My wounds ache at you" (III,v,95), compare "my wound aches at thee" in *A Chaste Maid in Cheapside*, V,i,13; there are various others.[4]

Overall, the best, simplest, most obvious explanation for the stylistic and textual profile of *Timon of Athens* is that the surviving text of the play is a combination of the work of Shakespeare and Middleton—perhaps, in the view favored by David Lake, a Shakespearean revision of a Middletonian original; or perhaps something closer to a simultaneous collaboration between the two men. Otherwise, I can't see how the play's Middletonian features can be adequately explained. Commentators who tend to reject the Middletonian hypothesis take refuge in the belief that the extant text of *Timon* is simply an unfinished work by Shakespeare[5]—but this hypothesis of incompletion, which may have some merit in and of itself, is hardly adequate to account for the play's Middletonian elements: a Shakespearean first draft would likely be less polished and less fully realized than a final version; but why would it be like the work of Middleton?[6] Incompletion might explain a certain unevenness of versification—but not overt Middletonian parallels. Unless a better hypothesis can be presented, we are justified in accepting the theory that *Timon of Athens* is some form of Middleton-Shakespeare joint work as the best explanation yet put forward.

A Yorkshire Tragedy

IT CAN BE ARGUED that this theory of *Timon of Athens* as a Shakespeare-Middleton work would be bolstered if we could point to similar works that show mixed Shakespearean and Middletonian characteristics. I believe we can do precisely that. In the same study of the Middleton canon to which we referred above, David Lake surveys the textual evidence in *A Yorkshire Tragedy*.[1] This short play, the only survivor of a quartet of playlets entitled *All's One*,[2] was first published in 1608, and since the Calverley murders on which the play is based took place in 1605, the play must have been written in 1605-8.[3] (*Timon*, too, is usually dated to 1605-8, with 1607 as perhaps the most likely single year.) That 1608 first quarto of the *Tragedy*, printed by Richard Braddock[4] for the bookseller Thomas Pavier,[5] claims on its title page that the *Tragedy* was "Acted by his Maiesties Players at the Globe," and that the play was "Written by W. Shakspeare." This ascription to Shakespeare also appears in the entry for the play in the Register of the Stationers Company (May 2, 1608; "written by Wylliam Shakespere"), where, as Lake points out, a false attribution could have no value as advertising. The assignment of the play to Shakespeare has met with virtually universal rejection—no one thinks that the play as a whole is the work of Shakespeare alone. A number of commentators have detected a Shakespearean contribution to the play's fourth scene—though often on impressionistic grounds that have failed to convince more skeptical readers. But David Lake concludes his discussion of the textual evidence in the *Tragedy* with the noteworthy verdict that "it is more than likely that *A Yorkshire Tragedy* is a play written mainly by Middleton with some help from others, who may include Shakespeare." It is true that in his view, the contribution of Shakespeare is decidedly minor: "Probably Shakespeare's part in the play (if it is not a mirage) is confined to a single insertion of a few lines" in the prose speech in iv,65-98, Lake concludes, noting that "many critics" have seen Shakespeare in this passage.[6] I believe that this conclusion is a step in the right direction—the direction of recognition of Shakespeare's hand in this play—but that it falls far short of the reality of the play's internal evidence. I will argue that the *Tragedy* offers us abundant evidence, both stylistic and textual, of Shakespeare's presence. Since Scene iv has drawn the most frequent recognitions of Shakespeare's hand, let's begin our survey there.

One of the more striking elements in Scene iv of the *Tragedy* is the existence of a version of Shakespeare's "hum" image cluster. A triple "Hum, vm, vm," similar to those in IV,v of *The Birth of Merlin*, is uttered by the Husband at line 17, and around it appear a number of the associations of "hum" usual in Shakespeare: death ("dead," 15, "kild," 18), spirit ("soules," 24 and 41, "spirit," 26), sleep ("quiet sleepes," 34), wealth or value ("bond executed for your debt," 13-14), ears and hearing ("sence ... sillables ... words," 42-3, "the worlds murmurs," 63). These associations are embedded in a scene that deals with the larger themes of bankruptcy and beggary, spiritual damnation, and murder, all of which are compatible with Shakespeare's "hum" cluster. (For a fuller discussion of this subject, see Chapter V of my study of *Merlin*.) There is also, in this scene, a notable frequency of word pairs—"plain and effectuall" (7-8), "pittious and lamentable" (9-10), "default and vnnaturall negligence" (12-13), "repentance and amends" (19-20), "pondorus and suddain" (20-1), "words and pains" (43-4), "Diuines and dying men" (104), "Slauery and mysery" (106). Some of these word pairs resemble phrasings in the Shakespeare canon: for "plain and effectuall," compare "pleasant, pithy and effectual" in *The Taming of the Shrew*, III,i,68, and "mighty, strong, and effectual" in *Titus Andronicus*, V,iii,43; for "pondorus and suddain," compare "ponderous and substantial" in *Measure for Measure*, III,ii,276, and "ponderous and settled" in *The Winter's Tale*, IV,iv,524.

There are various other features suggestive of Shakespeare in this scene: the phrase "good thought" (34) occurs nine times in plural form in the acknowledged Shakespearean works, while "better hopes" (38) occurs twice in singular form; for "quiet sleepes, contented walkes" (34-5), we can note "quiet sleep" in *Richard III*, V,iii,164, and "quiet walks" in *2 Henry VI*, IV,x,17. For "Brus'd with an execution" (49), we might compare "bruis'd with adversity" in *The Comedy of Errors*, II,i,34; for "sufficient answere" (60), compare "sufficient testimony" in *Cymbeline*, I,iv,149. The phrase "fully satisfied" (61) appears in *Henry VIII*, II,iv,149; for "pleasant sins" (65-6), compare "pleasant vices" in *King Lear*, V,iii,171 (a parallel noted by Lake and others). Various other features in this scene—"exceeding welcome," "assure your spirit," "prosperous hower," "desperate mysery," etc.—can be cited as conforming to Shakespearean patterns of usage. It can also be noted that the scene is written in a large and varied vocabulary, and that it concludes with what is for Shakespeare an ultimate horror, a murder between father and son.

The abundance of apparently Shakespearean features in Scene iv—in my view, the clearly Shakespearean writing in the scene—should prompt us to take a fresh look at the other scenes in the play. When we do so, we find some fascinating things.

Scene ii, for instance, begins with a soliloquy by the Wife,

which explains the situation in the family, delineates her character, and prepares the way for the coming action. At one point in
her speech (lines 15-18), the Wife describes her Husband's dis-
turbing mannerisms:

> He sits and sullenly lockes vp his Armes,
> Forgetting heauen looks downward, which makes him
> *Appeare soe dreadfull* that he *frights my heart*,
> Walks *heauyly*, as if his soule were earth . . .

compare *Richard III*, II,iii,38-40:

> Truly, the *hearts* of men are full of *fear*.
> You cannot reason (almost) with a man
> That *looks* not *heavily* and *full of dread*.

The parallel is contextual as well as verbal: both passages serve
to set moods of foreboding in preparation for the tragic actions
to follow—actions that involve the murders of two young
brothers. In *Richard III*, II,iii, the Citizens are worrying about
the consequences of King Edward's death and the ascension of
his young son to the throne; the new king and his brother are
murdered in the Tower in Act IV. In the second scene of the
Tragedy, the Wife is worrying about her Husband's altered state
of mind, which leads directly to the murders of her elder sons in
Scenes iv and v. Interestingly, both sets of brothers are slan-
dered with false charges of bastardy—*Richard III*, III,v,75-9;
Yorkshire Tragedy, ii,69 and after. Also, the line "You cannot
reason (almost) with a man" is strikingly appropriate to the
Wife's inability to deal with her Husband's mania. Finally, we
must note that the comparison is specifically with the First Folio
version of *Richard III*, and not with any of the quarto texts that
were in print when the *Tragedy* was written. *Richard III* had
gone through four editions by the time the *Tragedy* appeared—
Q1 in 1597, Q2 in 1598, Q3 in 1602, and Q4 in 1605—but in all of
these texts there is an alternative reading of the first line in the

relevant passage in II,iii: not "Truly, the hearts of men are full of fear" but "Truely, the soules of men are full of dread." (To be more specific, both Q1 and Q2 misprint "dread" as "bread.") Clearly, the passage in the *Tragedy* relates to the Folio text, not the quarto: not "frights my heart / soules of men are full of dread," but "frights my heart / hearts of men are full of fear." And the Folio text of *Richard III* did not appear until fifteen years after Q1 of *A Yorkshire Tragedy*. The argument that an imitator might have been influenced by *Richard III* is not, therefore, an adequate explanation for this parallel in *A York-shire Tragedy*.

Beyond this one parallel with *Richard III*, we can observe other interesting things about this opening soliloquy. It reveals, for instance, three subtle links to a single scene in *Titus Androni-cus*, III,i. For "that which kils me most" (10), note that Shake-speare uses similar "kills me" phrasings four times in his ac-knowledged works, one of which, "this object kills me," occurs in *Titus*, III,i,64. (The other three are in *Othello*, IV,i,105, *Cym-beline*, II,iv,108, and Sonnet 44,9.) For "recounts his Losses" (11), the closest Shakespearean parallel is "recount your sor-rows" in *Titus*, III,i,29; and for "looks downward" (16), com-pare "Looking all downwards" in *Titus*, III,i,124. *Titus*, III,i gives the same kind of atmosphere of bloody tragedy that is so important in the play we're considering; Shakespeare may well have recalled his earlier play while working on this soliloquy. Conversely, I find it hard to believe that this trio of subtle re-semblances could be the work of an imitator, or that they could be mere chance resemblances or coincidences. Also in the Wife's first speech, compare "consume his credit and his house" (3) with "pawn my credit and my honor" in *3 Henry VI*, III,iii,16; for "Ill beseeming / The auncient honor of his howse and name" (8-9), compare "ill beseeming any common man, / Much more a knight, a captain and a leader" in *1 Henry VI*, IV,i,31-2. The latter is an interesting commonality, in that *1 Henry VI* was not yet in print when the *Tragedy* was written.

The pattern of apparently Shakespearean features in Scene ii that we are beginning to perceive is not confined to the opening soliloquy, but rather extends throughout the scene. There are some striking commonalities of phrasing with the Shakespeare canon: "honest kindnes" (119) occurs in *Othello*, II,iii,328; "for fashion sake" (78) is found in *As You Like It*, III,ii,255; "the true cause" (60) appears in both *Julius Caesar*, I,iii,62 and *2 Henry IV*, II,i,110; "No, monster" (169) occurs in *The Tempest*, III,ii,134. The scene displays a complex relationship with canonical Shakespearean plays of the 1605-8 period: "see my reputation toucht to death" (167) is almost identical to "Seeing his reputation touch'd to death" in *Timon*, III,v,19, both lines occurring in dueling contexts; for "Hard fortunes" (182), compare "Hard fate" in the same scene in *Timon*, III,v,74. For "all societies" (84), the closest Shakespearean parallel is "All feasts, societies, and throngs of men" in *Timon*, IV,iii,21; "do proclaym" (115) appears only once in the collected works, in *Timon*, IV,iii,496—another double link to a single scene in that play. The phrase "for an earnest" (89) occurs in *MacBeth*, I,iii,104; for "sway so much with you" (119), the closest parallel is "sway with them" in *Coriolanus*, II,i,204; for "spit blood" (202), compare "spit forth blood," also in *Coriolanus*, I,iii,42. For "his Losses and false fortunes, / The weaknes of his state soe much deiected" (11-12), compare "The lowest and most dejected thing of fortune" in *Lear*, IV,i,3, while for "his state soe much deiected" compare "dejected state" in *Pericles*, II,ii,46; for "my hart / Would faine" (198-9), compare "the poor heart would fain" in *MacBeth*, V,iii,28, while for "vnable eene to speak" (203) compare "speech unable" in *Lear*, I,i,60.

Word pairs are common in the scene, and some are noteworthy: "plaine and right" (180) appears in *2 Henry IV*, IV,v,222; for "fond and peeuish" (140), compare Shakespearean usages like "hot and peevish," "strange and peevish," "wretched and peevish," etc.; for "landes and Credit" (141), compare "voice and credit," "worth and credit," "reputation and credit," etc., from various Shakespearean works. As for other features: in line 77 the Husband orders his Wife into silence with "Ha done"—compare Petruchio's "Ha' done with words" in *Shrew*, III,ii,116, in a similar dominant-husband context. (Also, "ha' done" occurs twice more in the acknowledged works, in *Henry V* and *Winter's Tale*.) "Ta's galde you" (168) might be compared with "a' has a little gall'd me" in *Shrew*, V,ii,60, again in a relevant marital context. For "spends with shame" (144), compare "spend mine honor with his shame" in *Richard II*, V,iii,68—both usages referring to a son dissipating the reputation and wealth amassed by preceding generations. Less distinctive but still relevant features can also be noted: for "in despight of ills" (22), note that 18 "in despite of . . ." phrasings occur in the collected works; for "vanish from my sight" (26), compare "vanish from our sight" in *Hamlet*, I,ii,220; for "so much vnlike / Him selfe" (37-8), compare "so unlike yourself" in *Shrew*, III,ii,104, and "how . . . unlike himself" in *2 Henry VI*, III,i,8; "vexed spirit" (38) is very close to "vex'd spirits" in *John*, III,i,17. Line 32 begins with "I do intreat you," as does the verse line in *Julius Caesar*, III,ii,60, with similar usages elsewhere in Shakespeare; "He beares himselfe more proudly" (56-7) resembles "I will bear myself proudly" in *Much Ado*, II,iii,225. "Base, slauish, abiect, filthie pouertie" (57-8) conforms to Shakespeare's habit of using such multiple-term phrases: compare canonical usages like "abject, base, and poor," "paltry, servile, abject," "in abject and in slavish parts," etc. "I neuer could abide" (79) compares with "'A could never abide" in *Henry V*, II,iii,33; for "Farewel Instructions, Admonitions" (121-2), note that Shakespeare's characters repeatedly say farewell to abstractions and personifications: "Contempt, farewell," "Farewell sour annoy," "Farewell nobility," etc. "Strike thine owne follies" (138) might be compared with "your follies fight against yourself" in *Richard II*, III,ii,182; for "Ile not indure thee" (158), note that "I'll not endure him" occurs once in the collected works, "I'll not endure it" twice; for "ignoble thought" (165), compare "ignoble mind" in *2 Henry*

VI, II,i,13. The phrase "rips thus my flesh" (201) is interesting: in
his acknowledged works Shakespeare uses the word "rip" exclusively in reference to the human body—"rip their hearts," "rips
my bosom," etc.

A number of other, more minor commonalities could also be
listed—but I think the above examples are adequate to make
the basic point. It's certainly fair to say that for a passage that is
denied Shakespeare by consensus opinion, the second scene in
the *Tragedy* is strikingly Shakespearean in style.

Scene iii continues the same apparently Shakespearean pattern. Perhaps the most arresting passage is this portion from
one of the Husband's speeches in mid-scene (lines 54-60):

> Thou pollitick whore, subtiller then nine Deuils, was this thy
> iourney to Nuncke, to set downe the historie of me, of my
> state and fortunes? Shall I that Dedicated my selfe to pleas-
> ure, be now confind in seruice to crouch and stand like an old
> man ith hams, my hat off?

For "the historie of me" (56), the closest Shakespearean parallel
is "my history" in *Pericles*, V,i,118; but note also usages like
"There is a history in all men's lives" in *2 Henry IV*, III,i,80, and
"his live's history" in *Julius Caesar*, V,v,40. For "state and fortunes" (56-7), compare "state of fortune" in both *Timon*, I,i,150,
and *Richard III*, III,vii,120, plus "fortune's state" in *Hamlet*,
II,ii,511, and "fortune did malign my state" in *Pericles*, V,i,89. "I
that Dedicated my selfe to pleasure" (57-8) compares with "I
dedicate myself to your sweet pleasure" in *Cymbeline*, I,vi,136,
another play of the relevant period (and one that was probably
written in 1609, the year after the *Tragedy* was first printed, so
that no imitator could have been influenced by it); compare also
"to greatness dedicate themselves" in *MacBeth*, IV,iii,75, and the
"dedication of yourselves to ..." phrasing in *Winter's Tale*,
IV,iv,566. For "Shall I ... crouch and stand" (57-9), compare
"Must I stand and crouch" in *Julius Caesar*, IV,iii,45—both passages expressing complaint about an assumption of a subservi-

ent role to a political superior. For "like an old man ith hams" (59), the closest Shakespearean parallel once again appears in a chronologically relevant work: "the French knight that cow'rs i'the hams" in *Pericles*, IV,ii,150.

One other element in this quoted passage demands attention: for "Thou pollitick whore, subtiller then nine Deuils" (54-5), compare "This is a subtile whore, / A closet lock and key of villainous secrets" in *Othello*, IV,ii,21-2. Later in Scene iii occurs the phrase "wretched fortunes" (92), which also occurs in singular form in the same scene in *Othello*, IV,ii,128. The commonalities are striking, since both of these scenes depict irrational men abusing their virtuous wives. The husbands in both scenes unjustly accuse their wives of infidelity. After the husbands exit, the wives justly complain of their "wretched fortune(s)."

Let's take a look at the context of the "wretched fortunes" line in this scene of the *Tragedy*. The Wife makes an extreme comparison of herself with all other wives, followed by a foreboding repetition of "nothing" (91-3):

> I maie Compare
> For wretched fortunes with all the wiues there are.
> Nothing will please him, vntill all be nothing.

In *Richard II*, V,v,1-41, we find a remarkably similarly constructed passage. Richard starts off with "I may compare" (the only use of this specific phrase in the acknowledged works), followed by a string of extreme comparisons, and a similar nihilistic "nothing" repetition: "Nor I, nor any man that but man is, / With nothing shall be pleas'd, till he be eas'd / With being nothing" (39-41). Again, we find a subtle and intricate resemblance unlikely to be the work of any conscious or unconscious imitator.

Other elements in Scene iii support the impression created by these features. The phrase "smal reason" (3) occurs in *Love's Labor's Lost*, I,ii,87. "I grant I had; but alasse" (4) compares with the "I grant I am a woman, but withal" lines in *Julius Caesar*, II,i,292 and 294; note too "I grant I cannot" in *2 Henry IV*, I,ii,167, and "I grant I never" in Sonnet 130,11. For "griefe enough within dores" (6), we might compare "rain within doors" in *2 Henry IV*, IV,v,9, the "rain" being tears of grief; for "withered with debts" (11), compare "debts wither 'em" in *Timon*, IV,iii,531 (another link to that particular scene); for "vsage and vnkindnes" (12), compare "unkind usage" in *1 Henry IV*, V,i,69. The usage "as I smoothd him / With all the skill I had" (16-17) is interesting: Shakespeare's consistent use of "smoothing" in verbal contexts was noted in my study of *Merlin* in connection with I,ii,128 of that play. Also, for "all the skill I had," the closest parallel in Shakespeare is "all the skill I have" in *Lear*, IV,vii,65. For "vglier then an vnshapte Bear" (18), compare "as ugly as a bear" in *Dream*, II,ii,94; note too that Shakespeare makes a similar allusion to the legend that mother bears licked their cubs into bear shape, in *3 Henry VI*, III,ii,161, "Like to . . . an unlick'd bear-whelp." For "his stooping fortunes" (21), compare "stoop with patience to my fortune" in *3 Henry VI*, V,v,6; "vouchsafe me hearing" (46-7) occurs in *1 Henry IV*, IV,iii,31, with "vouchsafe thee the hearing" in *Merry Wives*, II,ii,43.

For "I that neuer could abide" (60), recall the "'a could never abide" in *Henry V*, II,iii,33, quoted in connection with ii,79. In line 66 the word "possest" is used in the sense of "informed," as it is in *Coriolanus*, II,i,132, *Measure*, IV,i,43, and *Merchant*, IV,i,35. For "ile forget my selfe" (72), compare Shakespearean usages like "I shall forget myself," "I should forget myself," "I do forget myself," etc. For "quick, short" (81), compare "short, quick," in *Merry Wives*, IV,v,3; for "Was euer wife so wretchedlie beset" (86), compare "she is dreadfully beset" in *Lucrece*, 444; for "offerd violence" (88), compare "offer him no violence" in *3 Henry VI*, I,i,33. For "scarce be seene" (90) and "scarce see" (101), compare Shakespearean phrasings like "scarce seen," "scarcely see," and "scarcely look." For "my poore children . . . my prettie beggars" (96-7), the closest Shakespearean parallel is "babes and beggars" in *Antony*, V,ii,48, another play of the relevant era, where it occurs in a similar context of a woman's pre-death lament. In connection with the chronological relationship between the *Tragedy* and contemporaneous works in the Shakespeare canon, we can note the use of "Nuncke" for "uncle" in line 55; "nuncle" occurs seventeen times in the collected works, all seventeen instances being in *Lear*. The scene abounds in word pairs; one, "worth and credit" (50-1), occurs in *Measure*, V,i,244; others—"office / And place" (19-20), "good and sure" (20), "looks and modest words" (75)— have parallels in the Shakespeare canon.

We have already discussed the next scene, iv; the later scenes in the play, v-x, tend to show the same Shakespearean profile. Scene v is dominated by violent action, with little stylistic embellishment; of the thirty separate speeches in this scene of fifty-six lines, twenty-five consist of only a single line of dialogue. Yet Shakespeare's contribution remains traceable. In line 2 we find drowsiness described as "heauines"; compare "the heaviness of sleep" in *Lear*, IV,vii,20. And for the larger phrase in lines 1-2, "sorrow makes thy mother sleep: / It boades small good when heauines falls so deepe," compare "So sorrow's heaviness doth heavier grow, / For debt that bankrout sleep doth sorrow owe" in *Dream*, III,ii,84-5. For "thy hopes might haue been better" (3), we can refer back to the "better hopes" in iv,38, and the two instances of "better hope" in the Shakespeare canon noted in connection with it. For "Ruine and desolation" (7), compare "desolation, ruin, and decay" in *Richard III*, IV,iv,409, and "waste and desolation" in *Henry V*, III,iii,18; "out alas" (9) appears six times in the acknowledged works; "surest waie" (13) is found in *Richard II*, III,iii,201. For "charme a womans tongue" (also 13), we can cite various similar usages in Shakespeare— "charm your tongue" and "charm my tongue" in *Othello*, V,ii,183-4, plus "charm her chattering tongue" in *Shrew*, IV,ii,58 and "charm thy riotous tongue" in *2 Henry VI*, IV,i,64, among others.

As part of the complex relationship between the *Tragedy* and *Othello*, we might compare "Ha, whose that cride?" (16) with "ho? who is't that cried?" in *Othello*, V,i,74, in a similarly violent context. When the Husband's servant interrupts the Husband's attack on the Wife, the Husband says, "Comst thou between my fury" (39)—compare "Come not between the dragon and his wrath" in *Lear*, I,i,122. Note too the situational parallel with the servant who interposes himself between Cornwall and Gloucester in *Lear*, III,vii,72-82: both men attempt to prevent their masters from inflicting further injury on their victims, and both suffer bloody consequences for their interventions. For "you haue vndone vs all" (42), we can cite a range of similar Shakespearean usages—"we are all undone," "are we all undone," etc.; and we can note that Shakespeare uses "undone" repeatedly in violent contexts—as in *Othello*, V,i,54. For "My horse stands reddy" (54), compare "Your horse stands ready" in *3 Henry VI*, IV,v,19 (at the start of a verse line, as here); for "my brat at nurse, my sucking beggar" (55), the closest Shakespearean parallel is "brats and beggars" in *Cymbeline*, II,iii,119. For the Husband's direct address to the "Fates" in the scene's closing line (56), compare a similar address in *Julius Caesar*, III,i,98.

Scene vi is very short and perfunctory, only seven lines long; but it does show a continuity of Shakespearean style. For "you looke / Of a distracted colour" (1-2), we might compare "distraction in his aspect" in *Hamlet*, II,ii,555. "Please you walke in, Sir" (4) compares with several Shakespearean usages, most notably "I pray you, sir, walk in" in *Merry Wives*, I,i,281, but also "Will you walk in, my lord" and "Please you walk in, my lords" in *Troilus*, III,ii,60 and 99 and IV,iii,12, among others. For "Ile soone resolue you" (also 4), compare "I will resolve you herein presently" in *Richard III*, IV,ii,26, and "suddenly resolve me" in *Love's Labor's Lost*, II,i,110, among other such Shakespearean phrasings. The phrase "to make vp the som" (5) occurs in *Errors*, I,i,153 (at the end of a verse line, as here), and note also "Make up my sum" in *Hamlet*, V,i,271.

Scene vii is also brief and perfunctory, but it too shows signs of Shakespeare's hand. The word "bloud-hasty" (3) conforms to Shakespeare's habit of forming original and imaginative compound coinages—compare "blood-siz'd," "blood-bolter'd," "blood-bespotted," etc., in the collected works. For "damnation can make weake men strong" (6), compare "ye gods, you make the weak most strong" in *Julius Caesar*, I,iii,91; for "Oh, the most pitteous deed" (7), compare "O, the most pitious cry" in *Winter's Tale*, III,iii,90, plus "Alas, it was a pitious deed" in *3 Henry VI*, I,iv,163, and "The most arch deed of pitious massacre" in *Richard III*, IV,iii,2. The word pair "faint and bloudied" (13) compares with Shakespearean word pairs like "Breathless and faint," "faint and milky," "pale and faint," etc. The use of the word "mangled" for "maimed" or "wounded" (25) has precedents in Shakespeare—including *Othello*, V,i,79. For "thinking to preuent" (26), we can note that the single "thinking to . . ." phrasing in the collected works occurs in a chronologically relevant play—*Cymbeline*, III,iii,102; for "quick mischiefes" (also 26), note that "sudden mischief" appears twice in the acknowledged works. "I . . . rusht vpon him" (26-7) compares with "I rush'd upon him" in *Timon*, V,i,37, in a similar context of violent action, plus "rush upon us" in *1 Henry VI*, I,ii,28, among other comparable usages.

Scene viii continues in the same vein. Its most striking feature, in my opinion, is the Master's speech beginning at line 19:

> Vnnaturall, flintie, more then barbarous:
> The Scithians or the marble hearted fates
> Could not haue acted more remorselesse deeds
> In their relentlesse natures, then these of thine . . .

The first line in this speech exploits a rhythm that Shakespeare favors: compare "Lascivious, wanton, more than well beseems" in *1 Henry VI*, III,i,19, among other possible examples. As for specific parallels, perhaps the closest are "barbarous and unnatural" in *Cymbeline*, IV,iv,6, and "Unnatural, detested, brutish" in *Lear*, I,ii,76, though there are many others in the Shakespeare canon: "Erroneous, mutinous, and unnatural," "deeds inhuman and unnatural," "unnatural deeds," "carnal, bloody and unnatural," etc. For the "Scithians" in the second line, compare "barbarous Scythian" in *Lear*, I,i,116, and "never Scythia half so barbarous" in *Titus*, I,i,131; the "flinty Tartar's bosom" in *All's Well*, IV,iv,7 is also worth noting. For "marble hearted fates," compare "marble-hearted fiend" in *Lear*, I,iv,259, and also "marble heart" in *3 Henry VI*, III,i,38, and "marble-breasted tyrant" in *Twelfth Night*, V,i,124. For "their relentlesse natures," the closest Shakespearean parallels all occur in *Timon*: "our cursed natures," "Whose naked natures," and "Whose thankless natures" in IV,iii,19 and 228 and V,i,60, respectively. For "then these of thine," we can note that Shakespeare tends to indulge in this kind of alliteration; in the acknowledged works, compare "this is thine," "that is thine," "thee and thine," "thou and thine," etc. For the connection of "flintie" and "remorselesse," compare "flinty, rough, remorseless" in *3 Henry VI*, I,iv,142 (in a relevant child-murder context); for the linking of "flintie" and "relentlesse," compare "unrelenting flint" in *Titus*, II,iii,141 (in, again, a relevant context).

Other elements in Scene viii add to the Shakespearean impression. The word pair "ease and pleasure" (4) has various parallels in Shakespeare: "ease and idleness," "ease and gain," "sport and pleasure," "pleasure and affection," etc. "Dispatch that little begger and all's done" (12) might be compared to "A willing man dies sleeping, and all's done" in *Kinsmen*, II,ii,68; note too that Shakespeare repeatedly uses "dispatch" for "kill"—most notably, for our purposes, in *Titus*, IV,ii,86, where it similarly refers to the intended murder of an infant. (Other points of word usage in this scene are interesting and worth commenting upon. The past-tense verb "prisoned," 24, occurs three times in the collected works, in *Cymbeline* and *Venus*; for "blaze" in the sense of "spread news abroad," in "There shall his deeds be blazd," 31, compare "To blaze your marriage" in *Ro-*

meo, III,iii,151, and see also *Julius Caesar*, II,ii,31 and *Venus*, 219.)
"Oh, could I here reach to the infants heart" (17) may compare
with "But that my nails could reach unto thine eyes" in *Dream*,
III,ii,298.

Scene ix continues the Shakespearean pattern. The scene's
opening gives us a double connection with *Othello*. In a conversation between third parties about the Husband's attack on his
household, the Knight says, "I am sorry I ere knew him" (4); in
a similar third party conversation about Othello's striking of
Desdemona, Lodovico says, "I am sorry that I am deceiv'd in
him," in *Othello*, IV,i,282. This may not be a very strong parallel—but it is immediately followed by a more significant one:
for the Knight's assertion that the Husband takes his "life and
naturall being" from an ancient house (5), compare Othello's
statement that he takes his "life and being" from a race of kings,
in *Othello*, I,ii,21. Thus the special relationship between these
two plays continues to manifest itself. Other connections with
the Shakespeare canon can also be observed in Scene ix. For the
Knight's statement that the Husband comes "From such an
honoured stock, and fair dicsent" (6), compare "Come of a gentle kind and noble stock" in *Pericles*, V,i,68, plus "the stock and
honor of my kin" in *Romeo*, I,v,58; and for his further assertion
that this "stock" has been "without staine or blemish" (7), compare "a blemish'd stock" in *Richard III*, III,vii,122. Also, for
"staine or blemish," compare Shakespearean pairings like "spots
and stains" and "blots and stains."

The phrase "repeate it twice" (12) is a redundancy, a feature
typical of Shakespeare; compare "again repeat" in *Lucrece*, 1848.
For "Your fathers sorrows are aliue in me" (15), we might compare "if I die, my honor lives in thee" in *Lucrece*, 1032; for "monstrous cruelty" (16), compare the canonical usages "monstrous
treachery" and "monstrous villainy." "In a worde" (17) appears
four times in the collected works; for "knock my house oth
head" (20), the closest Shakespearean parallel is "knock'd i'th'
head" in *Troilus*, IV,ii,34, though similar usages recur in the

acknowledged works—"knock him about the sconce," "knock you o'er the mazzard," "knock'd out his brains," etc. ("Knocking out his brains" occurs in a key scene in *Othello*, IV,ii,230.) For "a cooler bloud" (21), compare "when the blood was cool" in *Cymbeline*, V,v,77, and "The blood is hot that must be cool'd" in *Richard II*, I,i,51; "Ruinous man" (35) occurs in *Timon*, IV,iii,459 (another key scene with many links to the *Tragedy*). The use of "blot" in line 36 is interesting: though it does not come with the associations found in Shakespeare's "blot" image cluster, it does partake of another pattern in the acknowledged works—for "the blot / Vpon his predecessors honord name" (36-7), compare "The blot and enemy to our general name" in *Titus*, II,iii,183, "blot that name" in *Much Ado*, IV,i,80, and "This blot that they object against your house" in *1 Henry VI*, II,iv,116. Also, while "honord name" may be a commonplace usage, it is interesting to note that Shakespeare's two canonical uses of the phrase both appear in *Tragedy*-era works—*All's Well*, I,iii,156, and *Pericles*, V,iii,96. For the "shame" repetition in the scene's closing line (38), compare similar repetitions in *Richard II*, II,i,112 and 135, and *3 Henry VI*, I,iv,20. (Note the continuing pattern of links to thematically relevant scenes: II,iii of *Titus*, I,iv of *3 Henry VI*.)

Scene x, the final scene in the play, carries on in the same style. "My greatest sorrow, my extreamest bleeding" (8) is a line similarly structured to "My purse, my person, my extremest means" in *Merchant*, I,i,138; also, for "my greatest sorrow," note that the closest Shakespearean parallel occurs in a play of the relevant era—"my greatest grief" in *All's Well*, III,iv,32. "Vnkindnes strikes a deeper wound then steele" (13) expresses the same thought as "The private wound is deepest" in *Two Gentlemen*, V,iv,71; also, among other usages in Shakespeare, we might note the "Unkindness" passage in *Othello*, IV,ii,159-60. For "deuiz'd / A fine way now to kill me" (17-18), compare "Devise strange deaths" in *2 Henry VI*, III,i,59, "I will devise a death as cruel for thee / As thou art tender to't" in *Winter's Tale*,

IV,iv,400-1, and "devise engines for my life" in *Othello*, IV,ii,216-17 (the special relationship with *Othello*, and especially with IV,ii of that play, reveals itself again and again). The word pair "Desperate and suddaine" (17) compares with Shakespearean word pairs like "forlorn and desperate," "fond and desp'rate," and "sudden and extemporal"; for "glides the deuill from me" (19), compare "gliding ghosts" in *Julius Caesar*, I,iii,63, and "his sprite, / In church-way paths to glide" in *Dream*, V,i,382. For "new torments" (21), compare "newer torture" in *Winter's Tale*, III,ii,177; "be assurde" (32) occurs fifteen times in the collected works, plus variants. For "to make a heart-string crack" (37), compare "till heart-strings break" in *Richard III*, IV,iv,365 (both lines referring to grief at the deaths of the sets of young brothers), plus "a crack'd heart," "my heart is ready to crack," "The tackle of my heart is crack'd," and "my old heart is crack'd, it's crack'd," from various Shakespearean works.

The Husband, standing over the bodies of his murdered sons, says, "Oh, were it lawfull that your prettie soules / Might looke from heauen into your fathers eyes" (38-9); in the second scene of *Richard III*, another mourner, standing over the body of another murder victim, makes a similar plea for the attention of the departed spirit—"Be it lawful that I invocate thy ghost," I,ii,8. As with *Othello*, the thematic relationship between the *Tragedy* and *Richard III* keeps attracting our attention. For "see the penitent glasses melt" (40), referring to the Husband's crying eyes, compare "the glasses of thine eyes" in *Richard II*, I,iii,208, and "The glasses of my sight" in *Coriolanus*, III,ii,117, among similar Shakespearean usages; and for the phrasings in lines 37 and 40 taken together, compare "broke mine eye-strings, crack'd them" in *Cymbeline*, I,iii,17. For "mine eyes so bleard" (48), compare "blear'd thine eyne" in *Shrew*, V,i,117, and "blear'd sights" in *Coriolanus*, II,i,205; for the Wife's "forget all other sorrowes" (51) and "former sorrows" (65), compare "forget all former griefs" in *Two Gentlemen*, V,iv,142—so that we see two parallels (refer back to line 13 above) between this final scene in the *Tragedy* and the closing scene in *Two Gentlemen*, a play that would not appear in print until 1623, fifteen years after the 1608 first quarto of our play. "Oh kinde wife, / Be comforted" (66-7) compares with "Be comforted, good madam" in *Lear*, IV,vii,77, and "Be comforted, dear madam" in *Antony*, IV,xv,2; "be comforted" usages also occur in *All's Well*, I,i,89 and *MacBeth*, IV,iii,213, so that all of Shakespeare's canonical uses of the phrase appear in works that date to the general period of the *Tragedy*. For "nomber vp all my friends" (72), compare "in number of our friends" in *Julius Caesar*, III,i,216, and note that "number up" occurs in IV,iii,208 of the same play. For "so kinde a creature" (74), we can observe that once again the closest Shakespearean parallels are in chronologically relevant works—"kindly creatures" in *Antony*, II,v,78, and "kind creatures" in *Cymbeline*, IV,ii,32. For "I shall bring newes weies heauier then the debt" (77), compare "Yonder is heavy news" in *All's Well*, III,ii,33, and "loaden with heavy news" in *1 Henry IV*, I,i,37.

With the end of Scene x we reach the conclusion of the play; but to make our survey of *A Yorkshire Tragedy* complete, we must double back to Scene i, which I have deliberately left to be considered last. This opening scene is discontinuous with the following scenes: it features a crew of servingmen in the house of an unknown family, the "young mistresse" of which was once betrothed to the Husband of scenes ii-x, before he married the Wife; a servant, Sam, returns from London with the news that their mistress' fiancé is now married to another, "beates his wife, and has two or three children by her" (52-3), thus setting up the main action of the extant playlet. With the end of Scene i the servants disappear, and the characters of the Husband-Wife plot take over; there is no other commonality between the two parts of the play. David Lake agrees with Baldwin Maxwell's opinion that Scene i may be a late addition to the *Tragedy*, perhaps by an alien hand; it has a link to one scene in George Wilkins' play *The Miseries of Enforced Marriage* (printed in 1607),

which concerns an earlier portion of Walter Calverley's life—
which has led some commentators to connect Wilkins with the
Tragedy as whole or part author, a theory Lake rejects on the
basis of textual evidence. (The relationship between Wilkins'
Miseries and the *Tragedy* is uncertain; but Wilkins' play may well
have been written in imitation of the successful *Tragedy*.) It is
possible, however, that the first scene of the *Tragedy* is not a late
addition at all; it may be representative of the kind of connect-
ing material that served to unite the four playlets of *All's One*
into a single presentable whole.

However that may be, we can note a few elements in Scene i
that give us some suggestion of Shakespeare's hand. The idea of
a play opening with otherwise unimportant characters would
not be unprecedented in Shakespeare: think of the servants at
the start of *Romeo and Juliet*, or the commoners at the beginning
of *Julius Caesar*; or consider the opening scene of *The Winter's
Tale*, where two supporting cast members set up the action, one
of them, Archidamus, then disappearing from the play like the
servants in the *Tragedy*. These servants tend to resemble their
counterparts in *Romeo*; they make plays on words ("beate" in
lines 54-7) similar to those of their Veronese compatriots (*Romeo*, I,i,1-29).

While there are no truly strong indicators of Shakespeare's
style that I can see, the prose of Scene i does show a fair measure
of consistency with what is usual for Shakespeare. The phrase
"passionate humor" (2) occurs in *Richard III*, I,iv,118; "Mass,
thou saiest true" (11) is in *2 Henry IV*, II,iv,4, "Neither of either"
(15) in *Love's Labor's Lost*, V,ii,459, "Honest fellow" (26) in
Othello, III,iii,5, and "ere he dyes" (40) in *Much Ado*, V,ii,78; "as
familiarly" (70) appears twice in the collected works, "thats well
sed" (42) seven times, "Is't possible" (68) twenty-one times. For
"is neither our young maister yet returned" (12-13), compare "is
my master yet return'd" in *Merchant*, V,i,34; for "my nose itches
... and so doe's mine elbowe" (17-19), compare "my elbow it-
ch'd" in *Much Ado*, III,ii,99; for "I were well serued, were I not"

(25), the closest Shakespearean parallel is "is it not then well serv'd" in *Romeo*, II,iv,81. For "after the truest fashion" (30-1), we might compare "after their fashion" in *Julius Caesar*, I,iii,34. In lines 43-4 Ralph says that his "young mistresse keeps such a puling for hir loue," to which Sam replies, "the more foole she" (45); in *Romeo*, III,v,183, Old Capulet calls Juliet a "puling fool" over her reluctance to marry Paris. "Ile tell you moreouer" (69) compares with "Tell me, moreover" in *Richard II*, I,i,8, and "I hear, moreover" in *2 Henry IV*, I,ii,107; for "speake in your conscience" (78), note that "speak my conscience" occurs twice in the acknowledged works; for "it holds countenance" (87), compare "he holds his countenance" in *1 Henry IV*, II,iv,392. For "Faith, that's excellent" (95), compare "Excellent, i'faith" in *Hamlet*, III,ii,93, "Most excellent, i'faith" in *2 Henry IV*, III,ii,107, and "Why, this is excellent" in *Twelfth Night*, V,i,24. For "all the degrees" (96), compare "all degrees" in *Winter's Tale*, II,i,85. Other phrasings in this scene have their closest Shakespearean parallels in works of the relevant period: for "pawnd his lands" (64), compare "pawn the moi'ty of my estate" in *Cymbeline*, I,iv,108; for "puld downe my breeches" (73-4), compare "put'st down thine own breeches" in *Lear*, I,iv,174.

The stylistic evidence of Shakespeare's hand in the *Tragedy* is verified by some arresting textual evidence. Perhaps the most interesting single such feature is the spelling "ceasd" for "seiz'd" in ii,76. In my study of *The Birth of Merlin* I made mention of Shakespeare's apparent habit of jumbling *c*'s, *s*'s and *z*'s; we find "ceaze" for "seize" in the 1634 quarto text of *The Two Noble Kinsmen*, at I,v,12 (a portion of that play generally conceded to be Shakespearean in authorship), and "cease" for "seize" in the First Folio text of *Antony and Cleopatra*, III,xi,47—Blakemore Evans, in the textual notes to the Riverside edition, calls the latter "a Shakespearean spelling." The presence of the same spelling here in the *Tragedy* should arouse our keenest attentions. We can also note several redundant *s* plurals in the play, another feature typical of Shakespeare: "apples ... makes so many fallings" (i,5-6), "farre fetcht is the best thinges" (i,82-3), and "their heirs may prosper, while mine bleeds" (x,63). These are the strongest orthographic features indicative of Shakespeare's hand in the play; but they are supported by others that also seem to partake of Shakespearean orthographic tendencies: "intreat" (ii,32) and "indure" (ii,158), "howse" (ii,9, iv,90 and x,39) and "hower" (iv,34), "discended" (ii,113) and "discent" (ix,6), and "deuiz'd" (x,17). The pattern of oaths, contractions, and linguistic alternatives in the play gives us a picture of a mixed text, with both Middletonian and Shakespearean elements. Lake, in his study of the play, cites a number of strong textual indicators of Middleton's hand, such as "Ta's" (ii,168), "vppot'h" (ii,48), and "puh" (i,67, ii,79, and iv,114), among a range of other features typical of Middleton, such as "Slidd" (for "'slid," i,16), "sfot" (for "'sfoot," viii,6), "y'aue" (iv,52), "em" (i,10 and 32, ii,104, iv,51, and viii,26) and "Ime" (twice in ii,27, once each in II,121 and 200, iii,53, and ix,9). Some of the textual elements in the play are problematical in that they are common to both Middleton and Shakespeare, and thus are useless as discriminators between the two men; "y'are," for instance, is typical of both playwrights' normal preference, so that the three examples of this contraction in the *Tragedy* (ii,65 and 188, and iv,1) could be signs of either man's hand, as could the instances of "thou'rt," "why," "faith," and "Mass," which Lake lists in Middleton's favor. Also, Lake cites features that are positively unlike Middleton, such as the "Hum, vm, vm" in iv,17 (which anchors the Shakespearean "hum" cluster in that scene) and the uses of "Oh god" in iv,28 and v,28 (a phrase that occurs thirty-seven times in the acknowledged Shakespearean works).

In addition to these textual features, Lake notes some stylistic parallels between the *Tragedy* and Middleton's works: "an vnderputter, a slaue pander" (ii,52-3), "broke custome" (ii,85), "Is the rubbish sold, those wiseakers your lands" (iii,37-8), "A sight able to kill a mothers brest" (vii,23), and "consumd all, plaid awaie long acre" (ix,17-18) all have significant parallels in

Middleton's undoubted works, and are unlike anything in Shakespeare. When we look at the distribution of Middletonian and Shakespearean features in the play, we find a very striking pattern: Middletonian elements are most common in the "evil" part of the play, in the Husband's ravings and threatenings; in the "good" parts of the play—the Wife's part, the parts of the Master and the other third parties, and the sections where the Husband is reflective (iv) or penitent (x)—Shakespearean elements predominate. The pattern is not rigid and absolute, and it would most likely be a mistake to suppose that it represents a deliberate division of the authorship task; the two dramatists may simply have been writing to their individual strengths. Insofar as the Husband's madness is the dominant aspect of the play, it is fair to say that the *Tragedy* is predominantly Middletonian in conception; and I would argue that it is this Middletonian and non-Shakespearean general nature that has been a barrier to the recognition of the true extent of Shakespeare's contribution.

I think that the evidence cited by David Lake of Middleton's contribution is obviously sound, and that the hypothesis of his participation in the authorship of the *Tragedy* is clearly correct. Yet by the same token, the evidence of Shakespeare's hand in the play is at least as strong as the evidence for Middleton. It is interesting to note that while Lake sees Shakespeare only in Scene iv (at most), he identifies other portions of the play—the second half of Scene iii, after line 62; all of Scene v; the second half of Scene x, after line 34—as the work of another collaborator, "who is neither Shakespeare nor Middleton," whom Lake identifies as "X." But as we have seen, these sections of the play are distinguished by Shakespearean features; Occam's razor and the law of parsimony should influence us to assign these scenes to Shakespeare before we postulate another unidentified collaborator.

The stylistic elements I have cited as Shakespearean vary widely in significance, from features that are strongly indicative of Shakespeare's hand ("see my reputation toucht to death"), to features that show simple consistency with Shakespeare's style ("be assurde"). I can imagine that some skeptical readers will wonder if this evidence is strong enough to justify an attribution to Shakespeare. I would remind such readers that it is not we who are to make the attribution—that attribution was made by Shakespeare's contemporaries. The question can logically be re-stated this way: Do we have any solid grounds for a total rejection of the attribution of *A Yorkshire Tragedy* to Shakespeare, an attribution that derives directly from the documentary record of the Jacobean age? As far as I can see, the answer to that question has to be, no, we don't.

This discussion of *A Yorkshire Tragedy* is certainly not meant to be exhaustive; a fuller analysis of the thematic relationships between the *Tragedy* and plays like *Othello* and *Timon* would be useful for placing this play within the thought world and value system of the Shakespeare canon. I hope that these paragraphs will at least be efficacious in re-directing some attention to this play, and in showing that the hypothesis of Shakespeare-Middleton collaboration in *A Yorkshire Tragedy* merits serious consideration.

The Puritan

THE PLAY *The Puritan, or the Widow of Watling Street*, sometimes known as *The Puritan Widow*, was first printed in 1607, and was most likely written in the previous year[1]—among other indications for such a dating, the play itself specifies July 13 as a Sunday (see III,v,290), which was true in 1606. The play, in other words, was contemporaneous with *Timon of Athens* and *A Yorkshire Tragedy*. The original quarto was both printed and sold by George Eld,[2] and claims on its title page that the play was "Written by W. S." Edward Archer, in his play list of 1656, was the first person to record a public identification of this W. S. as Shakespeare. As with *A Yorkshire Tragedy*, this attribution to Shakespeare has met with general rejection. Thanks to a good deal of insightful scholarship over the last century, we can say with a strong measure of certainty that Thomas Middleton is primarily responsible for *The Puritan*, but there is also ample justification (as we shall see) for the belief that *The Puritan* contains a contribution from Shakespeare.

The Middletonian nature of much of the writing in *The Puritan*, and of the general shape of the work, has been commented upon by many critics over the past hundred years and more, including individuals as diverse as Fleay, Bullen, W. D. Dunkel,

C. L. Barber, Mark Eccles, and Baldwin Maxwell; Maxwell gives a good concise summary of previous scholarship in his study of the play.[3] Samuel Schoenbaum, writing in 1966, also noted the strong opinion in favor of Middleton, but added that "the 1607 quarto has never been gone over for spelling, punctuation, and other textual clues to authorship; nor, for that matter, has it been studied for the related evidence of linguistic preferences."[4] These objections have largely been nullified by David Lake's textual analysis of the quarto in his 1975 study of the Middleton canon;[5] Lake concludes that "Middleton's authorship of *The Puritan* is now proved beyond reasonable doubt." I agree with that verdict—with the qualification that "authorship" may not in this case be "sole authorship." It is striking to note that Lake himself, in an earlier study of the play's authorship problem, entertained the idea of a "minor collaborator" on the basis of textual evidence;[6] it will be my contention that the stylistic evidence in the play supports Lake's original belief in the presence of a minor collaborator, and furthermore identifies that collaborator as Shakespeare.

Since the internal evidence of the contributions of both Middleton and Shakespeare is so abundant in this play, I intend to proceed through a scene-by-scene survey of its most salient features. Granting the presence of Middleton, I will not give too much attention to the evidence of his hand—it is the presence of Shakespeare that I wish to establish. But this survey will not come close to exhausting the evidence of Shakespeare's hand in the play, or achieving a complete and final definition of Shakespeare's contribution; I hope only to point out the most telling and most significant Shakespearean elements.

Act I, Scene i

The first scene in *The Puritan* offers an excellent illustration of the Middletonian style of much of the play; it is not too extreme to describe it as quintessential early Middleton. Schoenbaum has characterized Middleton's distinctive early comic prose style this way: "Middleton's best and most characteristic prose . . . is at once natural and stylized. It records faithfully, or with apparent faithfulness, the everyday speech of Jacobean London, and at the same time achieves the virtues of ease and buoyancy. In the realistic comedy of Middleton's contemporaries these qualities are rare. One does not find them in such routine works as *Northward Ho* or *Westward Ho*, and one misses them even in the great plays of Jonson."[7] Inevitably, the perception of "ease and buoyancy" rests on a subjective judgment, and the assertion that these qualities are present in the prose of *The Puritan* can carry little weight as evidence of authorship; but stronger and less subjective bonds between this play and Middleton's early comedies are readily apparent. Many commentators have remarked upon the preoccupation Middleton has with the idea of young men being glad of their fathers' deaths so that they can come into their inheritances—"so many laugh at their fathers' funerals," *A Mad World, My Masters*, I,i,51; "Are your fathers dead, gentlemen, you're so merry?", *Your Five Gallants*, IV,iii,288. The treatment of this controlling idea here in the first scene of *The Puritan* is very similar to that in IV,iv of *Michaelmas Term*, a play written by Middleton most likely in 1605 and printed in 1607, making it very closely contemporaneous with *The Puritan*. In the scene in *Michaelmas Term*, Ephestian Quomodo, the city merchant, had falsified his death and attends his own funeral disguised as a beadle, to observe his family's grief—only to be shocked by the callous reactions of his wife Thomasine and his son Sim. Sim Quomodo responds this way to his disguised father in IV,iv,31-43:[8]

> Prithee, beadle, leave thy lying; I am scarce able to endure thee, i'faith; what honesty didst thou e'er know by my father? Speak! . . . 'tis the scurviest thing i'th' earth to belie the dead so, and he's a beastly son and heir that will stand by and hear his father belied to his face; he will ne'er prosper, I warrant him. Troth, if I be not asham'd to go to church with him, I would I might be hang'd; I hear such filthy tales go on him.

> Oh, if I had known he had been such a lewd fellow in his life, he should ne'er have kept me company . . . But I am glad he's gone . . .

In the opening scene of *The Puritan*, a genuine funeral has just concluded, and Edmond and Mary Plus, the dead man's son and daughter, fulfill the roles of Sim and Thomasine Quomodo, the one displaying the same impertinent gleeful greed, and the other the same lubricity. Edmond Plus—a typical Middletonian foolish young tradesman's son, like Sim Quomodo, like Tim Yellowhammer in *A Chaste Maid in Cheapside*, unfeeling and selfish, redeemed from evil only by his folly—has this to say about his father's death (I,i,42-7, 62-4, 166-70):

> Troth, Mother, I should not weepe, I'me sure; I am past a childe, I hope, to make all my old Schoole fellowes laughe at me; I should bee mockt, so I should. Pray, let one of my Sisters weepe for mee. Ile laughe as much for her another time . . . Weep, quotha? I protest I am glad hee's Churched; for now hee's gone, I shall spend in quiet . . . So, a faire riddance! My fathers layde in dust; his Coffin and he is like a whole-meate-pye, and the wormes will cut him vp shortlie. Farewell, old Dad, farewell. Ile be curb'd in no more.

Both Edmond Plus and Sim Quomodo share the same tone of lighthearted callousness, the same expressions of satisfaction ("I'm glad he's gone"; "I am glad hee's Churched"), the same clipped and oath-filled style of speech; both express a desire to spend on pleasure the wealth their fathers amassed by cheating gentlemen of their lands. We might also compare Tim Yellowhammer's similar callousness toward his sister's (supposed) death in *A Chaste Maid*, IV,ii, to underscore the typically Middletonian nature of the material in the opening scene of *The Puritan*.

This first scene of the play, and the other Plus-family scenes that follow, bring us squarely into the world of Middleton's early city comedies. The satire on the mercenary middle class—with its intellectual and social pretensions, its Puritan hypocrisy, and its barely disguised licentiousness—that we find in *The Puritan* may not be unique to Middleton among the Jacobean dramatists. But there is in Middleton's comedies of the early 1600s a growing tone of amoral glee in the escapades of his characters, a tone that is never quite duplicated in the works of his contemporaries. Various critics have written about the evolving moral perspective in these comedies, and about the ways in which that moral perspective enhances or limits the dramatic effectiveness of the plays. Middleton's earliest venture in this form, *The Phoenix*, is the most morally conventional of his comedies, the most didactic, and the weakest; from there he begins his evolution toward the amoral masterpieces *A Trick to Catch the Old One* (1607) and *A Chaste Maid in Cheapside* (ca. 1613). In intermediate plays like *Michaelmas Term* and *A Mad World, My Masters*, Middleton indulges his amoral characters until the play's end, where he tries to restore a moral order with a sudden reversal; R. B. Parker has written of these plays that "the final judgments always demand from the audience too abrupt a switch from sardonic amusement to stern condemnation. . . . Having enjoyed the wiles of the rogues, it seems pompous, even hypocritical, for us to become suddenly indignant about them; yet without such indignation Middleton's punishments are too harsh and his indictments self-righteous."[9] *The Puritan* fits this description precisely: the reversal in the final scene is precipitous and unsatisfying; it denies the entire thrust of the play up to that point; indeed, it relies on the intrusion of a social authority previously unprecedented in the play. In this curious ending it merely conforms to the pattern of Middleton's work of the period. From first scene to last, the Plus family material in *The Puritan* displays Middleton's handiwork.

Act I, Scene ii

But if the play's first scene is wholly typical of Middleton's writing in 1606, the second scene strikes some surprising dissenting notes. This second scene introduces the play's "rogues," led by George Pye-boord, a disaffected scholar—a character modelled on George Peele, the Elizabethan poet and dramatist who died around 1597. (Some of the plot incidents in *The Puritan* derive from a jest book called *The Merry Conceited Jests of George Peele*, which was entered into the Stationers Register on December 14, 1605, and was in print by 1607.[10] "Peel" and "pieboard" are alternate terms for the tool that bakers use to move their wares into and out of their ovens.), The style of the prose in I,ii is noticeably different from that in I,i: the sentences are longer, and are structured with greater complexity; the pace is slower, the thought is more subtle and involved, and the vocabulary is richer, with a thicker texture of imagery and metaphor.

> Troth, and for mine owne part, I am a poore Gentleman, & a Scholler: I haue beene matriculated in the Vniuersitie, wore out sixe Gownes there, seene some fooles, and some Schollers, some of the Citty, and some of the Countrie, kept order, went bare-headed ouer the Quadrangle, eate my Commons with a good stomacke, and Battled with Discretion; at last, hauing done many slights and trickes to maintaine my witte in vse (as my braine would neuer endure mee to bee idle,) I was expeld the Vniuersitie, onely for stealing a Cheese out of Iesus Colledge ... I say as you say, and for my part wish a Turbulency in the world, for I haue nothing to loose but my wittes, and I thinke they are as mad as they will be: and to strengthen your Argument the more, I say an honest warre is better then a bawdy peace, as touching my profession. The multiplicitie of Schollers, hatcht and nourisht in the idle Calmes of peace, makes 'em like Fishes one deuoure another; and the communitie of Learning has so plaide vpon affections, and thereby almost Religion is come about to Phantasie, and discredited by being too much spoken off—in so many & meane mouths. ...

These passages, lines 35-47 and 60-74 of I,ii, are generally representative of the scene as a whole. Lake, noting the difference from Middleton's usual style, theorises that Middleton may deliberately have adopted a style of speech befitting a scholarly character—though we should note that Peter Skirmish, the uneducated soldier who is Pye-boord's companion in I,ii, tends to speak more like Pye-boord than like the Middletonian characters of I,i. Moreover, there are a number of specific features in this scene that point unambiguously to Shakespeare. One of the most telling of these, in my opinion, is the passage quoted above that culminates in "like Fishes one deuoure another"—telling because it is an example of a striking feature that recurs in Shakespeare's works. Consider *Coriolanus*, I,i,184-8:

> What's the matter,
> That in these several places of the city
> You cry against the noble Senate, who,
> (Under the gods) keep you in awe, which else
> *Would feed on one another*?

Also, compare *Troilus and Cressida*, I,iii,121-4:

> And appetite, an universal wolf
> (So doubly seconded with will and power),
> Must make perforce an universal prey,
> And last *eat up himself*.

And *King Lear*, IV,ii,49-50:

> Humanity must perforce *prey on itself*,
> *Like monsters of the deep*.

And the fragment of *Sir Thomas More* in Shakespeare's autograph, lines 84-7:

> For other ruffians, as their fancies wrought,
> With self-same hand, self reasons, and self right,
> Would *shark* on you, and men like *ravenous fishes*
> *Would feed on one another*.

And *Pericles*, II,i,26-32:

> *Third Fisherman:* ... Master, I marvel how the fishes live in the sea.
> *First Fisherman:* Why, as men do a-land; the great ones eat up the little ones. I can compare our rich misers to nothing so fitly as to a *whale*: 'a plays and tumbles, driving the poor *fry* before him, and at last *devour them all* at a mouthful.

The presence of this type of imagery in the *More* fragment is one strong indication of Shakespeare's authorship—Kenneth Muir has written that "this association of disorder and cannibalism is, as far as we know, peculiar to Shakespeare."[11] This key point can be illustrated by comparing a similar passage in a play by Philip Massinger, a writer who often uses Shakespearean phrasings. In the opening scene of *The Maid of Honor* (1621) appear these lines (I,i,210-13):[12]

> Not Sicily, though now it were more fruitful
> Than when 'twas styled the "granary of great Rome,"
> Can yield our numerous *fry* bread. We must starve,
> Or *eat up one another*.

The similarity is obvious—but so is the difference. Massinger has picked up Shakespeare's wording, but without the metaphorical context: his passage refers to literal starvation and literal cannibalism. With its inclusion of this metaphor, *The Puritan* offers us a priceless opportunity: we can compare this feature with, on the one hand, similar features in the Shakespeare canon, and on the other, with an instance of imitation by an author known to have been influenced by Shakespeare. We can plainly see that the "like Fishes one deuoure another" in *The Puritan* is like Shakespeare's work in a way that the imitation is not.

Coriolanus is one of the plays that shares the disorder-as-cannibalism imagery with *The Puritan*, and we can cite another important connection between the two plays rooted in the same passage. In *The Puritan*, the line about fishes devouring each other occurs in Pye-boord's "Argument" that "an honest warre is better then a bawdy peace"; this same argument is made by the servants at the end of IV,v of *Coriolanus*. Compare, from that play, IV,v,218-32:

> *Second Servingman:* Why then we shall have a stirring world again. This peace is nothing but to rust iron, increase tailors, and breed ballad-makers.
> *First Servingman:* Let me have war, say I, it exceeds peace as far as day does night; it's sprightly, waking, audible, and full of vent. Peace is a very apoplexy, lethargy, mull'd, deaf, sleepy, insensible, a getter of more bastard children than war's a destroyer of men.
> *Second Servingman:* 'Tis so, and as wars, in some sort, may be said to be a ravisher, so it cannot be denied but peace is a great maker of cuckolds.
> *First Servingman:* Ay, and it makes men hate one another.
> *Third Servingman:* Reason: because they then less need one another. The wars for my money!

We find the same sentiments given the same kind of comic expression in the second scene of *The Puritan*: "not to cogge with Peace, Ile not be afraide to say, 'tis a great Breeder, but a barren Nourisher: a great getter of children, which must either be Theeues or Rich-men, Knaues or Beggers" (79-83). It's a noteworthy parallel, especially when we consider that *Coriolanus* is generally dated to ca. 1607, and thus may well have been written after *The Puritan*, so that imitation of Shakespeare by another dramatist would not be an issue.

This scene is Shakespearean in other respects as well. There is a tremendously significant relationship between I,ii of this play and a scene in *King Lear*, a play that was written only a year or so before *The Puritan* and that was not yet in print when *The Puritan* appeared. At the close of I,ii Pye-boord and Skirmish have a short exchange about usurers; Pye-boord describes them as "our ancient Enimies; they keepe our money in their hands, and make vs to bee hangd for robbing of 'em" (154-6). In *Lear* we find the same thought expressed even more succinctly: "The usurer hangs the cozener" in IV,vi,163. But this verbal parallel is only the most obvious sign of a complex interconnection between the two scenes. The same elements occur in both: beggars (*The Puritan*, I,ii,23-4, 83; *King Lear*, IV,vi,68, 155), poverty (*The Puritan*, 84-8, *King Lear*, 29, 221), money (*The Puritan*, 17-18, *King Lear*, 28, 87, 131), and thieves and robbery (*The Puritan*, 82, 147-8, 156; *King Lear*, 152, 154); lechery and bawdry (*The Puritan*, 8-14, 66, 93-4; *King Lear*, 110 ff.); apprehension (*The Puritan*, 146; *King Lear*, 189) and imprisonment (*The Puritan*, 157; *King Lear*, 190); devils and hell (*The Puritan*, 113; *King Lear*, 69-79, 127-9); fools (*The Puritan*, 56, 120, 134; *King Lear*, 183, 191); eyes (*The Puritan*, 129; *King Lear*, 6, 12 ff., 136 ff.) and weeping (*The Puritan*, 126; *King Lear*, 176-80, 196); misuse and corruption of religion (*The Puritan*, 71-3; *King Lear*, 100); plots and strategems (*The Puritan*, 99-100 ff.; *King Lear*, 184); and killing (*The Puritan*, 152; *King Lear*, 187).

Beyond these specifics, it becomes blatantly obvious, when one compares the two scenes in full, that both are dominated by the same concerns with law and justice, crime and punishment, abuse of authority, economic hardship and inequality, and disruptions of the natural order. It is not an exaggeration to claim that in these two scenes we have alternative prose-comic and verse-tragic treatments of the same material, expressive of the same authorial world view and value system.

The structure of the two scenes is also remarkably similar; both depend upon a significant conversation between protagonist and supporting character, followed with an interruption that moves the plot along to the next development. In I,ii of *The Puritan* this pattern occurs in its simplest form: Pye-boord and Skirmish have a conversation of 140 lines that expresses the important themes and issues, and then they are interrupted by the sight of Captain Idle being taken to prison. In IV,vi of *Lear* we get a doubling of this pattern: first Gloucester and Edgar have their strange and momentous conversation, followed by the arrival of Lear; then Lear and Gloucester recapitulate the pattern, until new interruptions move the play on to its next action. (When Skirmish sees Idle being led away in custody, he says, "this sight kils me," *The Puritan*, 143; when Edgar sees Lear, he says, "O thou side-piercing sight," *King Lear*, 85.) I confess that I find this commonality between I,ii of *The Puritan* and IV,vi of *Lear* crucially important, and utterly persuasive of Shakespeare's authorship; I think it matches the most complex interrelations we find among the works of the acknowledged canon. (The links between these two scenes range from the most significant to the most trivial; both scenes, curiously enough, include a mention of cheese—*The Puritan*, 46, *King Lear*, 89.) One could hardly ask for more from this or any other play in terms of internal evidence of Shakespeare's authorship.

Yet there is more. Another of the plays that shares the disor-der-as-cannibalism metaphor with *The Puritan* is *Troilus and Cressida*—and here again we find a more complex relationship. Let's turn back to the Pye-board speech quoted above; for his description of war as "a Turbulency in the world" (61-2), com-pare "bloody turbulence ... shapes and forms of slaughter" in *Troilus*, V,iii,11-12 (this being the only use of "turbulence" in the collected works). For "the idle Calmes of peace" (68), compare "The ... married calm of states" in *Troilus*, I,iii,100, and for "communitie of Learning" (70) compare "communities, / De-grees in schools" in *Troilus*, I,iii,103-4—note the double link between a three-line passage in *The Puritan* and a five-line pas-sage in *Troilus*. And for "Religion is ... discredited" (71-2), com-pare "It would discredit the blest gods" in *Troilus*, IV,v,247. *Troilus* is another Shakespearean play that was not yet in print when *The Puritan* was written and published, thus complicat-ing any hypothesis of imitation; it did not appear in print until 1609 (when it was issued by George Eld, who also printed *The Puritan*).[13] *Troilus* is thought to have been written ca. 1598-1602, though a minority of scholars and critics has argued for a Shake-spearean revision of *Troilus* shortly before publication, based on the Epistle prefixed to the play in the 1609 quarto (second state), and on the similarity of its outlook with that of *Lear* and *Timon*. This hypothesis of revision is not taken very seriously in the present critical climate; but the relationship between *Troilus* and *The Puritan* makes me wonder if this idea of revision might have more merit than is generally allowed.

And still more: I,ii contains a version of Shakespeare's "hum" image cluster, comparable to the one we saw in the fourth scene of *A Yorkshire Tragedy*. Shakespeare tends to associate his uses of "hum" with ideas of illicit sexuality, like adultery or bastardy; here in I,ii Pye-boord refers to "Bawdes" who "stand ready charg'd to giue warning, with hems, hums, & pockey-coffs" (10-12). Death is another typical Shakespearean "hum" association; this scene is full of references to war, soldiering, guns, and hanging, and note Pye-boord's assertion that all his friends are "gone to Graues" (52-3). For associations of wealth or value, we have already noted the scene's thematic preoccupation with ideas of poverty and wealth, beggars, thieves, robbing, usurers, and money; we can also cite usages like "spent aboue a hundred crownes out a purse" (17-18), "Rich-men" (83), "siluer" (148), etc. For the food association, we can cite "eate my Commons with a good stomacke" (41-2), and "feede out of Flint" and "my belly beene much beholding to my braine" (57-9), in a general pattern of references to eating, starving, and surviving (the stolen cheese in line 46, the fishes devouring each other in 69). For the association of plotting, note that the central development in the scene is Pye-boord's plan to take up confidence tricks as a *modus vivendi* for himself and his friends (cf. "shiftes, wiles, and forgeries," 99-100, "deuice well managde," 129-30). For the spirit association, we can perhaps cite the mention of the Devil in line 113; for the association of ears and hearing, we can cite several relevant phrases: "put to silence" (4-5), "giue warning" (11-12), "ouerheard" (135), etc. Clearly, the use of "hum" in I,ii,12 occurs in a typically Shakespearean context.

Also in this scene we can observe a wide range of other commonalities with Shakespeare's acknowledged works—especially with Shakespearean works that employ similar general themes. While Pye-boord is a scholar, his compatriots, Peter Skirmish, Corporal Oath, and Captain Idle, are all discharged soldiers; they become involved in a scheme to cheat a family of hypocritical Puritans, the Plus family introduced in I,i. Shakespeare wrote two plays that can be considered, in some form, to some degree, anti-Puritan plays—*Twelfth Night* and *Measure for Measure*; he also wrote a number of plays that utilize themes or atmospheres of soldiering and soldiers—the Henrician trilogy and *The Merry Wives of Windsor*, *All's Well That Ends Well* and *Othello*, *Much Ado About Nothing* and the early histories, among others. In *The Puritan* we find parallels and commonalities with the whole range of Shakespeare's works—but we find them most frequently with the plays that share these themes of soldiering and anti-Puritanism. A few of these links have been noticed by other commentators—the resemblance between the duels in III,i of *The Puritan* and V,i of *Othello* is a good example;[14] but the entire pattern has not been fully perceived and appreciated. Some of the individual features may seem to be trivial resemblances, but I think they are worth noting as elements in the larger thematic relationships.

In the first line of I,ii, Pye-boord addressed Skirmish as "old lad of War"; the phrase recalls Prince Hal's moniker for Falstaff, "old lad of the castle," in *1 Henry IV*, I,ii,41 (Falstaff's name, of course, having originally been Sir John Oldcastle). Other Falstaffian echoes follow: when Pye-boord describes how he was expelled from the university "onely for stealing a Cheese," he adds that "there was one Welshman (God forgiue him) pursued it hard; and neuer left, till I turnde my staffe toward London" (49-51); the Welshman's proverbial love of cheese is exploited by Falstaff in *Merry Wives*, II,ii,303, and V,v,82 and 138-43. At the end of the scene, Pye-boord and Skirmish plan their con game on the Plusses, which takes the form of stealing a chain and then recovering it by "magic"; compare the similar material in *Merry*

Wives, IV,v,30-8, and note the mention of a "usurer's chain" in *Much Ado*, II,i,189. (It is interesting to observe how often Shakespeare uses this device, of plot developments hinging upon a change of possession of some personal article. The most famous example is of course the handkerchief in *Othello*, but there are also the rings in *Errors*, *All's Well*, *Merchant*, and *Cymbeline*, the chain in *Errors*, and the glove in *Henry V*. I don't find a similar pattern of such devices in Middleton's plays.) When Pye-boord speaks of "Bawdes" who "stand ready charg'd to giue warning, with hems, hums, & pockey-coffs" (10-12), we are reminded of the point in *Othello* where Othello calls Emilia a "bawd" and orders her to fulfill a bawd's function—"shut the door; / Cough, or cry 'hem,' if anybody come" (IV,ii,20, 28-9).

Indeed, the scene abounds with interesting and relevant phrasings. Pye-boord describes Skirmish as having been "as nimble as a fencer" (3), though the rest of his opening speech is couched in gunnery terms; compare "the nimble gunner" in *Henry V*, III,Pr,32. The phrase "put to silence" (4-5) occurs in *Julius Caesar*, I,ii,286; for "I haue beene a souldier any time this forty yeares" (18-19), compare "I have been thy soldier forty years" in *Titus*, I,i,193. The phrase "olde Courtier" (20) occurs in *All's Well*, I,i,156, in a similar context of negative comparison; for "turne both to hob-nayles" (21-2), compare "turn'd to hob-nails" in *2 Henry VI*, IV,x,59. For Pye-boord's "Troth, and for mine owne part, I . . ." (35), compare Slender's "Truly, for mine own part, I . . ." phrasing in *Merry Wives*, III,iv,62-3. In lines 55-7 we find "Sonnes and Heyres, and Fooles, and Gulls, and Ladyes eldest Sonnes," a collection of multiple terms typical of Shakespeare; compare "a gull, a fool, a rogue" in *Henry V*, III,vi,67, and "an ass-head and a coxcomb and a knave, a thin-fac'd knave, a gull" in *Twelfth Night*, V,i,206-7—and note that "my lady's eldest son" occurs in *Much Ado*, II,i,9. (David Lake, in his study of this play, cites the repeated uses of the phrase "son and heir" as evidence of Middleton's authorship, but the same phrase also appears eight times in Shakespeare's acknowledged works, not counting variants.)

For the word pair "hatcht and nourisht" (67-8) compare "hatch'd and born" in *Measure*, II,ii,97; for "not to cogge with Peace" (79-80), we can cite similar usages in the collected works, such as "I cannot cog" in *Merry Wives*, III,iii,48 and 70. (In lines 78-9 of this scene, we find "Greeke" and "cogge" within a line of each other; "cogging Greeks" occurs in *Troilus*, V,vi,11.) For the triplet "shiftes, wiles, and forgeries" (99-100), compare "treason, forgery, and shift" in *Lucrece*, 920; "well managde" (130) occurs in *Errors*, III,ii,19; for "it stands firme" (131), compare "to stand firm" in *Troilus*—the relationship between these two plays continues to manifest itself. The phrase "you haue my voyce" (132) appears in *Timon*, III,v,1, with variants elsewhere in Shakespeare; "I ouerheard 'em seuerally" (135) resembles "severally we hear them" in *Julius Caesar*, III,ii,10. "Nere doubt me" (139) compares with phrases like "doubt not," "without doubt," "no doubt," etc., which occur frequently in the acknowledged Shakespearean works; interestingly, though, the only use of "doubt me" in the collected works falls in *Timon*, I,ii,154, in the strongly Middletonian second scene.

For "teach me to coniure" (140), compare "I'll learn to conjure" in *Troilus*, II,iii,6; for "Ile perfect thee" (141), compare "I'll perfect him" in *Measure*, IV,iii,141. As we have already noted, Skirmish exclaims "O George! this sight kils me" (143) when he sees Idle on his way to prison; when Lucius sees the mutilated Lavinia, he says, "Ay me, this object kills me" in *Titus*, III,i,64. The phrase "sworne brother" (144) occurs six times in singular form in the collected works, and twice in plural; for "lackt siluer" (148), compare "lack'd gold" in *Othello*, II,i,50. In lines 149-50 Skirmish asserts that Idle would not "pawne his Buffe-Ierkin," the symbol of his profession of soldier; compare "pawn their swords" in *2 Henry VI*, V,i,113, and "lay their swords to pawn" in *Merry Wives*, III,i,110. The phrase "peepe out" (152) is interesting: while Caroline Spurgeon may have exaggerated somewhat when she called "peep" Shakespeare's favorite word, it is doubtlessly one that he found evocative; "peep(s) out" occurs five times in the collected works, with variants like "peep forth" and "peep through" also recurring. For "letts follow after to the prison" (157), compare "Go follow them to prison" in *Lear*, V,iii,27—and note that "follow after" is a redundancy, a feature typical of Shakespeare's style. For "know the nature of his offence" (157-8), compare "know the nature of your griefs" in *1 Henry IV*, IV,iii,42; for the oxymoronic "charitable Knaue" (160), compare "charitable murderer" in *Titus*, II,iii,178, and "charitable war" in *King John*, II,i,36.

In contrast to the abundant stylistic evidence of Shakespeare's hand in I,ii, stylistic evidence of a contribution by Middleton is very hard to find; it is logical to suppose that this scene is either primarily or totally the work of Shakespeare. David Lake does cite some textual evidence in I,ii that points toward Middleton, however. Some of this evidence may be misleading; the scene's repeated uses of "'em" for "them" (14, 69, 135, 156) suggest Middleton more than Shakespeare—but Shakespeare may have been trying deliberately for a more colloquial style with the use of this contraction, as he does at certain points in his undoubted works (see, for instance, *The Tempest*, III,ii,121-2). But some other features—Lake cites "licenc'st" (13), "she'as" (128), and "Sh'as" (133) as Middletonian—do seem to point toward the author of the play's opening scene. This gives us a curious dichotomy in I,ii: stylistic evidence pointing toward Shakespeare, but textual evidence favoring Middleton. The contradiction is resolved, however, if we postulate a Middletonian fair copy of Shakespeare's original draft. There is nothing inherently unlikely in such a hypothesis: one of Middleton's solo plays, *A Game at Chess*, exists in an authorial holograph presentation manuscript; and if the *More* fragment in Shakespeare's handwriting is at all representative of his foul papers, a fair copy of I,ii in his collaborator's hand would be perfectly sensible.

Taken together, the first two scenes in *The Puritan* set a pattern for much that follows: the Plus family material is strongly Middletonian in style, the Pye-board material strongly Shakespearean; but the textual evidence of both plots tends to favor Middleton. It would seem that when the two men set out to write the play (as I believe the sum total of the evidence indicates they did), they had two operating assumptions: the first was the division of authorship between the two basic plot segments, Middleton taking the Plus family characters, Shakespeare handling Pye-board and company; the second was that Middleton would prepare a fair copy of the resulting work. Curiously, it seems that both of these working assumptions were modified during the course of the collaboration; in later scenes we find more evidence of cross-writing between the parts and intimate collaboration between the dramatists, and we also find some textual indices of Shakespeare's hand to corroborate the abundant stylistic evidence.

Act I, Scene iii

If I,i is Middletonian in authorship and I,ii Shakespearean, then I,iii illustrates how the two plots blend together through the use of "bridge" characters, the minor characters from both plots who serve to glue the halves together. This scene depicts an encounter between Corporal Oath, one of the other soldier characters from the Pye-board subplot, and the three Puritan fools and Plus-family servants Nicholas St. Antlings, Simon St. Mary Overies, and Frailty. (The parishes of St. Antlings and St. Mary Overies, like the Watling Street of the play's subtitle, were areas of Puritan concentration in Jacobean London.) If the previous two scenes are any indication, we might expect to find a mixture of Shakespearean and Middletonian characteristics in I,iii.

Lake notes two features in this third scene that point to Middleton: the phrase "what an oth was there" (46) appears in *No Wit, No Help Like a Woman's*, V,i,183, with a close variant, "what a word was there," in *More Dissemblers Besides Women*, II,iii, 40; the phrase "wee shall all fall downe in a sowne presently" (41-2) has close parallels in three of Middleton's plays, *More Dissemblers*, *Your Five Gallants*, and *Hengist, King of Kent*. I do not dispute that these parallels are valid indicators of Middleton's contribution, but I believe we can note features that reveal a Shakespearean contribution with equal or greater clarity.

The character of Corporal Oath, described in the opening stage direction of I,iii as "a Vaineglorious fellow," is obviously similar to that of Pistol in *2 Henry IV* and *Henry V*; such broad resemblances in character type could be the result of imitation of Shakespeare by another playwright, rather than Shakespearean authorship, so let us note this commonality merely as a point of consistency—though it is certainly fair to say that the character type is more Shakespearean than Middletonian. But in lines 45-50, as part of a preoccupation in this scene with swearing, Oath and the fools have this bit of business:

> *Oath*: . . . by Vulcans Lether Cod-piece point—
> *Nicholas*: O Simon, what an oth was there.
> *Frailty*: If hee should chance to break it, the poore mans
> Breeches would fall downe about his heeles, for Venus
> allowes him but one point to his hose.

Shakespeare uses the same pun on "points," the laces used to hold up men's hose, twice in his acknowledged works; compare *Twelfth Night*, I,v,22-5:

> *Clown*: . . . I am resolv'd on two points—
> *Maria*: That if one break, the other will hold; or if both
> break, your gaskins fall.

And also *1 Henry IV*, II,iv,214-5:

> *Falstaff*: Their points being broken—
> *Poins*: Down fell their hose.

Note especially that the two plays in which these features appear share with *The Puritan* the themes of anti-Puritanism and soldiering. Similarly, when Corporal Oath exploits the old Elizabethan joke "we three" in line 11 (a picture of two fools captioned "we three," the viewer being the third fool), we can cite another use of the same joke in *Twelfth Night*, II,iii,17.

There are other clues of Shakespeare's presence in the scene. For "next our hearts" (2), compare "next his heart" in *Love's Labor's Lost*, V,ii,715, and "next my heart" in *Henry VIII*, III,ii,157. The phrase "I would you would do so much as forsake vs" (6-7) conforms to a Shakespearean pattern of such double "would" lines; to cite a few of many possible examples, compare:

> I would you would accept of grace and love,
> > *1 Henry IV*, IV,iii,112
>
> I would you were as I would have you be,
> > *Twelfth Night*, III,i,142
>
> I would my valiant master would destroy thee,
> > *The Tempest*, III,ii,46
>
> I would your Highness would depart the field,
> > *3 Henry VI*, II,ii,73
>
> I would your grace would give us but an hour,
> > *Henry VIII*, II,ii,79
>
> I would not tell you what I would, my lord,
> > *All's Well*, II,v,84
>
> And yet I would that you would answer me,
> > *1 Henry VI*, V,iii,87

It is interesting to note that these two features, the "next our hearts" and the "I would you would" phrasing, occur in the speeches of the Puritan fools, not Corporal Oath; it seems clear that the writing was not rigidly divided between the two collaborators in this scene. This, I think, is hardly surprising, since collaboration is by its very nature a cooperative enterprise. We could go on to cite other, less striking elements in the scene that are still consistent with Shakespeare's habits; but perhaps it would be better to concentrate only on the weightier indications of Shakespeare's hand, in order to avoid the appearance of overstating the case for his contribution. I believe it is clear that the signs of Shakespeare in this scene are at least as impressive as the signs of Middleton (I would say they are more impressive); if we accept the evidence of Middleton's authorship in I,iii, we cannot reject the evidence of Shakespeare's, unless we apply a double standard of judgment for which there is no rational justification.

Also in I,iii, there is some comic material on the subject of Corporal Oath's bad breath (27-34). We know that Shakespeare had a rather strong aversion to this particular human frailty. This may seem too vague and general a point to have much value as evidence of authorship; but it fits in well with a strikingly Shakespearean feature at the start of the play's next scene.

Act I, Scene iv

At the opening of the fourth scene in Act I, Pye-boord and Skirmish come to visit Captain Idle in Marshalsea Prison, and the following dialogue takes place (6-10):

> *Captain*: ...Y'are welcome to a smelling Roome here. You newly tooke leaue of the ayre; ist not a strange sauour?
> *Pye.*: As all prisons haue: smells of sundry wretches, Who, tho departed, leaue their sents behind 'em. By Gold, Captaine, I am sincerely sory for thee.

This passage combines two Shakespearean elements in a notable way. Caroline Spurgeon, writing about Shakespeare's strong dislike of offensive smells, especially "the smell of unwashed humanity," observes that "to his imagination sin and evil deeds always smell foully."[15] Elsewhere Spurgeon notes that Shakespeare's displays of sympathy for prisoners are very unusual for an Elizabethan dramatist.[16] In the passage quoted above, we find both of these tendencies combined into a single unified expression; taken with the bad breath of Corporal Oath in the preceding scene, I have to feel that the whole matter smells strongly Shakespearean. And consider the general structure of this scene: a character sympathetic to the audience is shown in his prison cell; to him come friendly visitors who commiserate with his misfortune, including the protagonist of the play, who will gain the prisoner's release through disguise and manipulation. This summary fits both I,iv of *The Puritan* and III,i of *Measure for Measure*, another play about Puritan hypocrisy.

Features of phrasing and word choice in this scene perpetuate the apparently Shakespearean patterns of the two previous scenes. The phrase "vaine breath" (64) occurs in *John*, III,i,8, "most tyrannically" (73) in *Hamlet*, II,ii,341, "breath onlie" (135) in *Coriolanus*, II,ii,150, "not regarded" (285) in both *2 Henry VI*, III,i,18, and *1 Henry IV*, III,ii,76. In lines 65-9 there is a passage worth noting: "Ile sooner expect mercy from a Vsurer when my bonds forfetted, sooner kindnesse from a Lawier when my mony's spent: nay, sooner charity from the deuill, then good from a Puritaine!" Compare "I will rather trust a Fleming with my butter, Parson Hugh the Welshman with my cheese, an Irishman with my aqua-vitae bottle, or a thief to walk my ambling gelding, than my wife with herself" in *Merry Wives*, II,ii,302-5, which gives us a similar progression of "sooner/ rather ... than" unlikelihoods; we can also cite comparable "sooner than" and "sooner but" progressions in *As You Like It*, V,ii,33-7, and *1 Henry IV*, II,i,77-9. For "hee lookes like a Monkey vpward, and a Crane downe-ward" (74-6), compare "as a German from the waist downward, all slops, and a Spaniard from the hip upward, no doublet" in *Much Ado*, III,ii,35-7.

For "desprate, vnsetled" (31), we might compare "unheedful, desperate" in *1 Henry VI*, IV,iv,7; for "publish't him" (82), compare "publish'd me" in *Winter's Tale*, II,i,98; for "my disgrace will dwell in his Iawes" (105-6), compare "notable scorns / That dwell in every region of his face" in *Othello*, IV,i,82-3. For "I would bee heartily glad" (109), compare "I am heartily glad" in *As You Like It*, I,i,159, and "As heartily as he is glad" in *John*, III,iv,124; for "nothing dangerous" (129-30), compare "something dangerous" in *Hamlet*, V,i,262; for "thou holdst my life at no price" (132), compare "If you hold your life at any price" in *Twelfth Night*, III,iv,230. For "broken & vnioynted offers" (133), compare "bald unjointed chat" in *1 Henry IV*, I,iii,65—both phrases referring to speech that is deficient in serious meaning. For "now borne, and now buried" (134), we might compare "born at sea, buried at Tharsus" in *Pericles*, V,i,196; for "helpe him in extremities" (146), compare "save your life in this extremity" in *Shrew*, IV,ii,103; for "too vnkinde a Kinsman" (156-7), note the similar "too unkind a . . ." phrasing in *Merchant*, V,i,175.

In lines 162-7 there is a play on words centering on the alternative uses of "steale," "rob," and "nim"—Nicholas St. Antlings will not "steale" Sir Godfrey Plus' chain, though he will "rob" or "nim" it. The same type of word play is found in *Merry Wives*, IV,v,36-8: "the very same men that beguil'd Master Slender of his chain cozen'd him of it." I think it is easy to see why there are so many points of commonality between *The Puritan* and *Merry Wives*; both plays concern ex-soldier con men and their victims—and both plays depend upon a very rich verbal texture for their comic effects. Pye-boord is only slightly inferior to Falstaff as a master manipulator of words; Corporal Oath's resemblance to Pistol has already been noted; and the verbal habits of other characters in *Merry Wives* are reflected in *The Puritan* as well. Three times in this scene (169, 229, 267) Pye-boord and Oath address or describe other characters as "bullie"; this appellation occurs twenty times in the canon of Shakespeare's acknowledged works, either simply or in hyphenated compound combinations ("bully-knight," "bully-doctor," etc.), and sixteen of these twenty usages fall in *Merry Wives*, in the mouth of the Host of the Garter Inn.

For "you shall not haue all your owne asking" (174), we find similar "your asking" usages in *Coriolanus*, I,vi,64-5, and *Henry VIII*, II,iii,52, and elsewhere in Shakespeare as well. The phrase "notable gullery" (182) resembles a group of Shakespearean usages—"notable contempt," "notable shame," "notable scorns," etc. For "three times thrice hunnie Couzen" (231-2), compare Shakespearean endearments like "honey monarch," "honey lord," and "honey Greek"—and note that "three times thrice" occurs in *Love's Labor's Lost*, V,ii,488 and 491, and in *2 Henry VI*, III,ii,358, with "thrice three times" in *Merchant*, I,iii,159. For "egregious Asse" (249), compare "egregious dog" in *Henry V*, II,i,46 (Oath and Pistol respectively); "my directions" (255) occurs in *Winter's Tale*, IV,iv,523, in singular form; "prompt me" (258) appears three times in the collected works. The phrase "knit strong" (265) echoes "strongly knit" in Sonnet 26,2; for "maintaine a quarrell" (272), compare "maintain such a quarrel" in *Titus*, II,i,47.

In addition, we can note a strong degree of consistency with Shakespeare's style, illustrated with less dramatic but still relevant features. In lines 19-20, for instance, Pye-boord has a short and rather nondescript speech: "Nay, prophecy not so ill; it shall go heard, / But Ile shift for thy life." We find several comparable usages in the acknowledged works: "It shall go hard but I'll . . ." in *Two Gentlemen*, I,i,85; "it shall go hard but I will . . ." in *Merchant*, III,i,72; "and't shall go hard but I'll . . ." in *2 Henry IV*, III,ii,329; and "an't shall go hard / But I will . . ." in *Hamlet*, III,iv,207-8, among other "go hard" usages. Also, for "shift for thy life" (20), we might compare "live by shifts" and "shift and save yourself" in *Errors*, III,ii,182, and V,i,168; for "prophecy not so ill" (19), we can observe that the closest Shakespearean parallel is "not prophesy so" in *Antony*, II,vi,117, a play of the relevant era. For "I protest at this instant" (290-1), we can note that "I protest" occurs thirty-three times in the acknowledged works, not counting variants, while "at this instant" occurs six times (twice in *Lear*), again not counting variants. If we paused to take note of all such elements, however, this study would be distended to an unmanageable (and unreadable) length; I can only ask the reader to remember that this survey only touches upon the most obvious and most significant Shakespearean features in the play, while passing over many other points consistent with Shakespeare's style, and relevant to the hypothesis of a Shakespearean contribution.

Inevitably, this study must be partial in another sense as well. It would be ideal if we could ascertain the degree of frequency with which similar features do or do not appear in the works of the Middleton canon, to achieve a more balanced perspective. In line 183 of I,iv, for example, the phrase "Ile come neerer to you" resembles several Shakespearean usages, such as "come a little nearer" in *Merry Wives*, II,ii,45 and 49, and "come something nearer" in *Winter's Tale*, II,ii,53; but the strongest parallel is with "I might come nearer to you" in *Timon*, I,ii,101, in the Middletonian second scene. A Middleton concordance would allow us to locate similar features in his undoubted plays; lacking such a resource, our study risks a Shakespearean bias that must always be kept in mind. Yet even as we remain mindful of such a bias, we can attain a basic level of confidence that our survey is leading us in the right direction. David Lake, in his discussion of I,iv, cites several features that are suggestive of Middleton—but he also notes other features that are positively unlike Middleton's normal usage. Lake cites the phrase "grace of God" (233), with its use of the "undisguised divine name," as being atypical of Middleton; but such uses of "God" are very common in Shakespeare, and this specific phrase, "grace of God," occurs five times in the collected works.

Act II, Scene i

With the beginning of the first scene in Act II, the Plus family characters return for the first time since I,i; and with them returns the style of the first scene, the style of early Middleton. Consider II,i,47-57:

> Nay, Sister, let Reason rule you, doe not play the foole; stand not in your owne light. You haue wealthy offers, larger tendrings; doe not with-stand your good fortune: who comes a wooing to you, I pray? no small foole; a rich Knight ath Citty, Sir Oliuer Muck-hill—no small foole I can tell you: and furthermore, as I heard late by your Maide-seruants, (as your Maide-seruants will say to mee any thing, I thanke 'em) both your Daughters are not without Suters, I, and worthy ones too!

At mid-scene (144) Pye-boord enters, and the prose shifts to the more complex, eloquent, thicker-textured style of I,ii. Consider lines 183-95:

> Well, Lady, in cold bloud I speake it; I assure you that there is a Purgatory, in which place I know your husband to recide, and wherein he is like to remaine, till the dissolution of the world, till the last generall Bon-fire, when all the earth shall melt into nothing and the Seas scalde their finnie labourers: so long is his abidance, vnlesse you alter the propertie of your purpose, together with each of your Daughters theirs; that is, the purpose of single life in your selfe and your eldest Daughter, and the speedie determination of marriage in your youngest.

And with the return to the style of I,ii we have a return of the pattern of apparently Shakespearean stylistic features, phrasings, and word choices. For "Ide not be troubled with you" (147), compare "I will not long be troubled with you" in *As You*

Like It, I,i,77; for "better welcome" (150), we can cite a group of similar usages in Shakespeare—"worser welcome," "good welcome, " "great welcome," etc. "Good bluntnesse" (153) might be compared with "Having been prais'd for bluntness" in *Lear*, II,ii,96 (the only use of "bluntness" in the collected works); the word pair "weight and feare" (170) fits with a Shakespearean pattern of word pairing—compare, for instance, "weight and worthiness" in *Henry V*, II,ii,35. In line 172 we find the phrase "vnregarded, and vneffected," while later in the scene (233-4) we come upon "vngarterd, vnbuttend ... vntrust"; such multiple uses of "un" prefix words are very much typical of Shakespeare —compare "undressed, unpolished, uneducated, unpruned, untrained, or rather unlettered, or ratherest unconfirmed" in *Love's Labor's Lost*, IV,ii,16-18, and "uneven and unwelcome" in *1 Henry IV*, I,i,50, and "untainted, unexamin'd" in *Richard III*, III,vi,9, among various other possible examples.

The phrase "sober toung" (181) can be compared to several similar Shakespearean usages, most notably the "sober eye" in *Antony*, V,ii,54; "cold bloud" (183) occurs five times in the acknowledged works, plus variants. For "the dissolution of the world" (187), compare "the world were all dissolv'd" in *Richard II*, III,ii,108; for "the last generall Bon-fire" (also 187), compare "everlasting bonfire" in *1 Henry IV*, III,iii,41, and *MacBeth*, II,iii,19. This speech of Pye-boord's about the end of the world puts us in mind of Prospero's famous "Our revels now are ended" speech in *The Tempest*; for Pye-boord's "melt into nothing" (188-9), compare Prospero's similar "melted into air" in IV,i,150 of his play. For Pye-boord's description of fish as "finnie labourers" (189-90), compare "finny subjects of the sea" in *Pericles*, II,i,48, a phrase that appears in conjunction with the disorder-as-cannibalism imagery in that scene. (In addition to this "finnie labourers" usage, we can note that in line 220 of II,i Pye-boord claims that the late Master Plus "would eate fooles and ignorant heires cleane vp." Thus we can see that the peculiar Shakespearean imagery of I,ii, the "Fishes one deuoure another," has echoes in a later scene of the play, and is not an isolated feature that can be dismissed as borrowing or chance resemblance.)

For "speedie determination" (194-5), compare "quick determination" in *Hamlet*, III,i,168; for "I know your determinations" (203-4), compare "They have acquainted me with their determinations" in *Merchant*, I,ii,102 (the only use of the plural form, "determinations," in the collected works). "This puts Amazement on me" (207) resembles "Put not yourself into amazement" in *Measure*, IV,ii,204; "to steale a marriage" (209) recalls "to steal our marriage" in *Shrew*, III,ii,140. For "would his tongue / Had dropt out when he blabt it" (209-10), compare Marcus Andronicus' description of Lavinia's severed tongue as "the delightful engine of her thoughts, / That blabb'd them with such pleasing eloquence" in *Titus*, III,i,82-3—both passages associate the word "blabb'd" with the idea of the tongue being separated from the mouth. For "Tis but meere folly now to guild him ore, / That has past but for Copper" (214-15), note that "mere folly" occurs in both *Antony*, III,xiii,43, and *As You Like It*, II,vii,181, and note too that Shakespeare has two references to gilded copper passing as gold in his acknowledged works, in *Troilus*, IV,iv,105, and *1 Henry IV*, III,iii,83-4 and 142-4.

For "he would scrape ritches to him" (223), compare "As thriftless sons their scraping fathers' gold" in *Richard II*, V,iii,69, which gives us a similar use of "scrape" for greedy accumulation—and note the sameness of context: Pye-boord is speaking of the late Master Plus, whose son Edmond is precisely the kind of thriftless son ready to spend his father's hoarded wealth that Shakespeare is describing in the line from *Richard II*. The phrase "most vniustly" (also 223) appears in *Othello*, IV,ii,184. In lines 244-6 Pye-boord asserts that "a Sermon's a fine short cloake of an houre long, and wil hide the vpper-part of a dissembler"; in *Twelfth Night*, IV,ii,1-6, Maria has Feste dress in a gown to masquerade as a curate, and Feste says, "Well,

I'll put it on, and I will dissemble myself in't, and I would I were the first that ever dissembled in such a gown"—giving us the same idea of religious garments hiding hypocrisy, and the same anti-Puritan mood, as the cited passage in *The Puritan*. The phrase "no more endure" (249) appears in *The Tempest*, III,i,61, while similar usages like "no longer endure" occur frequently in the Shakespeare canon. Pye-boord, playing the fortune-teller, assures Lady Plus, "You may belieue my straines, I strike all true" (253); we can cite a similar phrasing in "high strains / Of divination" in *Troilus*, II,ii,113-14.

The phrase "heauen for-fend" (259) may seem a common-place, but we can at least note that it falls within the range of Shakespeare's observable usage—it occurs in singular form in *1 Henry VI*, V,iv,65, and in plural in *Troilus*, I,iii,302. The phrase "more fearefull" (263) occurs four times in the collected works, including a use in *MacBeth* and two in *Coriolanus*, plays with close chronological relationships to *The Puritan*. The phrase "all beholders" (271-2) is almost identical to "all the beholders" in *As You Like It*, I,ii,131; "out, alasse" (276) occurs six times in Shakespeare, twice in *Merry Wives*; "Giue eare" (279) occurs five times, including uses in *Merry Wives* and *Lear*. For "past proba-tion" (281), compare "pass'd in probation" in *MacBeth*, III,i,79; "all sham'de" (283-4) is used in *Lear*, III,iv,66; "all vndon" (284) appears four times in the acknowledged works. The phrase "strange fortunes" (289) occurs in singular form in *Winter's Tale*, II,iii,179; for "accident of death and bloud-shedding" (290), compare "bloody accidents" in *Othello*, V,i,94, plus a use of "blood-shedding" in *2 Henry VI*, IV,vii,102. For "with all present speede" (293-4), compare "with all convenient speed" in *Merchant*, III,iv,56, and "With all good speed" and "With all swift speed" in *Richard II*, I,ii,66, and V,i,54, among similar Shakespearean usages.

For "meddle not with a husband" (295-6), compare "meddle not with her" in *Shrew*, II,i,25, and "not meddle with him" in *All's Well*, IV,iii,35 ("meddle not" occurs once in the collected works, "not meddle" six times, "never meddle" twice). The phrase "be-thinke your selues" (314) appears in singular form in both *Othello*, V,ii,26, and *Lear*, I,ii,159 ("bethink you" appears six times in the acknowledged works, "bethink thee" three times). The phrase "good happinesse" (328) is a redundancy, a feature typical of Shakespeare; compare "good outward happiness" in *Much Ado*, II,iii,183. In line 330 the word "neighbours" is used as a verb, an unusual usage that we also find in *Venus*, 259. For "some Cordiall to comfort him" (342-3), compare "cordial comfort" in *Winter's Tale*, V,iii,77; for "potion of a sleepy Nature" (343-4), compare "sleeping potion" in *Romeo*, V,iii,244 (an important contextual link, as we shall see in a moment). The phrase "seeme as dead" (344-5) occurs in *As You Like It*, IV,iii,118, while "beeing apprehended" (345-6) occurs in *Twelfth Night*, V,i,86; "see occasion" (353) is found in *Romeo*, II,iv,160; for "keepe true time" (354-5), note that "keep time" and "true time" appear within seven lines of each other in *Richard II*, V,v,42-8, while "keep time" also occurs in *Hamlet*, III,iv,140.

This long scene of 357 lines (one of the two longest in the play, the other being III,v) concludes with a 32-line soliloquy by Pye-boord, in which he carries further the plotting begun in earlier scenes, and explains how the confidence trick on the Plusses will work. A staged duel between Oath and Skirmish was discussed at the end of I,iv; here in II,i Pye-boord reveals that his plan also involves the use of a sedative that counterfeits death—a plot device that Shakespeare used previously in *Romeo and Juliet*, ca. 1595, and would use again a few years after *The Puritan* in *Cymbeline*, ca. 1609. There are several such large-scale plot elements in this play that provide obvious links to the works of either Shakespeare or Middleton, and that support the hypothesis that *The Puritan* is a collaboration between the two men. (Please note that I am not making any statement about the originality of such devices; both dramatists drew heavily upon their cultural tradition, as did all of their contemporaries. The sleeping-potion-that-mimics-death could no doubt be traced

through a long line of antecedents in literature and folklore—
think of Sleeping Beauty, for one. The point I wish to make here
is simply that this plot element is one that Shakespeare uses
more than once in his acknowledged works.)

In II,i of *The Puritan*, then, I argue that the first portion of
the scene, dealing with the Plus family characters, is in all likeli-
hood the work of Middleton alone; but with Pye-boord's entrance after line 143 we encounter a major Shakespearean contribution. I certainly would not insist that this second part of the
scene is "pure" Shakespeare; quite the contrary, it seems most
likely that the final 200 lines in II,i constitute a mixed text, the
product of both dramatists' hands. I do not, therefore, dispute
the evidence of Middleton's presence in II,i cited by David Lake
—though I would add a qualification to one small point. Lake
mentions the rare usage "can possible" (286), which he finds in
two of Middleton's early plays, *The Phoenix* and *Your Five Gallants*, but hardly anywhere else in the relevant literature. We can,
however, note an instance of the almost-identical "canst possible" in Shakespeare's *1 Henry VI*, I,ii,87.

Act II, Scene ii

This next scene is very short, consisting of a single speech in ten
lines of prose, in which Nicholas St. Antlings informs the audience that he has stolen Sir Godfrey Plus' chain and hidden it in
the rosemary bush in the Plusses' garden—that being the next
step in Pye-boord's plan. Since Nicholas is one of the Plus family servants, we might expect his part to be mostly or wholly the
work of Middleton; but since he is also one of the minor characters who functions as a "bridge" between the two groups of
characters, and since the two previous scenes in which he appeared (I,iii and iv) show clear Shakespearean elements, it may
be worthwhile to investigate this scene as well. And indeed this
short scene provides a fair amount of evidence of Shakespeare's
hand.

In the first line of his speech, Nicholas uses the phrase "excel-

lent aduantage"; compare Shakespearean usages like "rich advantage," "best advantage," "good advantage," "excellent device," "excellent endeavor," etc. For "by little & little" (4), we
can cite several repeat uses of "little" in Shakespeare's works—
"little little less than little" in *Troilus*, II,iii,13, "A very little little"
in *Henry V*, IV,ii,33, and "a little grave, / A little little grave" in
Richard II, III,iii,153-4. For "most Puritanically" (4-5), we can
observe that Shakespeare has a marked preference for this type
of "most __ly" phrasing, using no less than 120 of them in his
acknowledged works (a figure that counts only those cases in
which Shakespeare transforms a noun or adjective into an ad-
verb with the suffix "ly," and omits phrases like "most likely,"
"most lively," "most comely," and other similar usages). Also,
for comparison with "most Puritanically," we can note that
Shakespeare uses phrases like "most Christian-like," "most
Christian" and "most heathenish" in his collected works. "Wee
shal haue good sport anon" (5) echoes "you shall have sport"
and "you shall see sport anon" in *Merry Wives*, III,ii,81 and
III,iii,169, while "good sport" occurs in both *Lear*, I,i,23, and
Troilus, I,i,113. For "an honest man of my word" (7-8), compare
"an honest woman of her word" in *Merchant*, II,i,7. The phrase
"betweene Heauen & Earth" (9) may be a commonplace, but it
is one that lies within Shakespeare's range of usage: compare
"'twixt heaven and earth" in both *John*, IV,ii,216 and *Winter's
Tale*, V,i,132, and "between earth and heaven" in *Hamlet*,
III,i,127.

Before leaving this scene, we should note that David Lake
singles out two textual features in II,ii as suggestive of Middleton in their specific spellings: the contractions "ha's" for "he
has" (6) and "I'me" (8). This conforms well to my hypothesis of
a Middletonian fair copy of the text. It would seem sensible to
suppose that Middleton and Shakespeare composed this short
speech together, continuing their collaboration from the latter
part of II,i, and the pen that wrote the manuscript was held in
Middleton's hand.

Act III, Scene i

This scene contains the brawl that has reminded commentators of the fight in V,i of *Othello*. In both scenes, the manipulator character (Pye-boord, Iago) arranges a swordfight in which one combatant (Skirmish, Roderigo) wounds the other (Oath, Cassio) in the leg, and after which one of the participants is left "dead" (in the comedy, Corporal Oath has been given the sleeping potion and only appears dead; in the tragedy, Roderigo's death is real). Both scenes show the manipulator character rushing in after the brawl, offering "help" to the man with the leg wound (Pye-boord gives Oath a "Cordiall" to "comfort" him; Iago calls for a surgeon for Cassio), and insuring that the "death" occurs (Pye-boord with his sedative; Iago by killing Roderigo). These similarities might be interpreted as the result of imitation of Shakespeare by another playwright—Baldwin Maxwell calls them "parody"—but there are stylistic features in the scene that suggest a different interpretation.

While the prose of III,i is perfunctory and undistinguished, nothing more than functional, there are elements in the scene that indicate a continuation of the Shakespearean contribution evident in earlier scenes. Simon St. Mary Overies describes Lady Plus as "an honest, chast, and vertuous woman" (4-5), a triplet that compares well with a number of Shakespearean phrasings: "honest, chaste, and true" in *Othello*, IV,ii,17, "as continent, as chaste, as true" in *Winter's Tale*, III,ii,34, "Virtuous, wise, chaste, constant" in *Cymbeline*, I,iv,60, etc. Simon also asserts that widows require a "Coniunction Copulatiue" (10); in *As You Like It*, V,iv,66-103 we find a whole series of such pompous phrases in reverse noun-adjective order, spoken by a clown character for comic effect—"Countercheck Quarrelsome," "Quip Modest," "Retort Courteous," etc. And note too that just before this passage in *As You Like It*, we find a similar alliterative effect in "country copulatives," V,iv,55.

At line 18 the main business of the scene begins, with the entrance of Skirmish and his question, "whats a clock?" The brawl between Oath and Skirmish occurs over a deliberately false report of the time; compare a similar disagreement over another deliberately false report of the time in *Shrew*, IV,iii,187-95. (It is striking to note how often Shakespeare's characters ask or tell each other the time—several dozen instances appear in the acknowledged works. It would be interesting to compare Middleton's habits in this respect.) Having noted one link between III,i of *The Puritan* and IV,iii of *Shrew*, we can cite a second: in lines 12-14 Frailty mentions that "Master Pilfer the Tailor" is displaying his wares in the Plusses' house—with any luck he'll fare better than the unfortunate tailor who attends Petruchio and Katherine in IV,iii of *Shrew*.

As for other features: "baffle me" (31) appears in *1 Henry IV*, I,ii,101; for "By yon blew Welkin" (56), compare "By welkin and her star" in *Merry Wives*, I,iii,92; "lay hands vpon the villaine" (60-1) is almost identical to "lay hands on the villain" in *Shrew*, V,i,38, with similar usages elsewhere in Shakespeare. For "emptie creatures" (77), we can cite a number of empty creatures in Shakespeare's works: the "empty eagle" in *2 Henry VI*, III,i,248, *3 Henry VI*, I,i,268, and *Venus*, 55; the "empty tigers" in *Romeo*, V,iii,39; the "empty ass" in *Julius Caesar*, IV,i,26; and the "infants empty of all thought" in *Troilus*, IV,ii,6. Finally in III,i, we can note Pye-boord's closing line, "Now to my patient; here's his potion" (80). In *2 Henry IV*, I,ii,126-31, Falstaff has these lines: "I am as poor as Job, my lord, but not so patient. Your lordship may minister the potion of imprisonment to me in respect of poverty...." The similarity here extends beyond the mere conjunction of the words "potion" and "patient"; the idea of being sent to prison because of poverty, of indebtedness, is crucial to this portion of *The Puritan*, and leads to another significant link between Pye-boord and Falstaff in a coming scene in this play.

Act III, Scene ii

This scene is dominated by the Plusses, and appears to be mostly Middletonian, but we do find a few elements in it that suggest a Shakespearean contribution, even in the speeches of the Plus characters—as the play progresses we begin to detect a departure from the fairly clear division of authorship in the first two scenes. (As the two plots became more intimately entangled, the collaborators likely found it harder to separate the tasks of authorship, and simply continued to compose the play together. This seems to be true for much of what follows—though not for everything in the last three acts, as we shall see.) The phrase "beyond our thoughts" (1) occurs in *Coriolanus*, I,iv,26, and compare also "beyond the mark of thought" in *Antony*, III,vi,87, and "beyond thought's compass" in *Henry VIII*, I,i,36. For "luckie faire euent" (2), compare "fair and lucky war" in *Henry V*, II,ii,184; "yet liuing" (6) occurs three times in the collected works, not counting variants like "living yet" and "yet is he living." For "a wondrous fellow, surelie" (13), compare "a sweet gallant, surely" in *Much Ado*, IV,i,317, and "a good matter, surely" in *Shrew*, I,i,251. For "be patient" (26), "if he would be patient" (78-9) and "I will be patient" (82), note that the latter phrase occurs verbatim in both *Merry Wives*, II,i,126, and *Troilus*, V,ii,47, with similar usages throughout the canon—"I'll be patient," "I'll be as patient," "I must be patient," etc., with "be patient" a total of fifty-one times in the collected works. For "goodly godly sister" (39), we might compare a similar assonant-alliterative effect in "goodly portly man" in *1 Henry IV*, II,iv,422.

For the triplet "strangers, Theeues, and Catch-poles" (47), compare "knaves, thieves, and treachers" in *Lear*, I,ii,123; for the reference to "a cold Capons" corpse (55), compare "a cold Capon's leg" in *1 Henry IV*, I,ii,116; for "it cannot chuse but come to light" (72), note that similar "cannot choose but . . ." phrasings appear twenty-one times in Shakespeare's acknowledged works, not counting variants like "canst not choose but," "shalt not choose but," and "should not choose but." The phrase "stole away" (76) occurs once in the Shakespeare canon, with "stol'n away" eight times and "stolen away" twice. For "shew your selfe a man" (77), note that "show yourself" occurs in present or past tense in *Merry Wives*, II,iii,53, and in *Hamlet*, IV,vii,125—and compare "be a man" in *Othello*, IV,i,65, a similar injunction to regain self-control after an emotional outburst. The phrase "a Trifle" (96) appears ten times in the collected works.

Before quitting this scene, let's pause to note an interesting feature that has some potential, I think, for clarifying a point of difficulty in the recognized Shakespearean works. At line 81, Nicholas St. Antlings says that Captain Idle will be able to fetch Sir Godfrey's missing chain "with a Sesarara." George Steevens was the first to note that "Sesarara" derives from the legal term "Certiorari"—"a writ for transference of hearing to superior court, or calling for production before superior court of records of a lower court"; though in the context of the scene it is clear that in its popularized form the phrase "with a Sesarara" does not mean "with a writ," but rather "in a hurry," "in an instant," or words to that effect—equivalent to more recent colloquialisms like "in a flash" or "at the snap of a finger." David Lake notes that Middleton uses similarly corrupt forms of "Certiorari"—"Sursurrara," "Sursurarers," and "Sursararaes"—three times in his early play *The Phoenix*, so that the "Sesarara" here in *The Puritan* is most likely his as well. Yet this particular spelling, "Sesarara," may help to explain the mysterious word "sessa," which Shakespeare uses three times in his acknowledged works, in *Shrew*, In,i,6, and in *Lear*, III,iv,100 and III,vi,74. The meaning and derivation of "sessa" is uncertain; but since the word seems to be, in essence, a hunting cry, its range of meaning is limited. Blakemore Evans, in the Riverside edition of Shakespeare's works, glosses "sessa" as "perhaps equivalent to 'let it go' (from Spanish 'cesar,' 'cease')."[17] But if the phrase "with a Sesarara" was current in Shakespeare's time, as a cant phrase for quick action—as the usage here in *The Puritan* certainly seems to suggest—it seems at least possible that the word might have been further corrupted into, perhaps, a general exclamation often used while hunting. This, I think, would give us a reasonable explanation for the word as it is used by Edgar and by Christopher Sly, as well as a (more plausible?) native English derivation for the term rather than a foreign one. At the very least, I think it's an idea worth considering. This minor point has no direct relevance to the authorship of *The Puritan*, but it does show that renewed study of the plays of the Apocrypha may help to clear away some lingering uncertainties in the canonical Shakespearean texts.

Act III, Scene iii

In connection with the final line in III,i, I made mention of a commonality between Pye-boord and Falstaff, based on the idea of being imprisoned for debt; this linkage becomes clear in III,iii. Both the third and fourth scenes of Act III are devoted to an interlude in the larger plot of the play, a miniature plot that concerns Pye-boord's encounter with three officers intending to arrest him for unpaid debts (one of these officers is a constable named Dogson—a blend of Dogberry in *Much Ado* and Abhorson in *Measure*). Here in III,iii, Pye-boord is accosted by the officers, who intend to arrest him for debt at the suit of the hostess of the inn where he resides—which is precisely what happens to Falstaff in *2 Henry IV*, II,i. In that scene, one of the officers, Snare, is described as a "yeoman," as is Dogson in III,iii of *The Puritan*. In lines 29-33, the sergeants Puttock and Ravenshaw are concerned about whether Pye-boord wears a sword; when they're reasonably sure he doesn't, Ravenshaw says, "if I clutch him once, let me alone to drage him if he be stiff-necked" (33-5). In the parallel scene in *2 Henry IV*, Snare and Mistress Quickly have a similar exchange about whether Falstaff "will stab" when arrested (II,i,11-17); Fang claims that "If I can close with him, I care not for his thrust" (18-19)—the two passages handle their similar material in very similar ways.

As for other features in the scene: for "trust him no longer" (1-2), compare "no longer trust thee" in *1 Henry VI*, III,iii,84; for "if you will accompany me" (3), compare "Unless you will accompany me" in *Shrew*, I,ii,106; for "desperate or swift" (5), compare "venturous or desperate" in *1 Henry VI*, II,i,45. The phrase "good Angell" (6), with the pun on the coin so called, is of course a commonplace of the era—yet it is interesting to note that Shakespeare's three uses of the phrase in canonical plays all occur in works with thematic connections to *The Puritan*; see *Measure*, II,iv,16, *1 Henry IV*, III,iii,178, and *2 Henry IV*, II,iv,335. The phrase "imperfections, Knaueryes, and Conuayances" (13-14) conforms to Shakespeare's habit of using such multiple terms; compare, for instance, "jests, and gipes, and knaveries, and mocks" in *Henry V*, IV,vii,49. For "he weares no weapon" (30,31), compare "Thou hast no weapon" and "he had no weapon" in *Othello*, V,ii,256 and 360; "I am right glad" (32) occurs four times in the collected works, all in later plays, *Timon, Cymbeline, The Tempest*, and *Henry VIII*. The fishing metaphor in line 43-7 suggests Shakespeare, I think, more than Middleton; for "caught many a foole" (47), compare "fools are caught" in *Othello*, IV,i,45. The phrase "be crost" (52) appears five times in the collected works; for "I spoke truer than I was a ware" (56), compare "you have spoken truer than you propos'd" in *The Tempest*, II,i,20, and "Far truer spoke than meant" in *2 Henry VI*, III,i,183.

The phrase "little less" (63) occurs four times in the canon, including a use in *Troilus*, II,iii,13; the unusual word "rablement" (73, 74) is found in *Julius Caesar*, I,ii,244. For "hees tame" (79), compare "I am tame" in *Hamlet*, III,ii,310, "you are a tame man" in *Dream*, III,ii,259, and "A most poor man, made tame" in *Lear*, IV,vi,221. In lines 106-10 Pye-boord addresses a series of rhetorical questions to himself as he casts about for a new strategy; in *Henry VIII*, II,ii, Cardinal Wolsey, another

Shakespearean manipulator character, similarly asks himself rhetorical questions as he searches for a way out of his predicament—compare Pye-boord's "no deuice to . . ." line (109) with Wolsey's "No new device to . . ." usage in III,ii,217 of his play. (Wolsey is "undone" by a "paper," III,ii,210; Pye-boord is able to rescue himself because he has a "paper" with him, 111.) For "haue most need of" (108-9), compare "had most need of" in *Macbeth*, II,ii,29, and "have most need" in *Richard III*, II,i,36; for "Extremity is the Touch-stone vnto wit" (112-13), compare "Extremity, that sharpens sundry wits" in a certainly Shakespearean scene in *Kinsmen*, I,i,118. More minor features in the scene add to the Shakespearean impression: the phrase "halfe an hower hence" (125) occurs in *The Tempest*, III,i,91, with "some half hour hence" in *Cymbeline*, I,i,176 and similar usages throughout the canon; for "if you had not crost me" (126), compare "But hadst thou not cross'd me" in *Shrew*, IV,i,72-3; for "great ioy" (127), it may be worth noting that the closest single Shakespearean parallel occurs in a play that's closely contemporaneous with *The Puritan*—"great sea of joys" in *Pericles*, V,i,192. At the end of the scene the officers tell Pye-boord that he is "a good Scholler" (150-1) who has "proceeded very well"; "a good scholar" occurs in *2 Henry IV*, III,ii,10, while for "proceeded very well" compare "Proceeded well" in *Love's Labor's Lost*, I,i,95, a usage that occurs in a scholarly context. (We might also cite the "well proceeded" in *Richard III*, III,v,48.)

We can also note that III,iii is rich in other minor features that show strong measures of consistency with Shakespeare's normal habits of usage, supporting the impression created by the more distinctive and noteworthy elements: "of a sodaine" (45), "spent his rage" (49), "great Admiration" (50), "I protest" (117), "at this instant" (119), and "well said" (134,144), among others, can be cited in this category.

Also in this scene, we find, for the first time in this play, redundant *s* plurals, a textual feature definitely suggestive of Shakespeare. (See the third chapter of my study of *Merlin* for more on this point.) To be accurate, we must recognize that this type of plural does occasionally occur in the works of other playwrights—including Middleton: "that's the worst words" in *The Second Maiden's Tragedy*, IV,i,11.[18] Yet it also seems clear that this kind of defective plural form is more characteristic of Shakespeare than it is of any of his contemporary dramatists. When, therefore, we read "All my meanes is confounded" (105-6) and "has my wits serued me so long" (106-7), we have to be struck by the presence of two redundant *s* plurals in the space of three lines.

The location of these plurals is also striking: as noted earlier, III,iii introduces an interlude in the larger plot of the play, a miniature plot from which all the Middletonian Plus-family characters are excluded. In considering this episode with the officers, we may be dealing with something close to purely Shakespearean material, with little or no Middletonian contribution. It is true that other pieces of textual evidence in III,iii appear to point toward Middleton more than Shakespeare— but some of these elements are open to interesting qualification. The contractional oath form "Sfoot" (114), for instance, is more frequent in Middleton than in Shakespeare—indeed, it occurs only once in the latter poet's works; but that single instance falls in *Troilus* (II,iii,5), a play with so many links to *The Puritan*. (The usage belongs to Thersites: "'Sfoot, I'll learn to conjure and raise devils," a usage very *apropos* to the play that is the subject of our investigation.) Similarly, "Slid" (121, 139) occurs only twice in the acknowledged Shakespearean works—but those two uses are in *Merry Wives* (III,iv,24) and *Twelfth Night* (III,iv,391), other plays with significant relationships to *The Puritan*. (For Shakespeare, "'Slid" is a gull's oath, used by characters who end up on the short end of life's battles of wit: Abraham Slender uses it, Sir Andrew Aguecheek too—and so does Puttock, one of the sergeants in III,iii.) For the apparently Middletonian contraction "'tas" (33), we can note that Shakespeare's few similar usages occur in a relevant work: see the "'tas" and "'tad" in *Pericles*, III,ii,4 and IV,iii,11, a play written most likely within a year or so of *The Puritan*. It may well be that this scene was not, or not completely, transcribed from foul papers into fair copy by Middleton, so that Shakespearean textual features like the redundant *s* plurals were preserved in the copy text from which the 1607 quarto was set in type. I am sure that in some readers' minds the absence of clear textual evidence of Shakespeare's contribution in the first half of the play will stand as a significant barrier to the acceptance of the hypothesis of partial Shakespearean authorship. But I assert that in the second half of *The Puritan* we do find some sound textual evidence (there's more to come) to support the stylistic and external evidence of Shakespeare's contribution.

Act III, Scene iv

This is the second and final scene of the mini-plot in the middle of Act III, depicting Pye-boord's encounter with the officers; and it contains a feature that must, I believe, be taken as a very strong indicator of Shakespeare's authorial presence. In lines 58-61, Pye-boord states:

> . . . if I fall into the *hungrie swallow* of the *prison*, I am like *vtterly to perish*, and with *fees* and *extortions* be *pincht cleane to the bone*.

Compare *Timon of Athens*, IV,iii,527-31:

> Hate all, curse all, show charity to none,
> But let the *famish'd flesh slide from the bone*
> Ere thou relieve the beggar: give to dogs
> What thou deniest to men; let *prisons swallow* 'em,
> *Debts wither 'em to nothing* . . .

The parallels of thought and expression are very striking; and if the usual dating of *Timon* to ca. 1607 is sound, then the canonical play was likely written after *The Puritan*, so that imitation of

Shakespeare by another playwright could not be a factor. We can also cite usages from other Shakespearean works to show that the quoted passage in *The Puritan* conforms to Shakespeare's habits of expression: "swallow up his life" in *3 Henry VI*, V,vi,25, "pinch'd to death" in *The Tempest*, V,i,276, and "lank and lean with thy extortions" in *2 Henry VI*, I,iii,129, can all be listed among various other possible examples. (The usage of the word "pinch" in this context also conforms well to the pattern of associations that Edward Armstrong has detected in Shakespeare's uses of the word.[19])

This parallel with *Timon* is set in a scene that shows many other signs of Shakespeare's presence. The opening of the scene may seem quite unremarkable: the Gentleman's servant answers Pye-boord's knock at the door with "Who knocks? whose at doore?" (1); when Pye-boord and his captors enter, Pye-boord asks, "is the Gentleman your maister within" (3-4). Prosaic as it is, we can observe that this opening is typical of the way Shakespeare gets his characters onstage; compare "Who knocks so loud at door?" in *2 Henry IV*, II,iv,352, "Who's that at door?" in *Troilus*, IV,ii,35, and "Who's there that knocks?" in *Cymbeline*, II,iii,77, among similar Shakespearean usages, and also "is Signor Lucentio within" in *Shrew*, V,i,18, and "is thy lady within" in *Twelfth Night*, III,i,48, plus a half-dozen other comparable lines elsewhere in the collected works.

Of all the specific parallels and Shakespearean phrasings in III,iv, perhaps the most distinctive is "labour his deliuerie" (204), which occurs in *Richard III*, I,iv,246; but there are many others, which, taken altogether, show a strong degree of consistency with Shakespeare's style. The phrase "haue you forgot me" (7) appears in *Timon*, *Hamlet*, and *Shrew*, with close variants elsewhere in Shakespeare; "all happinesse" (41) occurs six times in the acknowledged works, including uses in *Timon* and *Cymbeline*; "make bold" (77) occurs seven times in the present tense in the collected works, and three times in the past tense; "excellent deuice" (86, 87) occurs three times, "better pleasde"

(95) twice, "good witte" (95-6) nine times, "goe thy wayes" (101) fourteen times, "too busie" (116) twice. "I can assure you" (172) occurs three times, as does "Why, whats the matter" (178); "make known" (183) occurs seven times in the acknowledged canon. The phrase "kindly welcome" (43) appears in *Cymbeline*, I,vi,41, with "be dooing" (105) and "so finely" (133) in *Henry V*, III,vii,99 and II,ii,137 respectively, "little villaine" (108) in *Twelfth Night*, II,v,13, and "Faith, like enough" (128) in *Much Ado*, II,iii,103 (with eight other "like enough" usages elsewhere in Shakespeare).

The phrase "bee remembred" (24) appears seven times in the acknowledged works, along with variants like "rememb'red be" and "be you rememb'red," and two instances of "be remembered" in the non-contracted form. We can note in passing that the contractional form "rememb'red" is favored by Shakespeare; it occurs 28 times in the collected works, while the un-contracted form "remembered" is used only three times, and the alternative "remember'd" is not used at all. We can make the same observation about other contractional forms used in III,iii-iv—they tend to by typical of Shakespeare's habits. For the instance of "vpont" in III,iii,49, for example, we can observe that "upon't" occurs twenty-eight times in the acknowledged works, "upon it" only eighteen times; also, it seems worth noting that "upon it" is Shakespeare's preferred usage in plays written in the 1590s, while he favors "upon't" after 1600. Other contractions used in III,iii-iv partake of similar chronological patterns—the "hate" (for "ha't") in III,iii,141, and the "with't" in III,iv,187, are two good examples among various others. Lacking a Middleton concordance, it is hard to say how often Middleton does or does not use the same forms, so that it would be unwise to lay too much emphasis on this consistency, but its existence is worth noting nonetheless.

For "pritty comfortable roome" (25) and "pritty painted things" (115), compare a range of similar Shakespearean phrasings: "pretty knavish page," "pretty sweet wit," "pretty slight drollery," "pretty vaulting sea," "pretty hollow cage," etc. The word "dog-holes" (28, 29) occurs in singular form in *All's Well*, II,iii,274; for "haue my Chamber here shortly, nay, and dyet too" (30-1), we can note a pattern of such "this, nay, that too" phrasings in Shakespeare—see *Troilus*, I,i,23-6, *Winter's Tale*, I,ii,422-3, *Dream*, III,ii,313, and *2 Henry IV*, V,ii,85-9 for some examples. For "the most free-hartedst Gentleman" (31-2), the obvious parallel is "complete, free-hearted gentleman" in *Timon*, III,i,10; but note too that Shakespeare has a habit of constructing such "most __est" redundancies: "most bravest," "most heaviest," "most stillest," and "most unkindest," among others, can be found in the acknowledged works. The "most fairest and comfortablest" in line 79 of this scene conforms to the same pattern. The phrase "maps, and pictures, and deuices, and things" (38-9) is typical of Shakespeare's list-making propensity—we might compare "maps for ports and piers and roads" in *Merchant*, I,i,19. For "the Gentleman makes great account of him" (45-6), compare "The princes make high account of you" in *Richard III*, III,ii,69. For "my extreames makes me the boulder" (51-2), we can cite "my extremes" in *Romeo*, IV,i,62, and "makes me the bolder" in both *2 Henry VI*, I,i,29, and *Two Gentlemen*, II,i,83—and, perhaps most important, we can note that "extreames makes" constitutes another redundant *s* plural.

For "the fangs of vnmercifull officers" (54-5), compare "fangs of malice" in *Twelfth Night*, I,v,184. (Twice in this scene, in lines 54 and 205, the "fangs" of the officers are mentioned; recall that one of the officers who attempts to arrest Falstaff in *2 Henry IV*, II,i is named Fang.) Also, the use of the words "vnfortunately" and "vnmercifull" within a line of each other (54-5) reminds us of Shakespeare's habit of abundant use of such "un" prefix words, noted earlier in reference to II,i,172 and 233-4; "vnlettered" (71) and "vnpittying" (205) partake of the same tendency. In "lands, money, and friends" (57) we have another instance of

Shakespeare's list making; "His plate, his goods, his money and his lands" in *Richard II*, II,i,210, is only one of many possible comparisons. For "if euer pitty had interest in the bloud of a Gentleman" (61-2), compare "If ever love had interest in his liver" in *Much Ado*, IV,i,231. "Goe forward" (65) occurs thirteen times in the collected works; it is used as a succinct command, as it is here, in *Henry VIII*, I,ii,177, where it appears, as here, in conjunction with a "beseech you" usage, in a scene with some interesting structural and atmospheric commonalities with III,iv of *The Puritan*.

For "giddy, and doubtfull what to doe" (68), we might compare "Giddy in spirit, still gazing on a doubt" in *Merchant*, III,ii,144; "labouring thoughts" (69) compares with "our brains . . . laboring for invention" in Sonnet 59,2-3, with similar usages elsewhere. In line 123 Dogson suggests that the officers should look at the "back-side" of a map to find the Counter Prison; it is interesting to observe that the single use of "back-side" in the collected works occurs in a similar urban-geographical context—"o'th' backside the town" in *Cymbeline*, I,ii,13. In line 140 Ravenshaw explains his plan to "close with" the hostess at whose suit they've arrested Pye-boord, and make a financial settlement that will yield the officers a nice profit; compare "close with him, give him gold" in *Winter's Tale*, IV,iv,800, and note that "close with" also occurs in the parallel arrest scene in *2 Henry IV*, II,i,18. "It was my hap to helpe him" (201) can be compared with the "it was their hap to . . ." phrasing in *Errors*, I,i,113, and the "it is their hap / To . . ." usage in *The Tempest*, V,ii,101-2.

Beyond these cited features, we could list a wide array of other stylistic elements in III,iv that conform to Shakespeare's habits, or that have precedents in his acknowledged works—to take only one example, compare "God you good den, sirs,— would you speake with me?" (163-4) to "Gentlemen, good den, a word with one of you" in *Romeo*, III,i,38 (with a "God ye good den" in II,iv,110 of the same play). Recurrences of features noted earlier, like "peepe out" (131) and "bullies" (146), are also worth noting.

And in addition to the stylistic evidence, the textual evidence here in III,iv, as in III,iii, allows the possibility that the manuscript source for the 1607 printed text was Shakespearean holograph. The presence of three redundant *s* plurals in these two scenes is very significant, as is the lack of any truly strong evidence of Middleton's hand. The two features in III,iv that Lake cites as indicative of Middleton—the "masse, here he comes" in line 39 and the "You're kindly welcome" in line 43—both have parallels in the Shakespeare canon. For the former, compare "By the mass, here comes Bardolph" in *2 Henry IV*, II,ii,69. In regard to the latter, Lake writes that "Adverbs in *-ly* followed by *welcome* constitute another collocation of which Middleton is unusually fond, especially in his early period."[20] But Shakespeare uses such phrasings as well—"truly welcome," "entirely welcome," "dearly welcome," "fairly welcome," "respectively welcome"; and since "kindly welcome" appears verbatim in *Cymbeline*, as noted above, I can't see that it can be regarded as more Middletonian than Shakespearean. Overall, I have to regard III,iii and iv as key aspects of the Shakespearean contribution to *The Puritan*.

(In making such specific and perhaps even trivial-seeming discriminations with the details of David Lake's study of the play, I hope I don't appear to be taking an unfair advantage of his published work or engaging in nitpicking criticism. In actuality I have found his work to be an indispensible resource, and I feel a strong admiration for the remarkable scope, ambition, and detail of his achievement, and the thoroughness, precision, and discipline that are so abundantly displayed throughout his survey of problems in the Middleton canon. I do disagree with Lake on the question of the best basic approach to take toward attribution study, since I believe that textual analysis divorced from more traditional literary and stylistic considerations does not always lead to wholly sound conclusions—*The Puritan* being an obvious case in point. But I prize his book highly, and I would be delighted if any readers of this book turn to David Lake's work in response.)

Act III, Scene v

This scene is, with II,i, one of the two longest scenes in the play; it depicts Pye-boord's liberation of Captain Idle from prison and the final stage in the preparation of the confidence trick they intend to play on the Plusses. We have already noticed the substantial relationship between *The Puritan* and *Merry Wives*, based on the two plays' similar subject matter of discharged soldiers turned thieves and con men. We can note another relationship between these plays, one that comes into focus very clearly in this scene. In Sir Godfrey Plus, Edmond Plus, and Nichoas St. Antlings, we have the same constellation of foolish uncle, foolish nephew, and foolish servant that we find in Robert Shallow, Abraham Slender, and Peter Simple in *Merry Wives*. (To be wholly accurate, Shallow and Slender address each other as "cousin," but their status as relations of an older and a younger generation is essentially the same as that of Sir Godfrey and Edmond.) The pattern of specific parallels between the two plays continues here in III,v: for "how the Play goes forward" (92-3), compare "let our plot go forward" in *Merry Wives*, IV,iv,12; for "marke the end on't" (95), compare "mark the sequel" in III,v,107; for "simply tho I stand here" (270), compare "simple though I stand here" in I,i,219; for "I desire more acquaintance on you" (333-4), compare "I desire more acquaintance of you" in II,ii,162. Both Edmond and Nicholas partake of Slender's habit of saying "la"—"truely, la" (356-7) recapitulates the "truly la" in I,i,309 of the canonical play. (Also, note that "in truth la" occurs in both *Troilus*, III,i,75, and *Coriolanus*, I,iii,89.)

Other signs of Shakespeare's hand in III,v abound. One of the best, I think, is "Speake big words, and stampe and stare" (96-7); compare "look not big, nor stamp, nor stare" in *Shrew*,

III,ii,228, along with other usages like "brag and stamp and swear" in *John*, III,i,122, "stamp'd and swore" in *Shrew*, III,ii,167, "stamp, rave, and fret" in *3 Henry VI*, I,iv,91, and even "speak parrot, and squabble, swagger, swear" in *Othello*, II,iii,279-80. In my study of *The Birth of Merlin* I made mention of Shakespeare's habit of putting tag-lines of identity into the mouths of his protagonists; when Pye-boord answers Idle's "whose that" (1) with "The same that I should be" (2), he participates in this Shakespearean pattern. For "why camst thou in halfe fac'd, muffled so?" (4), compare "Is not that his steward muffled so?" in *Timon*, III,iv,41, and note that "half-fac'd" occurs four times in the collected works, "half-face" once. The hunting metaphor in lines 11-18, in which Pye-boord pictures himself set upon like a bear by dogs in a bear-baiting ring, is typical of Shakespeare's animal imagery—compare, for instance, the "as a bear, encompass'd round by dogs" image in *3 Henry VI*, II,i,15-17. The phrase "scapt by miracle" (21) occurs in *1 Henry IV*, II,iv,165, while "a conscience" (132) appears (as "a' conscience") in *Pericles*, IV,ii,22, "vtterly denyed" (159) in *2 Henry IV*, IV,v,217, and "Boystrous storme" (294) in *Richard III*, II,iii,44. "Let it suffice" (20) occurs three times in the acknowledged Shakespearean works, "by my fay" (31), "siluerd ore" (81), "nay, faith" (129) and "in regard of" (155) occur twice each, "may easily" (105) and "within the compass" (293) four times each, "I warrant thee" (114, 212) ten times, "at length" (152) twelve times, "crie you mercy" (153) fourteen times, "in hast" (187) twenty-one times, "good comfort" (190) eleven times. The expression "Looke you" (78) is used over a hundred times in the Shakespeare canon; and while "look you," like some of the other usages just noted, is a commonplace, such phrases have some potential for distinguishing Shakespeare's style from the styles of other dramatists who do not use the same phrases with comparable frequencies; and on that basis such phrasings can be worth noting as consistent with Shakespeare's style. In the same spirit, we can pause to note that versions of "A pax of" (185) occur sixteen times in the collected works, and, for "Ber-lady" (187), that "by'r lady" is used fifteen times in the Shakespeare canon.

For "the time is busie" (19), compare "busy time" in *Much Ado*, I,ii,27 and III,v,4; for "What rests is all in thee" (29), we find similar "what rests" phrasings three times in *3 Henry VI*, in III,ii,45, IV,ii,13, and V,vii,32. "High-wayes, Heath, or Cunny-groues" (57-8) is a typical Shakespearean triplet; for the association between discharged soldiers and thieves, cheats and highwaymen in Pye-boord's speech (49-66)—no doubt a valid one in Shakespeare's era—we might compare "soldiers, not thieves" in *Timon*, IV,iii,413. (Also, for the "Cunnygroues," note that Falstaff and company are "coney-catching rascals" in *Merry Wives*, I,ii,4.) For "far better booties" (58), we can cite a similar "far better" usage in *2 Henry VI*, V,i,28, and we can note other "far __er" phrasings in the collected works, like "far poor-er" in *Antony*, I,ii,142, and "far truer" in *Richard III*, I,ii,190. For "geld fooles" (61), we can observe that Shakespeare repeatedly uses "geld" to mean "rob": "geld a codpiece of a purse" in *Winter's Tale*, IV,iv,610, "Bereft and gelded of his patrimony" in *Richard II*, II,i,237, "gelded the commonwealth" in *2 Henry VI*, IV,ii,165. For the triplet "perfect you, direct you, tell you the trick on't" (71-2), we can cite triplets with similar rhythms in the collected works—"Prevent it, resist it, let it not be so" in *Richard II*, IV,i,148 being a good example; and for "tell you the trick on't," compare usages like "I see the trick on't," "I smell the trick on't," "he has the trick on't," and "the very trick on't," from various Shakespearean works.

The hyphenated compound word "stalking-stamping" (84-5) is suggestive of Shakespeare, since Shakespeare has a knack for creating such compounds, sometimes very imaginative ones; from a vast list, let's cite only a few examples that are similar in sound, in meaning, or in their exploitation of alliterative and assonant effects: "deadly-standing," "mortal-staring," "gallant-springing," "shrill-shriking," "merchant-marring," "grim-grinning," "loud-howling." Also, for the larger phrase, "a stalking-stamping Player," we might compare "a strutting player" in *Troilus*, I,iii,153. The phrase "peepe fearefully" (91) occurs in the seventeenth poem of *The Passionate Pilgrim*, line 28, and also gives us the play's fourth usage of "peep"; for "Masse, that's well remembred" (113), we might cite "Marry, well rememb'red" in *Merchant*, II,viii,26. The description of the "Pothecaries shop" with all its strange furnishings (120-5) reminds us of the picture of the apothecary's shop in *Romeo*, V,i,37 ff. The word "fortunde" is used as a verb in line 157, as it is in *Two Gentlemen*, V,iv,169. For "tis a passing good one" (276), compare "This is a passing merry one" in *Winter's Tale*, IV,iv,288, and "'tis passing good" in *Shrew*, IV,iii,18. For "will the Curse of the beggar preuaile so much" (283), compare "Did York's dread curse prevail so much" in *Richard III*, I,iii,190; for "make all whole agen" (342), compare "make it whole again" in *Troilus*, III,i,51. Finally, while not significant as evidence of authorship, it is still interesting to note that references to "Stonie-stratford" (341) and "Brownists" (355) occur in *Richard III*, II,iv,1, and *Twelfth Night*, III,ii,31, respectively.

Other more minor features in III,v could also be considered, but I believe we have achieved a basic demonstration of Shakespeare's contribution. Lake cites several features in this scene indicating Middleton, and I do not dispute their accuracy. The almanac trick introduced in this scene (line 287 ff.) is re-used in Middleton's *No Wit, No Help Like a Woman's* (1611); and the phrases "Troth, and you say true" (122) and "lin laughing" (110) (the rare word "lin" for "leave" in the context of a death-of-father joke) can be taken as Middletonian features. It is interesting to note that both of these usages occur in the speeches of Captain Idle, a character of the Pye-boord hemisphere of the play; again, as we continue through the play, we find more evidence of cross-writing between the parts. But if we accept these indications of Middleton's hand in this scene, I don't see how we can reject the many similar signs of Shakespeare's presence.

Act IV, Scene i

This scene provides a good illustration of the cross-writing just mentioned. This short and rather perfunctory scene of forty-four lines of prose (the longest speech being only eight lines long) consists entirely of a conversation between Moll Plus and her suitor, Sir John Penny-dub. Since these are characters in the Plus-family plot, we might expect this scene to be of Middletonian authorship; and we do find that IV,i is written in that clipped, compressed, colloquial style that is typical of early Middleton, the style of I,i. But there are also a few elements in this scene that suggest a minor Shakespearean contribution. For "let it be deferd awhile" (6-7), compare "let it be conceal'd awhile" in *All's Well*, II,iii,266; for "as bigge a heart" (7), compare "a big heart" in *All's Well*, I,iii,95, "a heart as big" in *Cymbeline*, IV,ii,77, "no woman's heart / So big" in *Twelfth Night*, II,iv,95-6, "as big heart as thou" in *Coriolanus*, III,ii,128, and "thy heart is big" in *Julius Caesar*, III,i,282. For "crosse my loue thus" (12), we might cite "cross me thus" in *Merry Wives*, V,v,36, with similar usages elsewhere in Shakespeare; for "what case I was in" (13), compare "What case stand I in" in *Winter's Tale*, I,ii,352, and "in what case" in *All's Well*, I,iii,22, among similar phrasings. "And then hee told mee more-ouer" (15) compares with "and I hear, moreover" in *2 Henry IV*, I,ii,107, and "I understand, moreover" in *Measure*, I,iii,19; the phrase "sure together" (43) appears in *As You Like It*, V,iv,135, in a similar nuptial context. Thus, it seems fair to say that while IV,i is mainly the work of Middleton, it quite likely contains some traces of a Shakespearean contribution as well. I would assert that this makes simple sense at this point in the play: IV,i is a short Plus scene nestled between two long scenes in which Pye-boord plays a major part; there would have been little reason for Shakespeare to refrain from participation in the composition of IV,i merely to adhere to a predetermined division of the authorship task.

Act IV, Scene ii

This scene delivers one of the most important plot developments in the play, the conjuring trick through which the con game on the Plusses is brought to a successful end. Pye-boord and Idle pretend to conjure up devils as a means of recovering Sir Godfrey's "lost" chain, Idle roaring out nonsensical conjuring words for the benefit of the eavesdropping Plusses in the next room, to the accompaniment of the thunder and lightning predicted by the almanac. As David Lake observes in his study of this play, Middleton uses a pseudo-conjuring plot device in his early *The Family of Love*, which dates from ca. 1602-5; also, the nonsense-language trick reappears in the later *More Dissemblers Besides Women* of ca. 1615, with a little bit of the nonsense language from *The Puritan* repeated almost verbatim (in *The Puritan*, "Rumbos-ragdayon," IV,ii,123; in *More Dissemblers*, "Rumbos stragadelion," IV,i,129).[21] But if a Middletonian usage of nonsense language can be cited in a play that postdates *The Puritan*, we can also cite a Shakespearean usage of a very similar nonsense-language trick in a play that predates *The Puritan*—that being, of course, *All's Well That Ends Well*. The trick played on Parolles in IV,i and iii of that play has obvious affinities with Pye-boord's and Idle's trick here in *The Puritan*; and since *All's Well* is generally dated to ca. 1602-4, or a few years before *The Puritan*, its precedence demands consideration. Nonsense language can certainly be found in various dramatic works of the Elizabethan-Jacobean era (Rowley's roaring talk in the comic subplot of *A Fair Quarrel* is one example; Massinger's pseudo-Indian language in *The City Madam* is another), but the nonsense language in both *All's Well* and *The Puritan* seems unusual in its volubility and in its reliance on assonant and alliterative effects. In *The Puritan* the nonsense language reads this way:

> Rumbos—ragdayon, pur, pur, colucundrion, Hois-Plois...
> Beniamino,—gaspois—kay—gosgothoteron—vmbrois...

Flowtse—Kakopumpos—dragone—Leloomenos—
hodge—podge ... Gog de gog, hobgoblin, huncks,
hounslow, hockley te coome parke ... Nunck—Nunck—
Rip—Gascoynes, Ipis, Drip—Dropite ... O Sulphure
Sooteface—

In *All's Well*, we find this:

Throca movousus, cargo, cargo, cargo. Cargo, cargo, cargo,
villianda par corbo, cargo ... Boskos thromuldo boskos ...
Boskos vauvado ... Kerelybonto ... Manka revania dulche
... Oscobidulchos volivorco ... Accordo linta ... Bosko chi-
murcho ... Boblibindo chicurmurco.

Note the same assonant-alliterative effects, especially with o's
and s's, l's and c-k sounds—"Kakopumpos" and "Oscorbi-
dulchos," "colucundrion" and "chicurmurco." Insofar as nonsense language can be said to conform to a style, we have in
these two plays the same style of nonsense. Overall, it seems
likely that if certain elements of the plot, such as the conjuring
trick and the use of the almanac, are mainly Middletonian in
inspiration, the use of the nonsense language is contrastingly
Shakespearean. The later reuse by Middleton of the same device, and even some of the same language, in *More Dissemblers* (a
play written about a decade after *The Puritan*) does not contra-
dict such a conclusion.

IV,ii is a mixed Pye-boord/Plus scene, and as we might expect, it shows evidence of contributions by both dramatists.
Concerning Shakespeare, one of the stronger indications of his
hand in the scene is "So faire, and yet so cunning: that's to bee
wonderd at" (23-4); compare "so cunning and so young is wonderful" in *Richard III*, III,i,135, plus "so young and so untender"
in *Lear*, I,i,106, among similar Shakespearean usages. Also, we
can cite "Plots some device ... / To make us wonder'd at" in
Titus, III,i,134-5, and "the breed of wits so wondered at" in
Love's Labor's Lost, V,ii,266—giving us the same essential idea,
of cunning, plots, wit to be "wonder'd at." For "the feskewe of

the Diall is vpon the Chrisse-crosse of Noone" (84-5), compare
"The bawdy hand of the dial is now upon the prick of noon" in
Romeo, II,v,113; note too that the rare word "fescue," the name
for a teacher's pointer, is found in *Kinsmen*, II,iii,34. For "my
shirt sticks to my Belly already" (215), compare "The child brags
in her belly already" in *Love's Labor's Lost*, V,ii,677—I doubt that
anyone could regard the phrase "belly already" as a commonplace of the era.

The phrase "wondrous rare" (7) occurs in *1 Henry VI*, V,v,1,
with "spit fire" (92) in *Lear*, III,ii,14, "why, when" (118) in
Shrew, IV,i,143, "much beholding" (170) in *Henry VIII*, V,iv,70,
"pittifull case" (189) in *Romeo*, IV,v,99, and "new dropt" (196) in
Kinsmen, IV,i,88; "walke inuisibile" (243) occurs in *1 Henry IV*,
II,i,87, with "walking invisible" three lines later in the same
scene; "roaring tempests" (139) occurs in singular form, and
"makes mee giddy" (294) in the past tense, in *John*, III,iv,1 and
IV,ii,131 respectively. The phrase "much to blame" (34-5) appears four times in the collected works, "to bee rid of" (63) three
times (with "be rid of" four more times), "if hee chance to" (95),
"nothing remaines" (177), "I remember mee" (266) and "abusde
me" (266-7) twice each. The exclamations "Fooh" (18), "Fuh"
(91, 211), and "foh" (216) can be noted profitably: "foh" occurs
seven times in the acknowledged works, and "fough" once, all
in plays written in the 1599-1605 period, from *Henry V* and *Merry Wives* through *Lear*. For "neither smoake-dryed, nor scorcht,
nor black, nor nothing" (18-19), we can observe that Shakespeare frequently uses such "neither ... nor" and "nor ... nor"
formulations: "neither sad, nor sick, nor merry, nor well" in
Much Ado, II,i,293-4, "neither wit, nor words, nor worth, / Action, nor utterance, nor the power of speech" in *Julius Caesar*,
III,ii,221-2, and "Nor wink, nor nod, nor kneel, nor make a
sign" in *Titus*, III,ii,43, are only a few of the scores of such
phrasings distributed throughout the Shakespeare canon.

For "sincere loue" (44), compare "love sincere" in *Two
Gentlemen*, II,vii,76; for "maintain you gallantly" (55-6), com-

pare "gallantly maintain'd" in *Henry V*, III,vi,91; for "faire society of ladies" (57), compare "sweet society of fair ones" in *Henry
VIII*, I,iv,14. The phrase "simplie tho it lies here" (74-5) echoes
the "simply tho I stand here" in III,v,270, as well as the "simple
though I stand here" in *Merry Wives*, I,i,219, quoted earlier. For
"fayrest Roome" (75), compare "fairest chamber" in *Shrew*,
In,i,46, and "fairest house" in *Measure*, II,i,241; for "put by your
chattes" (83), compare "leave this chat" in *Love's Labor's Lost*,
IV,iii,280, "no more of this unprofitable chat" in *1 Henry IV*,
III,i,62, and "leave this idle theme, this bootless chat" in *Venus*,
422 ("chats" in plural form occurs once in the collected works,
in *Coriolanus*).

In lines 162-4 we find two connections with *Venus and
Adonis*: for "shuddering and shaking" (162), compare "shake
and shudder" in *Venus*, 880; for "as if an Earth-quake were in
their kidneyes" (163-4), compare "My boding heart pants . . . /
Like an earthquake" in *Venus*, 647-8. For "put thee to paine"
(178), compare "put me to present pain" in *Pericles*, V,i,191;
"to'th venture" (187) is almost identical to "to the venture" in *2
Henry IV*, Ep,7. For "All's past" (181), compare "all's spent" in
both *Timon*, I,ii,162, and *MacBeth*, III,ii,4, while for "all's quieted" (194) compare "all's hushed" in *The Tempest*, IV,i,207. For
"without danger" (210), compare "without the taste of danger"
in *1 Henry IV*, III,i,173, among many other "without . . ." formulations in the collected works: "without desert," "without
cause," "without limit," "without addition," "without control-
ment," "without delay," "without observance," etc.

For "taste correction" (287), compare "taste of much correction" in *Henry V*, II,ii,51; for "let me embrace you, hug you"
(292-3), compare "embrace and hug" in both *Timon*, I,i,44, and
More, III,ii,16 (or line 16 or Addition III; this is not the long
addition about the May Day riots that is virtually certainly in
Shakespeare's autograph, but rather the soliloquy by More that
is also widely accepted as Shakespearean in authorship; see pp.
1694-7 of the Riverside edition). For "Ile pawne my life" (312),

compare "I dare pawn down my life" in *Lear*, I,ii,86. Characters in this scene continue to manifest the verbal traits they displayed in earlier scenes—"Nuncle" (92,111), "looke you" (248), "truely la" (300), etc.; and the scene is rich in less distinctive phrases that nonetheless are consistent with Shakespeare's usage, "ile requite your kindnes" (244) being only one of the many possible examples.

Lake, in discussing this scene, notes a variety of Middletonian features, primarily, though not exclusively, textual in nature; and I of course accept these as valid indicators of Middleton's contribution. Here again, as in some earlier scenes, it seems that the dramatic material was created by Shakespeare and Middleton in an intimate collaboration, and also that the pen that set the words down on paper was held in Middleton's hand.

Act IV, Scene iii

In IV,iii we witness the completion of the sleeping-potion-that-mimics-death plot device: Pye-boord interrupts Corporal Oath's funeral so that he can appear to bring the Corporal back from the dead. This spectacular stage effect of a supposedly dead body rising from its coffin occurs repeatedly in the dramas of the period; it is found in Marston's *Antonio and Mellida* (ca. 1600), in Beaumont's *The Knight of the Burning Pestle* (1607), and in several of the plays of Fletcher and his collaborators; Middleton gives us a simultaneous double resurrection in *A Chaste Maid in Cheapside* (ca. 1613); and no doubt many other examples could be cited from the dramatic and literary traditions, and from the folklore sources that underly them (remember Sleeping Beauty). For the use of this device in *The Puritan*, IV,iii, the essential comparison is with the awakening of Thaisa in *Pericles*, III,ii; the uses of the device in these two plays display various common features that set them apart from the other plays mentioned. One obvious similarity between these two plays, a similarity not shared by the other works cited, is the presence of a kind of magician figure who is responsible for returning the supposedly dead person to consciousness. (I say "a kind of magician figure" because Pye-boord is of course a fraud, while Cerimon in *Pericles* is much closer to being a magus, as the term is used by Francis Yates—though he does not actually perform magic in the way that Prospero does. This dichotomy between negative and positive portrayals of magus figures is precisely what we should expect from Shakespeare; it is a symptom of the shift in viewpoint that is displayed in his works with his adoption of the romance form around 1608.)

We find many specific links between the awakenings in *The Puritan* and *Pericles*; despite the different dramatic uses of this stage device in the two plays (the first being realistic, comic, and satiric; the second serious, spiritual, and romantic), the handling of the incidents is very similar. In both scenes the magician figure demands that the body in the coffin be given air (*Puritan*, IV,iii,34-5; *Pericles*, III,ii,91); fire and warmth are called for (*Puritan*, 53-5; *Pericles*, 80); both "bodies," upon waking, instantly ask "where am I?" (*Puritan*, 48; *Pericles*, 105). Both scenes contain the phrase "most strange" (*Puritan*, 26; *Pericles*, 24 and 64), and both feature bystanders who speak in superlatives of amazement (the Sheriff's "I do more then admire you," *Puritan*, 75-6; the First Gentleman's "increase our wonder," *Pericles*, 96); in both, the first motion of the body is described with the word "stir" ("he stirs—he stirs agen," *Puritan*, 43; "How thou stirr'st," *Pericles*, 91), and the event is spoken of with forms of the word "rare" ("rarest," *Puritan*, 79; "Most rare," *Pericles*, 106). Both scenes describe the person in the coffin as "recover'd" (*Puritan*, 25; *Pericles*, 87), both allude to music ("all's in tune," *Puritan*, 82; "rough and woeful music," *Pericles*, 88), and in both scenes the recovered person is borne offstage to a room ("Kitchin," *Puritan*, 58; "the next chamber," *Pericles*, 107). The similarities in the treatments of these two awakenings are numerous and particular—and they serve to set these two scenes apart from other uses of the same device in the plays mentioned above; the "recoveries" in *The Puritan* and *Pericles* resemble each other to a degree that is most easily explained by common authorship. And since *The Puritan* likely predates *Pericles*, imitation of Shakespeare by another writer is not a sound alternative explanation.

The scene also shows the other apparently Shakespearean features we might justifiably expect, at this point in our study, in a Pye-boord scene. "Gentles all" (11) occurs in *Henry V*, Pr,8, "vouchsafe mee audience" (11-12) in *Love's Labor's Lost*, V,ii,313, "under fauour" (17) in *Timon*, III,v,40, "more giddy" (47) in both *Twelfth Night*, III,iv,33, and *As You Like It*, IV,i,152-3, "I cannot abide" (64) in both *Merry Wives*, I,i,286, and *2 Henry IV*, II,iv,109 (with "cannot abide" five more times in the collected works, including two more instances in *Merry Wives*). For "lamentable seeing" (5), we may compare "lamentable to behold" in *Henry V*, II,i,119; "cur'd and safe" (18) compares with Shakespearean word pairs like "sure and safe," "secure and safe," "politic and safe," etc. For "proper health" (24), we might compare Shakespearean usages like "proper life," "proper deformity," and "proper harm," among others. We have already noted that "most strange" (26) occurs twice in *Pericles*, III,ii; the phrase also occurs once earlier in that play, in III,Ch,22, with nine more instances in other canonical works. For "the freedome of the ayre" (34-5), compare "have the air at freedom" in *The Tempest*, IV,i,265; for "wake betime" (37), compare "rise betime" in *Antony*, IV,iv,20, along with the "to be up betimes . . . to go to bed betimes" passage in *Twelfth Night*, II,iii,2-9. For "making a property on him" (40), compare "talk of him / But as a property" in *Julius Caesar*, IV,i,39-40; "Oh, oh defend vs" (45) can be classed with usages like "O, defend me" in *The Tempest*, II,ii,88, "O, God defend me" in *Much Ado*, IV,i,77, and "O, yet defend me" in *Hamlet*, V,ii,324; for "reades his lecture" (96), compare "read lectures" in both *Coriolanus*, II,iii,235 and *Lucrece*, 618, and "read many lectures" in *As You Like It*, III,ii,347. The word "Mum" (11) appears twelve times in the acknowledged works, including three uses in *Merry Wives* and two in *Lear*; the alternative spelling "mun" (86) occurs once in the canon, in *Lear*, III,iv,99.

Finally, there is one other feature in IV,iii that demands attention. When the "corpse" of Corporal Oath is revived, he is spoken of as a "Ghost" (65); at the end of the scene, when Sir Godfrey invites everyone present to a banquet, he says that "in stead of a Iester, weele ha the ghost ith white sheete sit at vpper end a'th Table" (89-91). Critics since Farmer have recognized this as an allusion to *Macbeth*, comparable to other allusions in Marston's *Sophonisba* of 1606 and Beaumont's *The Knight of the Burning Pestle* of 1607, and consistent with the normal dating of *MacBeth* to 1606. Critics and commentators have also tended to cite this allusion as evidence that *The Puritan* is non-Shakespearean, on the natural assumption that Shakespeare would not allude to his own work in this manner. The point has some validity—but it loses much of its force when we conceive of the play as a Shakespearean collaboration rather than a work by Shakespeare alone. Note that the allusion occurs in the speech of a Plus character, and can thus be assigned plausibly to Middleton rather than to Shakespeare; the latter playwright would merely have had to accept its inclusion. I don't find this inherently unlikely—the allusion to *MacBeth*, after all, is not mocking or belittling. Even if one rejects this view, and insists on interpreting this allusion as a piece of negative evidence of a Shakespearean contribution to *The Puritan*, this single datum of evidence would not be weighty enough, I don't think, to counterbalance all the many and varied indications of Shakespeare's hand in the play.

Act V, Scene i

The final act of *The Puritan* is comprised of four scenes, the first three rather brief (fifty-seven, twenty-two, and forty-two lines long, respectively), and the fourth only moderately longer (127 lines). All four scenes display mixed features as far as the two dramatists are concerned. The first two seem mostly Middletonian but with possible minor Shakespearean contributions. In the final two scenes, Shakespeare's hand is more clearly evident.

In V,i, perhaps the most interesting element is "may wee steall vpon 'em, thinkst thou, Maister Edmond?" (45-7); compare "Shall we steal upon them, Ned, at supper?" in *2 Henry IV*, II,ii,158. The phrase "out of ioynt" (32) occurs three times in the collected works, including usages in *2 Henry IV* and *Troilus*; for "are the Brides stirring" (45), compare "Is thy master stirring" and "Is the King stirring" in *MacBeth*, II,iii,42 and 45. The phrase "by the same token" (50) appears in *Troilus*, I,ii,281, with variants in other Shakespearean works; "tumbled downe" (also 50) occurs in present or past tense four times in the collected works. For the use of "licquour" as a verb (54), we can cite similar uses in *Merry Wives*, IV,v,98 and *1 Henry IV*, II,i,85.

Act V, Scene ii

In V,ii: for "Whewh" (1), we can note that the single use of "Whew" in the canonical works occurs in a relevant play, *1 Henry IV*, II,ii,28; for "so rare a stirrer" (6), we can cite the synonymous "An early stirrer" in *2 Henry IV*, III,ii,2, the only use of the word form "stirrer" in the acknowledged works. For "the nature of the Climates" (13), compare "the quality o'th'climate" in *The Tempest*, II,i,200. And for Moll Plus' comments on the young ages of brides (13-17), see the similar lines on the same subject in *Romeo*, I,ii,8-13.

Act V, Scene iii

This scene gives us an excellent demonstration of the play's Shakespearean style, contrasting with the more simple and colloquial style of Middleton: the longest speech in the scene, Sir Oliver Muck-hill's fifteen-line speech (12-26), is a single compound sentence. As for specifics: "honourable personage" (16) occurs in plural form in *All's Well*, II,iii,261, while "much indebted" (17) appears in *Kinsmen*, II,v,30; "good words" (20) occurs eleven times in the collected works, including two instances in *Troilus* and single uses in *Timon* and *Coriolanus*, among other works; "bee it spoken" (27-8) occurs twice, as does "come already" (39); "good hope" (42) occurs three times, including a use in *Lear*. "Sir, my Lord is newly lighted from his Coache" (37-8) resembles "Sir Walter Blunt, new lighted from his horse" in *1 Henry IV*, I,i,63, with another "new lighted" in *Hamlet*, III,iv,59. For "knauishly abusd" (8), compare Shakespearean usages like "mightily abused," "notoriously abus'd" and "rankly abus'd"; for "aduance their selues" (9), compare "advance ourselves" in *2 Henry IV*, I,iii,7; for "made onely properties on's" (8-9), recall the "making a property on him" in IV,iii,40. Variants of "vpon our shoulders" (10) occur fourteen times in the Shakespeare canon, with three in *Merry Wives*—see III,iii,13, III,v,100, and IV,ii,109 of that play. For "besotted on slights and forgeries" (13), we find a similar "besotted on . . ." phrasing on *Troilus*, II,ii,143; for "in priuate to you" (15-16), compare "in private to him" in *2 Henry IV*, V,v,77, and "in private / With you" in *Henry VIII*, II,iv,207-8. For "needfull occasions" (21), compare "compelling occasion" in *Antony*, I,ii,137, with similar usages elsewhere; "without soothing" (27) is another of those "without . . ." phrasings that are so common in Shakespeare. Other more minor features in the scene show consistency with Shakespearean usage: to take one example, "How now, fellow?" (36) appears in *Julius Caesar*, III,ii,261, with "How now, good fellow?" in *Winter's Tale*, IV,iv,628.

Act V, Scene iv

The play's final scene begins with a feature singled out by David Lake as a Middletonism: "your honour is most chastly welcome" (2-3); and the abrupt intrusion of the anonymous Nobleman is entirely typical of the radical about-face endings of Middleton's early comedies. But the style of the scene is Shakespearean to a surprising degree. (Although, upon reflection, perhaps it is not so surprising: noblemen characters need to talk like noblemen and not like their social inferiors, and Shakespeare's Pye-boord style is much better suited to that task than is Middleton's Plus style.)

One fascinating feature in V,iv is the use of "blot" in line 6; examination shows that it is accompanied by some of the associations we would expect with a Shakespearean "blot" usage. We know that Shakespeare tends to link his uses of "blot" with words like "sun," "moon," "night," and "heaven"; "Moone" occurs twice in this scene (23, 49), along with "euilly planeted" (19). Another Shakespearean "blot" association is "eyes"; "eys" appears in line 59, along with "blind" (8) and "blinded" (58). Other Shakespearean "blot" associations are present thematically in this scene: the idea of "disguise" is inherent in the exposure of Pye-boord's and Idle's masquerade as fortune teller and conjurer; ideas of "constancy" and "sovereignty" also appear in lines about the "state of an vnheaded woman thats a widdow" (8-9) and "maintenance of credit, state, and posterity" (12-13) and similar usages. Shakespearean "blot" cluster associations are not as prominent here in V,iv as they are in some verse passages in the undoubted works—but it would be surprising if they were; given the fact that we are discussing a prose passage in a play that is half-Shakespearean at most, the "blot" associations here seem quite telling to me. (Remember, too, that not all of Shakespeare's canonical uses of "blot" yield major displays of his image-clustering habits. As Kenneth Muir has noted, there are only "traces" of the cluster in eleven of Shakespeare's "blot" uses in the acknowledged works.[22])

These "blot" associations appear in speeches that show many other signs of Shakespeare's style. Triplets and multiple terms are common: for "credit, state, and posterity" (12-13), compare "Of years, of country, credit" in *Othello*, I,iii,97, and "honor, state and seat" and "what state, what dignity, what honor" in *Richard III*, I,iii,111 and IV,iv,247, among similar phrasings; for "accurst, disastrous, and euilly planeted" (19), compare "Accurs'd, unhappy, wretched, hateful" in *Romeo*, IV,v,43, plus "planets evil" in *Troilus*, I,iii,92, among similar phrasings; for "meere knauery, deceit, and coozenage" (38-9), compare "such patchery, such juggling, and such knavery" in *Troilus*, II,iii,72, and "avaricious, false, deceitful" in *MacBeth*, IV,iii,58, plus a use of "mere cozenage" in *Merry Wives*, IV,v,63; "holy, pure, religious" (82) and "worship, state and credit" (92) conform to the same tendency. For "amongst ten thousand millions" (17-18), compare "amongst a whole million" in *Kinsmen*, IV,iii,37, in a similar context of extreme evil and degeneracy, plus "many mortal millions," also in *Kinsmen*, V,iii,24, and "many millions" in *Coriolanus*, III,iii,71. For "whome Fortune beates most, whome God hates most" (19-20), we can cite a wide range of such "most . . . most" constructions in the Shakespeare canon; see *Lear*, I,i,251 and IV,ii,43, *Timon*, I,i,96, and *Measure*, II,ii,119 for a few examples.

Similarly, for "An Impudent fellow best wooes you, a flattering lip best wins you" (23-5), such "best . . . best" formulations can also be found in Shakespeare, as, for instance, in *Antony*, V,i,6-7, and in *Kinsmen*, I,iv,46-7. For "all societies" (21)—a phrase that also occurs in *A Yorkshire Tragedy*, ii,84—the closest Shakespearean parallel is "All feasts, societies, and throngs of men" in *Timon*, IV,iii,21. For "the peeuish Moone that rules your bloods" (22-3), compare "Our bloods / No more obey the heavens" in *Cymbeline*, I,i,1-2; for "a flattering lip best wins you" (24-5), compare "That flattering tongue of yours won me" in *As You Like It*, IV,i,184. For "who talkes roughliest is most sweetest" (25-6), we find a similar contrast of extremes in "sweetest things turn sourest" in Sonnet 94,13; and note too that "most sweetest" is another example of a kind of redundancy that Shakespeare uses repeatedly in his works, as we noted in connection with the "most free-hartedst Gentleman" in III,iv,31-2.

"O wonderfull" (40) occurs four times in the collected works; for the progression of wonder in lines 40-6, "I wondred . . . I more wonder . . . I wondred most of all," we may compare "O wonderful, wonderful, and most wonderful wonderful" in

As You Like It, III,ii,191-2. For "faire wether on our side" (49), compare "Fair weather after you" in *Love's Labor's Lost*, I,ii,144, in a similar amorous context. The phrase "euery euill" (50) occurs in *Kinsmen*, I,ii,38; "full of Spleene" (54) occurs in *Shrew*, III,ii,10, while for the larger phrase, "full of Spleene and enuy," compare "full of envy" in *Troilus*, II,i,33, plus word pairs like "spite and envy" and "spleen and fury" in *Troilus*, I,ii,139 and III,v,112, and "cruelty and envy" in *Coriolanus*, IV,v,74. For "so suddaine aduancements" (55), compare "so sudden business" in *Romeo*, IV,iii,12; "vnder fauour" (63) appears earlier in *The Puritan*, in IV,iii,17, and also in *Timon*, III,v,40. For "truely lost" (64), compare "truly find" in *Cymbeline*, V,v,188; "Resolue him of that" (66) resembles "resolve me that" in *Shrew*, IV,ii,7, along with similar usages elsewhere in Shakespeare, "resolve me this," "resolve me now," etc. "In few words" (67) is found in *Timon*, III,v,96, and in *3 Henry VI*, IV,vii,53 ("few words" also appears in the preceding scene, V,iii,29, and eight times more in the collected works, including uses in *Lear*, *MacBeth*, *Troilus*, and *Measure*). For the coinage "arch-gull" (68), compare "arch-mock" in *Othello*, IV,i,70; "all this while" (71) occurs sixteen times in the collected works; for "O vilainy of vilanies" (76), compare "he hath out-villain'd villainy" in *All's Well*, IV,iii,273, both usages referring to the tricks in the two plays. "Ile rend my lyon from thy back" (85) compares with "from thy burgonet I'll rend thy bear" in *2 Henry VI*, V,i,208, both lines referring to someone being stripped of a heraldic symbol worn on his apparel.

The phrase "great pitty" (90) appears in *1 Henry IV*, I,iii,59; the coinage "vncharity" (also 90) conforms to Shakespeare's habit of using, and of coining, such "un" prefix words (note that "uncharitably" occurs in *Richard III*, I,iii,274, while "incharitable" is found in *The Tempest*, I,i,41). For "forged shapes" (94), compare "forgery of shapes" in *Hamlet*, IV,vii,89. For "worthy and deseruing parts" (97-8), we can observe that Shakespeare has a habit of linking word pairs with "parts"—consider "still and mental parts," "his mental and his active parts," and "spacious and dilated parts," all in *Troilus*, I,iii,200, and II,iii,174 and 250 respectively, plus "sick and feeble parts," "stubborn and uncourteous parts," and "choice and rarest parts" in other Shakespearean works. For "cherrish fruitfull Vertues" (98), compare "cherish'd by our virtues" in *All's Well*, IV,iii,74, and "cherish such high deeds" in *1 Henry IV*, V,v,30; "men of estimation" (101) occurs in *1 Henry IV*, IV,iv,32, and note "man of no estimation" in *Henry V*, III,vi,14; "great creddit" (106) occurs in *Othello*, II,i,287. For "applaud your choyce" (122), compare "applaud my choice" in *Titus*, I,i,321, in an identical choosing-a-mate context.

In line 108 we find a striking feature: Lady Plus, confronted with the deceitfulness of her intended husband, Captain Idle, and pressured from all sides to accept Sir Oliver Muck-hill in his place, is finally left speechless, and her silence is interpreted as consent by the males in the scene ("her scilence does consent too't"). A lead female character finds herself confronted with a surprise husband in the final scene of her play, after having established a negative position toward marriage earlier, and has her silence accepted as consent by socially powerful males—Lady Plus has a good deal in common with Isabella in *Measure for Measure* (at least in these respects). In this connection, it is interesting to quote Baldwin Maxwell on the "un-Middletonian generosity to the Puritan women" that is shown in this play; Middleton's treatment of his female Puritan characters tends to be harsher and more satirical than what we find in *The Puritan*.[23] Shakespeare does not share Middleton's apparent harsh attitude. After Lady Plus has yielded to Sir Oliver and has even asked his forgiveness for having resisted him, Sir Oliver tells her that she is "pardon'd" (114); similarly, the Duke of Venice tells Isabella that she is "pardon'd" in *Measure*, V,i,387.

Before leaving this final scene and bringing our survey of the play to a close, we must pause to note a few other features in V,iv—textual rather than stylistic features. A few readers may already have noticed a key feature when it was quoted above: the "sc" spelling of "scilence" in line 108. This spelling is very close to the "scilens" that is found eighteen times in the speech prefixes of the first quarto of *2 Henry IV*, and also in the fragment of *Sir Thomas More* in Shakespeare's handwriting, and "apparently nowhere else in the literature of the period."[24] Admittedly, the two spellings, while very close, are not identical, and if "scilens" may be unique to Shakespeare, "scilence" is not: examples can be found in some of the plays of the Beaumont-Fletcher corpus,[25] and perhaps elsewhere in the relevant literature. Yet, since Shakespeare seems to have had a habit of making such initial "sc" spellings—"Sceneca" for "Seneca," "Scicion" for "Sicyon," and "Scicinius" for "Sicinius" can all be found in the original texts—this "scilence" in *The Puritan* seems well worth noting.

Similarly interesting is the spelling "straingly" for "strangely" (64), which compares with the instances of "straing" and "straingers" in the *More* fragment and in the original 1609 text of *A Lover's Complaint*, 303. (The spelling "chaingd" for "chang'd" in V,iv,50 is comparable.) Also, the "in" spelling of "inough" (127) and the contractional form "gotst" (72) seem consistent with Shakespearean usage. Thus it appears quite possible that V,iv, like III,iii and iv, may have been set into type from Shakespearean holograph manuscript. And of course, such textual evidence is valuable confirmation of the stylistic evidence of Shakespeare's contribution to the play.

To venture a summation: the features in *The Puritan* that I have selected for comment vary widely in importance; and further study may show that some of them are of limited use as Middleton-Shakespeare discriminators. On the other hand, it should be remembered that this general and introductory survey exploits only a few of the potential avenues of exploration into the authorship of the play. I have chosen to concentrate heavily on the most basic kind of stylistic evidence, because I think that

such a basic approach is the most direct way of reaching a fundamental understanding of the play's authorship; but stylistic evidence is held in so little favor currently that I fear that much of
the material presented in the above paragraphs will not receive
the consideration it merits. (The present prejudice against this
kind of study is amply illustrated by the reception given to Gary
Taylor's arguments in favor of Shakespeare's authorship of the
poem "Shall I die?" Taylor has cited, among other evidence, a
wide variety of parallels, links, and commonalities between the
poem and Shakespeare's acknowledged works—while recog-
nizing that the individual elements so cited differ greatly in im-
port and significance.[26] Donald Foster, in his response to Taylor's arguments,[27] ignores the stronger pieces of stylistic
evidence, and condemns the weaker for being weak!) I certainly
do not consider features like "looke you" or "I warrant thee" or
"sincere loue" to be strong evidence of Shakespeare's contribution to The Puritan; I have noted them only as individual consistencies with Shakespeare's style as displayed in his acknowledged works. Such consistencies are worth noting, I believe, in
the context of other features in the play that definitely do constitute strong stylistic evidence of Shakespeare's part-authorship.
The strongest of these, to my mind, is the complex and subtle
relationship between I,ii of The Puritan and IV,vi of King
Lear—but there are various others, as we have seen. It is in the
context of these stronger features that the weaker can have a
legitimate confirmatory and supportive function.

The use of stylistic evidence to demonstrate authorship can
never be wholly objective; to the degree that it involves us in
subjectivity and ambiguity, I can understand why scholars
would want to eschew it for the apparent objectivity of textual
analysis. Yet stylistic evidence, for all its inherent difficulties, has
a fundamental and irrefutable place in authorship studies. External evidence, after all, can be simply wrong; textual evidence
can be complicated, obscured, and compromised by various
types of scribal and compositorial intervention (as happened to

some degree, I believe, in the case of *The Puritan*). The stylistic evidence of an author's hand could only be effaced by an overt rewriting of his work. The value of stylistic evidence is also relative to the distinctiveness of a given author's style—as Schoenbaum has observed, a writer with a nondescript style is a poor candidate for such investigation. Conversely, when the styles in question are as distinctive as those of Middleton and Shakespeare, stylistic evidence is more than justified—it is required.

And there remains the key point that the stylistic evidence is confirmed and verified by the textual and the external evidence. If the textual profile of *The Puritan* strongly favors Middleton, it also departs from Middleton's norm in certain specifics, and in what we can call Shakespearean directions. Also, there is the attribution of the play to "W. S." on the title page of the 1607 quarto. If we think back to Samuel Schoenbaum's eight guidelines for attribution studies (quoted in my book on *Merlin*), we recall that the primary guideline states that "external evidence cannot be ignored." I feel no need to ignore the external evidence in this case, or to dismiss it as false or misleading, or to try to conjecture it away with speculative explanations; to the contrary, I argue that an objective and open-minded study of *The Puritan* shows that the external evidence is valid, in a way and to a degree that has not been generally recognized—that the play was indeed written, in significant part, by a "W. S.," and that this "W. S." was William Shakespeare. If we accept the evidence of Middleton's hand in the play, as I think we must, I can't see how we can reject the comparable evidence for Shakespeare; the fact remains that the initials on the title page of the 1607 quarto are "W. S.," not "T. M."

One other point about *The Puritan*: Baldwin Maxwell has argued that the Plus family servants Nicholas St. Antlings and Simon St. Mary Overies derive their names from the contemporary Puritan preachers Nicholas Felton and William Symonds, clergymen who were associated with the parishes of St. Antlings and St. Mary Overies respectively, and that this blatant ridicule of actual clergymen helped lead to the collapse or suppression of the Children of Paul's, the company of child actors that performed the play and that passed out of existence soon after, in late 1606 or 1607.[28] If this argument is sound, it would mean that *The Puritan* had a greater impact upon contemporary theater conditions than did other "scandalous" plays like *The Isle of Dogs* and *Eastward Ho*, and deserves more attention from scholars and critics on that basis.

Conclusion

SOME OF THE POINTS I made in my study of *The Birth of Merlin* have, I think, relevance here. As with *Merlin*, I think that *A Yorkshire Tragedy* and *The Puritan* can be characterized as intimate collaborations between Shakespeare and another dramatist—plays in which Shakespeare's contribution tends to be disguised, obscured, watered down by the participation of another writer, thus making the Shakespearean aspects less immediately apparent and harder to recognize. This is not to say that distinctions cannot be made; I believe there is a clear Middleton-Shakespeare dichotomy in *The Puritan* based on the contrasting Plus family and Pye-boord materials, just as I believe that the Clown's part in *Merlin* shows itself to be the work of Rowley with little input from Shakespeare. Yet in each of these plays I see a significant degree of blending of the contributions, so that the schematic divisions shown in other collaborative plays (where, for instance, one participant writes the main plot and the other the subplot) are less useful in understanding the genesis of the *Tragedy* and *The Puritan*.

Indeed, I will go as far as to suggest that intimate collaboration seems to be the usual way in which Shakespeare collaborated: in plays like *Pericles* and *The Two Noble Kinsmen*, the sections that are often considered non-Shakespearean are in reality mixed texts, with Shakespearean and non-Shakespearean contributions intermingled. (I have already made the same argument in regard to the supposedly Fletcherian portions of *Henry VIII*; see the Appendix to my book on *Merlin*.) I find nothing inherently surprising, then, in the mode of collaboration that is evinced in *The Puritan* and *A Yorkshire Tragedy*; and that mode of collaboration has been the crucial factor preventing more general recognition of Shakespeare's contribution to these plays.

Secondly, I find it unsurprising that these plays were left out of the First Folio; I would argue that they were logically omitted because they are collaborative efforts rather than solo works, just as *Kinsmen, Pericles, More*, and *Merlin* were omitted as mixed texts—and as *Timon of Athens* was nearly omitted too, winning inclusion only late in the publishing process when it appeared that *Troilus and Cressida* would be unavailable. Their exclusion from the First Folio in no way "proves" that *The Puritan* or *A Yorkshire Tragedy* is wholly non-Shakespearean in authorship, any more than the similar exclusion of *Pericles* or *Kinsmen* does. And just as Philip Chetwind was correct in adding *Pericles* to the Third Folio, so, we can see now, he was correct in adding *A Yorkshire Tragedy* and *The Puritan*.

I would argue, too, that just as Shakespeare's late collaborations with Fletcher help us to comprehend his collaboration with Rowley in *Merlin*, and vice versa, so too can we take these two other Apocryphal plays with *Timon of Athens* to attain a better understanding of a specific phase of collaborative playwriting in Shakespeare's career. In light of this sustained phase of Middleton-Shakespeare collaboration in 1605-8, there is one other work that merits mention: *MacBeth* is the one play in the canon of Shakespeare's acknowledged works that is recognized by consensus scholarship as having some of Middleton's writing in it.[1] *Macbeth*, as noted earlier, appeared on the stage for the first time almost certainly in 1606, but it was not printed until it was included in the First Folio in 1623. Between those dates, *MacBeth* is thought to have been cut considerably, the extant text (the fifth shortest in the Folio, and the briefest of the tragedies) showing the resultant discontinuities; it also endured interpolation of non-Shakespearean materials. Middleton wrote a play called *The Witch* around 1615; a few years later, around 1618, Middleton apparently added some material originally written for *The Witch* to *MacBeth*, as part of a revision of Shakespeare's play for a new performance—Middleton functioning as something close to a house dramatist for the King's Men at this point in his career. Middleton's interpolations were contained in the text of *MacBeth* that was used as copy text for the first Folio; the Hecate material and the witches' songs in III,v and IV,i are Middletonian and not Shakespearean in authorship. Clearly, this Shakespeare-Middleton connection is of a different kind, and dates from a different era, than the truly collaborative efforts of the 1605-8 period. Yet it is striking to see that the one connection between the two playwrights recognized by consensus opinion occurs in a play that originated in the years when the two men were actively working together. It would no doubt be a mistake to read too much into this circumstance, or to lapse too far into speculation regarding it; but it is consistent with the overall argument of this book.

Finally, as with my study of *The Birth of Merlin*, let me stress at the end, as at the beginning, that this volume is meant to be introductory in nature and not definitive; it will, I hope, be a viable first step in a reconsideration of the plays in question. Obviously, there is much more that can be said about these two apocryphal plays and their relationship with the Shakespeare canon; among other approaches, a more detailed and thorough analysis of the intellectual, moral, and social values of the plays, and their commonalities with the works of the Shakespeare canon in these respects, would be very useful. I think, however, that the surveys of the plays in this volume do show that such commonalities exist—that it is not simple happenstance, for instance, that both of the Apocryphal plays have significant links with a single passage in *Timon of Athens* (see *Timon*, IV,iii,527-31, *The Puritan*, III,iv,58-61, and *A Yorkshire Tragedy*, iii,11). Rather, such linkages show that the three plays share the same thematic interest in debtors and bankruptcy; and the same point can be made in regard to other plays of the acknowledged canon (like *King Lear*). On a basic level, then, this study is designed to challenge the first assumption that most modern students of Shakespeare have about *A Yorkshire Tragedy* and *The Puritan*—that these plays are almost certainly non-Shakespearean. If this volume prompts at least a few readers to question that assumption, it will begin to achieve its goal.

Notes

INTRODUCTION

1. I rely on the standard assignment of shares of authorship in the plays of the Beaumont-Fletcher canon, based on the work of Cyrus Hoy and other scholars.

2. The numbers derive from the section on Thomas Dekker, by M. L. Wine, in *The Popular School: A Survey of Recent Studies in English Renaissance Drama*, Vol. II, edited by Terence P. Logan and Denzell S. Smith (Lincoln, University of Nebraska Press, 1975), pp. 19-39.

3. The claim is made by Heywood in his preface to *The English Traveller* (1633); quoted here from a secondary source, F. E. Halliday's *A Shakespeare Companion 1564-1964* (Baltimore, Penguin, 1964), p. 226.

4. John C. Meagher, "Hackwriting and the Huntingdon Plays," in *Elizabethan Theatre: Stratford-upon-Avon Studies 9*, edited by John Russell Brown and Bernard Harris (New York, St. Martin's Press, 1967), pp. 197-8.

5. Edward B. Partridge, "Ben Jonson: The Making of the Dramatist (1596-1602)," in *Elizabethan Theatre* (see note 4 above), pp. 221-2.

6. The seven additional plays: *Pericles, A Yorkshire Tragedy, The Puritan, Locrine, Sir John Oldcastle, Thomas Lord Cromwell*, and *The London Prodigal*.

7. E. A. J. Honigmann, *Shakespeare's Impact on His Contemporaries* (Totowa, NJ, Barnes & Noble, 1982), pp. 91-108.

8. Ibid., p. 93.

9. Cyrus Hoy, "The Shares of Fletcher and his Collaborators in the Beaumont and Fletcher Canon" (I), in *Evidence for Authorship*, edited by David V. Erdman and Ephim G. Fogel (Ithaca, NY, Cornell University Press, 1966), pp. 205-6.

TIMON OF ATHENS

1. Samuel Schoenbaum, *Middleton's Tragedies* (New York, Columbia University Press, 1955), p. 218.

2. Samuel Schoenbaum, *Internal Evidence and Elizabethan Dramatic Authorship* (Evanston, IL, Northwestern University Press, 1966), pp. 88-95, etc.

3. David J. Lake, *The Canon of Thomas Middleton's Plays* (Cambridge, Cambridge University Press, 1975), pp. 279-86.

4. Samuel Schoenbaum, *Middleton's Tragedies*, pp. 219-21.

5. Ibid., pp. 222-3.

6. Lake makes a similar point: *Middleton's Plays*, pp. 279-80.

A YORKSHIRE TRAGEDY

1. David Lake, *Middleton's Plays*, pp. 163-74.

2. Baldwin Maxwell, *Studies in the Shakespeare Apocrypha* (New York, Greenwood Press, 1969), pp. 169-73.

3. Ibid., pp. 138-9, 175-82.

4. Braddock also printed the first quarto of *A Midsummer Night's Dream* (for the stationer Thomas Fisher) in 1600, and the fourth and fifth editions of *Venus and Adonis* (for William Leake) in 1599 and 1602(?).

5. Pavier published the first quarto of *Sir John Oldcastle*, another play of the Shakespeare Apocrypha, in 1600, but without any attribution to Shakespeare (or anyone else); he was also associated with William Jaggard in the so-called "false folio" printings of Shake-

spearean works in 1619. Halliday calls him "A publisher of dubious reputation"; one of those dastardly stationers!

6. David Lake, *Middleton's Plays*, pp. 171-3.

THE PURITAN

1. Baldwin Maxwell, *Shakespeare Apocrypha*, pp. 113-14; David Lake, *Middleton's Plays*, p. 110.

2. In 1609, two years after the first quarto of *The Puritan*, Eld would print the first quarto of *Troilus and Cressida* for the booksellers Richard Bonian and Henry Walley, and the first edition of Shakespeare's Sonnets for Thomas Thorpe.

3. Baldwin Maxwell, *Shakespeare Apocrypha*, pp. 134-7.

4. Samuel Schoenbaum, *Internal Evidence*, pp. 182-3.

5. David Lake, *Middleton's Plays*, pp. 109-35.

6. Ibid., p. 113 n. 1.

7. Samuel Schoenbaum, "*A Chaste Maid in Cheapside* and Middleton's City Comedy," in *Studies in the English Renaissance Drama*, edited by J. W. Bennett, et. al. (New York, New York University Press, 1959), p. 295.

8. Thomas Middleton, *Michaelmas Term*, edited by Richard Levin (Lincoln, University of Nebraska Press, 1966), p. 109.

9. R. B. Parker, "Middleton's Experiments with Comedy and Judgement," in *Jacobean Theatre*, edited by John Russell Brown and Bernard Harris (New York, Capricorn, 1967), p. 183.

10. Baldwin Maxwell, *Shakespeare Apocrypha*, pp. 118-21.

11. Kenneth Muir, *Shakespeare as Collaborator* (New York, Barnes & Noble, 1960), p. 7.

12. The quotation from *The Maid of Honor* is from the text of that play in *Elizabethan and Stuart Plays*, edited by C. R. Baskerville, et. al. (New York, Holt, Rinehart and Winston, 1934).

13. One might wonder whether these commonalities between *Troilus* and *The Puritan* might be traceable to their common printer, George Eld, but I cannot see any sensible hypothesis for this—certainly it is less plausible than a connection based on common

authorship. Printers, after all, do not write the plays they print; playwrights do.

14. Baldwin Maxwell, *Shakespeare Apocrypha*, pp. 130-2.

15. Caroline Spurgeon, *Shakespeare's Imagery and What It Tells Us* (Cambridge, Cambridge University Press, 1935), pp. 78-80.

16. Ibid., pp. 33-5.

17. *The Riverside Shakespeare*, G. Blakemore Evans, textual editor (Boston, Houghton Mifflin, 1974), p. 110 n. 6.

18. Obviously, I accept the attribution of *The Second Maiden's Tragedy* to Middleton, deriving from the work of scholars like Oliphant, Barker, and Schoenbaum, among others; I think that the internal evidence is so overwhelmingly in favor of that conclusion that it overrides any objection.

19. Edward Armstrong, *Shakespeare's Imagination* (Lincoln, University of Nebraska Press, 1963), pp. 42-9.

20. David Lake, *Middleton's Plays*, p. 115.

21. Ibid., pp. 116-17.

22. Kenneth Muir, *Shakespeare as Collaborator*, p. 23.

23. Baldwin Maxwell, *Shakespeare Apocrypha*, p. 137.

24. *The Riverside Shakespeare*, p. 1689 n. 50.

25. An instance of "scilence" occurs in *The Maid's Tragedy*, I,ii,203; see: Fredson Bowers, general editor, *The Dramatic Works in the Beaumont and Fletcher Canon*, Vol. II (Cambridge, Cambridge University Press, 1970), p. 42. I have also found one other instance of "scilence" in the literature of English Renaissance drama, but I regret to admit that the reference has eluded me.

26. Gary Taylor, "Shakespeare's New Poem," *The New York Times Book Review*, Dec. 15, 1985.

27. Donald W. Foster, "'Shall I Die' Post Mortem: Defining Shakespeare," *Shakespeare Quarterly* 38 (1987), pp. 58-77; see especially pp. 63-5.

28. Baldwin Maxwell, *Shakespeare Apocrypha*, pp. 123-8.

CONCLUSION

1. David L. Frost, *The School of Shakespeare* (Cambridge, Cambridge University Press, 1968), pp. 262-7.

A YORKSHIRE Tragedy

Not so New as Lamentable and true.

Acted by his Maiesties Players at the *Globe.*

VVritten by VV. Shakspeare.

AT LONDON
Printed by *R. B.* for *Thomas Pauier* and are to bee sold at his
shop on Cornhill, neere to the exchange.
1608,

```
Q 1 = Quarto of 1608
Q 2 =    „      „  1619
F 1 = (Third) Folio Shakespeare, 1664
F 2 = (Fourth)  „                1685
  R = Rowe, 1709
  M = Malone, 1780
 St. = Steevens, ibid.
 Th. = Theobald, ibid.
 Kn. = Knight, 1839-41
  S = Simms, 1848
  T = Tyrrell, 1851
Haz. = Hazlitt, 1852
Molt. = Moltke, 1869
Col. = Collier, 1878
pr. ed. = present editor
```

ALL'S ONE,

OR, ONE OF THE FOURE PLAIES IN ONE, CALLED

A YORK-SHIRE TRAGEDY

AS IT WAS PLAID BY THE KINGS MAIESTIES PLAIERS.

⟨Dramatis Personae.

Husband.	Other Servants, and Officers.
Master of a College.	Wife.
Knight, a Justice of Peace.	Maid-servant.
Oliver, ⎫	A little Boy.⟩[1]
Ralph, ⎬ Serving-men.	
Samuel ⎭	

⟨SCENE I. *A room in Calverly Hall.*⟩
Enter Oliuer *and* Ralph, *two seruingmen.*

Oliu. Sirrah *Raph,* my yong Mistrisse is in
such a pittifull passionate humor for the long
absence of her loue—   3
Raph. Why, can you blame her? why,
apples hanging longer on the tree then when
they are ripe makes so many fallings; viz.,
Madde wenches, because they are not gathered
in time, are faine to drop of them selues, and
then tis Common you know for euery man to
take em vp.   10
Oliu. Mass, thou saiest true, Tis common
indeede: but, sirah, is neither our young
maister returned, nor our fellow Sam come
from London?   14
Ralph. Neither of either, as the Puritan
bawde saies. Slidd, I heare *Sam: Sam's* come,
her's! Tarry! come, yfaith, now my nose itches
for news.
Oliue. And so doe's mine elbowe.
[*Sam calls within.* Where are you there?] 20
Sam. Boy, look you walk my horse with
discretion; I haue rid him simply. I warrand
his skin sticks to his back with very heate:
if a should catch cold & get the Cough of the
Lunges I were well serued, were I not?   25

⟨*Enter* Sam.⟩ *Furnisht with things from
London.*

What, Raph and Oliuer.
Am⟨bo⟩. Honest fellow *Sam,* welcome,
yfaith! what tricks hast thou brought from
London?   29

¹ *Add. R* Scene I. *etc. add. M* S. D. and Raphe *Q 2*
6 viz.] so *Haz.*   8 drop off *M*   10 em] them *Q 2, etc.*
17 heere tarry *Q 2, Ff*: here he is; tarry *M*   25 S. D.
Enter Sam *add. M*   Furnisht, *etc. follows* 28 *Qq, Ff*

Sa. You see I am hangd after the truest
fashion: three hats, and two glasses, bobbing
vpon em, two rebato wyers vpon my brest,
a capcase by my side, a brush at my back, an
Almanack in my pocket, & three ballats in
my Codpeece: naie, I am the true picture of a
Common seruingman.   36
Oliuer Ile sweare thou art. Thou maist
set vp when thou wilt. Ther's many a one
begins with lesse, I can tel thee, that proues
a rich man ere he dyes. But whats the news
from London, *Sam?*   41
Ralph. I, thats well sed; whats the newes
from London, Sirrah? My young mistresse
keeps such a puling for hir loue.
Sam. Why, the more foole shee; I, the
more ninny hammer shee.   46
Oli. Why, *Sam,* why?
Sam. Why, hees married to another Long
agoe.
Ambo. Ifaith, ye Iest.   50
Sam. Why, did you not know that till
now? why, hees married, beates his wife,
and has two or three children by her: for you
must note that any woman beares the more
when she is beaten.   55
Raph. I, thats true, for shee beares the
blowes.
Oliu. Sirrah Sam, I would not for two
years wages, my yong mistres knew so much;
sheed run vpon the lefte hand of her wit, and
nere be her owne woman agen.   61
Sam. And I think she was blest in her
Cradle, that he neuer came in her bed: why,
hee has consumed al, pawnd his lands, and
made his vniuersitie brother stand in waxe

61 her] here *Q 1*   62–3 was..that..came] were
..had..come *conj. Percy*

for him—Thers a fine phrase for a scriuener!
puh, he owes more then his skins worth. 67
Oli. Is't possible?
Sa. Nay, Ile tell you moreouer, he calls
his wife whore as familiarly as one would cal
Mal & Dol, and his children bastards as
naturally as can bee.—But what haue we
heere? I thought twas somwhat puld downe
my breeches: I quite forgot my two potingsticks. These came from London; now any
thing is good heer that comes from London.
Oli. I, farre fetcht you know.   77
Sam. But speak in your conscience, yfaith,
haue not we as good potingsticks ith Cuntry
as need to be put ith fire. The mind of a
thing is all. The mind of a thing's all, and
as thou saidst eene now, farre fetcht is the
best thinges for Ladies.   83
Oliu. I, and for waiting gentle women to.
Sam. But, Ralph, what, is our beer sower
this thunder?
Oli. No, no, it holds countenance yet.
Sam. Why, then, follow me; Ile teach you
the finest humor to be drunk in. I learnd it
at London last week.   90
Am⟨bo⟩. I faith, lets heare it, lets heare it.
Sam. The brauest humor! twold do a man
good to bee drunck in't; they call it knighting
in London, when they drink vpon their knees.
Am⟨bo⟩. Faith, that's excellent. Come,
follow me: Ile giue you all the degrees ont in
order.   [*Exeunt.*

⟨SCENE II. *Another apartment in the
same.*⟩

Enter wife.

Wife. What will become of vs? all will
awaie.
My husband neuer ceases in expence,
Both to consume his credit and his house;
And tis set downe by heauens iust decree,
That Ryotts child must needs be beggery.   5
Are these the vertues that his youth did pro-
mise?
Dice, and voluptuous meetings, midnight
Reuels,
Taking his bed with surfetts: Ill beseeming
The auncient honor of his howse and name!
And this not all: but that which killes me
most,   10
When he recounts his Losses and false for-
tunes,

The weaknes of his state soe much deiected,
Not as a man repentant but halfe madd,
His fortunes cannot answere his expence:
He sits and sullenly lockes vp his Armes, 15
Forgetting heauen looks downward, which
makes him
Appeare soe dreadfull that he frights my heart,
Walks heauyly, as if his soule were earth:
Not penitent for those his sinnes are past,
But vext his mony cannot make them last:—
A fearefull melancholie, vngodly sorrow.   21
Oh yonder he comes, now in despight of ills
Ile speake to him, and I will heare him speake,
And do my best to driue it from his heart.

Enter Husband.

Hus. Poxe oth Last throw! it made   25
Fiue hundred Angels vanish from my sight.
Ime damnd, Ime damnd: the Angels haue
forsook me.
Nay, tis certainely true: for he that has
No coyne is damnd in this world: hee's gon,
hee's gon.
Wi. Deere husband.   30
Hus. Oh! most punishment of all, I haue
a wife.
Wi. I doe intreat you as you loue your
soule,
Tell me the cause of this your discontent.
Hus. A vengeance strip thee naked! thou
art cause,
Effect, quality, property, thou, thou, thou! 35
[*Exit.*
Wife. Bad, turnd to worse! both beggery
of the soule,
As of the bodie. And so much vnlike
Him selfe at first, as if some vexed spirit
Had got his form vpon him.—
[*Enter Husband againe.*
He comes agen.   40
He saies I am the cause; I neuer yet
Spoke lesse then wordes of duty, and of loue.
Hus. If mariage be honourable, then
Cuckolds are honourable, for they cannot be
made without marriage. Foole! what meant
I to marry to get beggars? now must my
eldest sonne be a knaue or nothing; he can-
not liue vppot'h foole, for he wil haue no land
to maintaine him: that mortgage sits like a
snaffle vpon mine inheritance, and makes me
chaw vpon Iron. My second sonne must be
a promooter, and my third a theefe, or an
vnderputter, a slaue pander.   53

73 somwhat *Q 1* : something *Q 2, etc.*   74, 79
poking sticks *R*   78–80 Sam. But speak . . fire *add.*
to Oliver's speech *M, etc.*   91 Faith *Q 2*   96 ont
Q 1 : of it *Q 2, etc.*   Scene II. *etc. add. M.*

14 *Placed after* 9 *Haz.*   25–7 *End* angels, damn'd,
Nay it is *M*   28 *Ends* coyne *Qq, etc. : corr. pr. ed.*
36–40 *Six lines Qq, ending* worse, bodie, first, spirit,
him, agen   37 As] And *M*

Oh beggery, beggery, to what base vses dost
thou put a man! I think the Deuill scornes
to be a bawde. He beares himselfe more
proudly, has more care on's credit. Base,
slauish, abiect, filthie pouertie!   58
  Wi. Good sir, by all our vowes I doe
    beseech you,
Show me the true cause of your discontent.
  Hus. Mony, mony, mony, and thou must
    supply me.   61
  Wi. Alas, I am the lest cause of your dis-
content,
Yet what is mine, either in rings or Iewels,
Vse to your own desire, but I beseech you,
As y'are a gentleman by many bloods,
Though I my selfe be out of your respect,   66
Thinke on the state of these three louely
  boies
You haue bin father to.
  Hu. Puh! Bastards, bastards, bastards;
begot in tricks, begot in tricks.   70
  Wi. Heauen knowes how those words
    wrong me, but I maie
Endure these griefes among a thousand more.
Oh, call to mind your lands already morgadge,
Your selfe woond into debts, your hopefull
  brother
At the vniuersitie in bonds for you,   75
Like to be ceasd vpon; And—
  Hu. Ha done, thou harlot,
Whome, though for fashion sake I married,
I neuer could abide; thinkst thou thy wordes
Shall kill my pleasures? Fal of to thy friends,
Thou and thy bastards begg: I will not bate
A whit in humor! midnight, still I loue you,
And reuel in your Company. Curbd in,
Shall it be said in all societies,   84
That I broke custome, that I flagd in monie?
No, those thy iewels I will play as freely
As when my state was fullest.
  Wi. Be it so.
  H. Nay I protest, and take that for an
    earnest,   [*spurns her*
I will for euer hould thee in contempt,   90
And neuer touch the sheets that couer thee,
But be diuorst in bed till thou consent,
Thy dowry shall be sold to giue new life
Vnto those pleasures which I most affect.   94
  Wi. Sir, doe but turne a gentle eye on me,
And what the law shall giue me leaue to do
You shall command.
  Hu. Look it be done: shal I want dust &
like a slaue

Weare nothing in my pockets but my hands
To fil them vp with nailes?   100
    [*holding his hands in his pockets.*
Oh much against my blood! Let it be done.
I was neuer made to be a looker on,
A bawde to dice; Ile shake the drabbs my
  selfe
And made em yeeld. I saie, look it be done.
  Wi. I take my leaue: it shall.   [*Exit.*
  Hu. Speedily, speedily. I hate the very
howre I chose a wife: a trouble, trouble!
three children like three euils hang vpon me.
Fie, fie, fie, strumpet & bastards, strumpet
and bastards!   110

    Enter three Gentlemen heering him.

  1 Gent. Still doe those loathsome thoughts
    Iare on your tongue?
Your selfe to staine the honour of your wife,
Nobly discended! Those whom men call
  mad
Endanger others; but hee's more then mad
That wounds himselfe, whose owne wordes
  do proclaym   115
Scandalls vniust, to soile his better name:
It is not fit; I pray, forsake it.
  2 Gen. Good sir, let modestie reproue you.
  3 Gen. Let honest kindnes sway so much
    with you.
  Hu. God den, I thanke you, sir, how do
you? adeiue! Ime glad to see you. Farewel
Instructions, Admonitions.   [*Exeun⟨t⟩ Gent.*

    Enter a seruant.

  Hu. How now, sirra; what wud you? 123
  Ser. Only to certifie you, sir, that my mistris
was met by the way, by them who were sent
for her vp to London by her honorable vnkle,
your worships late gardian.   127
  Hus. So, sir, then she is gon and so may
you be: But let her looke that the thing be
done she wots of: or hel wil stand more
pleasant then her house at home.   131
    ⟨*Exit seruant.*⟩

    Enter a Gentleman.

  Gen. Well or ill met, I care not.
  Hus. No, nor I.
  Gen. I am come with confidence to chide
    you.
  Hu. Who? me?   135
Chide me? Doo't finely then: let it not moue
  me,
For if thou chidst me angry, I shall strike.

---

57 on's *Q 1*: on his *Q 2, Ff*: of his *M*   65 you
are *Q 2, etc.* . 71 I maie *Q 1*: I'll *Q 2, Ff*   73
morgadge *Qq*: mortgag'd *Ff, etc.* 98, 99 *End* dust,
pockets *M*

99 my bare hands *M* 106–10 *Verse M* 108 vpon]
on *M* 128–31 *Verse M* 129 that *om. F 2, etc.* *S. D.*
Exit seruant *add. Q 2* 135–7 *Prose Qq*: *corr. M*

Gen. Strike thine owne follies, for it is they
    deserue
To be wel beaten. We are now in priuate:
Ther's none but thou and I. Thou'rt fond &
    peeuish,   140
An vncleane ryoter: thy landes and Credit
Lie now both sick of a consumption.
I am sorry for thee: that man spends with
    shame
That with his ritches does consume his name:
And such art thou.   145
    Hus. Peace.
    Gent. No, thou shalt heare me further:
Thy fathers and forefathers worthy honors,
Which were our country monuments, our
    grace,
Follies in thee begin now to deface.   150
The spring time of thy youth did fairely pro-
    mise
Such a most fruitfull summer to thy friends
It scarce can enter into mens beliefes,
Such dearth should hang on thee. Wee that
    see it,
Are sorry to beleeue it: in thy change,   155
This voice into all places wil be hurld:
Thou and the deuill has deceaued the world.
    Hus. Ile not indure thee.
    Gent. But of all the worst:
Thy vertuous wife, right honourably allied,
Thou hast proclaimed a strumpet.   161
    Hus. Nay, then, I know thee.
Thou art her champion, thou, her priuat friend,
The partie you wot on.
    Gent. Oh ignoble thought.
I am past my patient bloode: shall I stand
    idle   166
And see my reputation toucht to death?
    Hu. Ta's galde you, this, has it?
    Gent. No, monster, I will proue
My thoughts did only tend to vertuous loue.
    ⟨*Hus.*⟩ Loue of her vertues? there it goes.
    Gent. Base spirit,   172
To laie thy hate vpon the fruitfull Honor
Of thine own bed.
        [*They fight and the Husbands hurt.*
    Hu. Oh!
    Ge. Woult thou yeeld it yet?   176
    Hu. Sir, Sir, I haue not done with you.
    Gent. I hope nor nere shall doe.
                                [*Fight agen.*
    Hu. Haue you got tricks? are you in
    cunning with me?
    Gent. No, plaine and right.   180

He needs no cunning that for truth doth
    fight.   [*Husband falls downe.*
    Hu. Hard fortune, am I leueld with the
    ground?
    Gent. Now, sir, you lie at mercy.
    Hu. I, you slaue.
    Ge. Alas, that hate should bring vs to our
    graue.   185
You see my sword's not thirsty for your life,
I am sorrier for your woonde then your selfe.
Y'are of a vertuous house, show vertuous
    deeds;
Tis not your honour, tis your folly bleedes;
Much good has bin expected in your life, 190
Cancell not all mens hopes: you haue a wife
Kind and obedient: heape not wrongfull
    shame
On her ⟨and⟩ your posterity, ⟨nor blame
Your overthrow;⟩ let only sin be sore,
And by this fall, rise neuer to fall more. 195
And so I leaue you.   [*Exit.*
    Hu. Has the dogg left me, then,
After his tooth hath left me? oh, my hart
Would faine leape after him. Reuenge, I
    saye,
Ime mad to be reueng'd. My strumpet wife,
It is thy quarrel that rips thus my flesh, 201
And makes my brest spit blood, but thou shalt
    bleed.
Vanquisht? got downe? vnable eene to speak?
Surely tis want of mony makes men weake.
I, twas that orethrew me; Id'e nere bin downe
    els.   [*Exit.*

⟨SCENE III.   *The same.*⟩

*Enter wife in a riding suite with a
        seruingman.*

    Seru. Faith, mistris, If it might not bee
    presumtion
In me to tell you so, for his excuse
You had smal reason, knowing his abuse.
    Wi. I grant I had; but, alasse,
Whie should our faults at home be spred
    abroad?   5
Tis griefe enough within dores. At first
    sight
Myne Vncle could run ore his prodigall life
As perfectly, as if his serious eye
Had nombred all his follies:
Knew of his morgadg'd lands, his friends in
    bonds,   10

138 *Ends* they *Qq*: corr. *M*   follies *Q 2, etc.*: follie
Q 1   144 does *Q 1*: doth *Q 2, etc.*   149 county's
Haz.   154 on] upon *M*   169 will *om. Q 2, Ff*
171 *Prefix om. Q 1*   173 *Ends* fruitfull *Qq*

192-3 *The compositors appear to have corrupted two
lines into one*   and *add. Q 2* 193-4 nor .. overthrow
conj. pr. ed.   198 left] gor'd *conj. St.*   Scene
III. Another room in the same *M*   1 might *Q 1*:
may *Q 2, Ff*

Himselfe withered with debts: And in that
   minute
Had I added his vsage and vnkindnes,
Twould haue confounded euery thought of
   good:
Where now, fathering his ryots on his youth,
Which time and tame experience will shake
   off,   15
Gessing his kindnes to me (as I smoothd him
With all the skill I had) though his deserts
Are in forme vglier then an vnshapte Bear,
Hee's reddy to prefer him to some office
And place at Court, A good and sure reliefe
To al his stooping fortunes: twil be a meanes,
   I hope,   21
To make new league between vs, and redeeme
His vertues with his landes.
   Ser. I should think so, mistris. If he should
not now be kinde to you and loue you, and
cherish you vp, I should thinke the deuill
himselfe kept open house in him.   27
   Wi. I doubt not but he will now: prethe,
leaue me; I think I heare him comming.
   Ser. I am gone.   *[Exit.*
   Wife. By this good meanes I shal pre-
   serue my lands,   31
And free my husband out of vserers hands:
Now ther is no neede of sale, my Vncle's kind,
I hope, if ought, this will content his minde.—
Here comes my husband.   *[Enter Husband.*
   Hu. Now, are you come? wher's the mony?
lets see the mony Is the rubbish sold, those
wiseakers your lands? why, when? the mony!
where ist? powr't down, down with it, downe
with it: I say powr't oth ground! lets see't,
lets see't.   41
   Wi. Good sir, keep but in patience and I
   hope
My words shall like you well: I bring you
   better
Comfort then the sale of my Dowrie.
   Hu. Hah, whats that?   45
   Wi. Pray, do not fright me, sir, but vouchsafe me hearing: my Vncle, glad of your kindnes to mee & milde vsage—for soe I made it to
him—has in pitty of your declining fortunes,
prouided a place for you at Court of worth &
credit, which so much ouerioyd me—   51
   Hu. Out on thee, filth! ouer and ouerioyd, *[spurns her]* when Ime in torments?
Thou pollitick whore, subtiller then nine
Deuils, was this thy iourney to Nuncke, to set
downe the historie of me, of my state and

fortunes? Shall I that Dedicated my selfe to
pleasure, be nowe confind in seruice to crouch
and stand like an old man ith hams, my hat
off? I that neuer could abide to vncover my
head ith Church? base slut! this fruite beares
thy complaints.   62
   Wife. Oh, heauen knowes
That my complaintes were praises, and best
   wordes
Of you and your estate: onely my friends
Knew of our morgagde Landes, and were
   possest   66
Of euery accident before I came.
If thou suspect it but a plot in me
To keepe my dowrie, or for mine owne good
Or my poore childrens: (though it sutes a
   mother   70
To show a naturall care in their reliefs)
Yet ile forget my selfe to calme your blood:
Consume it, as your pleasure counsels you,
And all I wishe eene Clemency affoords:
Giue mee but comely looks and modest wordes.
   Hu. Money, whore, money, or Ile—   76
   (*Draws his dagger.*)

      Enters a seruant very hastily.
What the deuel? how now? thy hasty news?
                    [to his man.
   Se. Maie it please you, sir—
               [Seruant in a feare.
   Hu. What? maie I not looke vpon my
dagger? Speake villaine, or I will execute the
pointe on thee: quick, short.   81
   Ser. Why, sir, a gentleman from the
Vniuersity staies below to speake with you.
   Hu. From the Vniuersity? so! Vniuersity—
That long word runs through mee.   *[Exit.*
   Wi. Was euer wife so wretchedlie beset?
                 [Wif. alone.
Had not this newes stept in · between, the
   point   87
Had offered violence vnto my brest.
That which some women call greate misery
Would show but little heere: would scarce be
   seene   90
Amongst my miseries. I maie Compare
For wretched fortunes with all wiues that are.
Nothing will please him, vntill all be nothing.
He calls it slauery to be preferd,
A place of credit a base seruitude.   95
What shall become of me, and my poore
   children,
Two here, and one at nurse, my prettie
   beggers?

---

14 on *Q 2, etc.*: one *Q 1*   17 had)] *Parenthesis
continued to* Bear *M*   40 oth *Q 1* : on the *Q 2, etc.*
42-4 *Prose M*   49 has *Q 1* : hath *Q 2, etc.*   53
torment *Q 2, etc.*   56 of my *Q·1* : my *Q 2, etc.*

75 comely *Q 1* : pleasant *Q 2, etc.*   76 *S. D. add.*
Q 2   85 *S. D.* Exit *Q 2, etc.* : Exeunt *Q 1*   88
vnto *Q 2, Ff* : to *Q 1*   91 Among *Q 2, etc.*

I see how ruine with a palsie hand
Begins to shake the auncient seat to dust:
The heauy weight of sorrow drawes my liddes
Ouer my dankishe eies: I can scarce see: 101
Thus griefe will laste; it wakes and sleeps with
    mee.   ⟨*Exit.*⟩

⟨SCENE IV.   *Another apartment in the
        same.*⟩

*Enter the Husband with the master of the
        Colledge.*

Hu. Please you draw neer, sir, y'are exceeding welcome.
Ma. Thats my doubt; I fear, I come not to
be welcome.
Hus. Yes, howsoeuer.   5
Ma. Tis not my fashion, Sir, to dwell in
long circumstance, but to be plain, and
effectuall; therefore, to the purpose. The
cause of my setting forth was pittious and
lamentable: that hopefull young gentleman,
your brother, whose vertues we all loue
deerelie, through your default and vnnaturall
negligence, lies in bond executed for your
debt, a prisoner, all his studies amazed, his
hope strook dead, and the pride of his youth
muffled in theis dark clowds of oppression.
Hus. Hum, vm, vm.   17
Mr. Oh, you haue kild the towardest hope
of all our vniue⟨r⟩sitie: wherefore, without repentance and amends, expect pondorus and
suddain Iudgements to fall grieuosly vpon you.
Your brother, a man who profited in his diuine
Imployments, mighte haue made ten thousand
soules fit for heauen, now by your carelesse
courses caste in prison, which you must answere for, and assure your spirit it wil come
home at length.   27
Hu. Oh god! oh!
Mr. Wise men think ill of you, others
speake ill of you, no man loues you, nay, euen
those whome honesty condemnes, condemne
you: and take this from the vertuous affection
I beare your brother; neuer looke for prosperous hower, good thought, quiet sleepes,
contented walkes, nor any thing that makes
man perfect til you redeem him. What is
your answer? how will you bestow him? vpon
desperate miserye, or better hopes? I suffer,
till I heare your answere.   39
Hu. Sir, you haue much wrought with mee.

I feele you in my soule, you are your artes
master. I neuer had sence til now; your
sillables haue cleft me. Both for your words
and pains I thank you: I cannot but acknow-
ledge grieuous wronges done to my brother,
mighty, mighty, mighty wrongs.—Within
there!   47

Enter a seruingman.

Hu. Sir, Fil me a bowle of wine. Alas,
poore brother,
Brus'd with an execution for my sake.
        [*Exit seruant for wine.*
Mr. A bruse indeed makes many a mortall
sore   50
Till the graue cure em.

Enter with wine.

Hu. Sir, I begin to you, y'aue chid your
welcome.
Mr. I could haue wisht it better for your
sake.
I pledge you, sir, to the kind man in prison.
Hu. Let it be soe. Now, Sir, if you so please
        [*Drink both.*
To spend but a fewe minuts in a walke   56
About my grounds below, my man heere shall
Attend you.
I doubt not but by that time to be furnisht
Of a sufficient answere, and therein   60
My brother fully satisfied.
Mr. Good sir, in that the Angells would be
pleasd,
And the worlds murmures calmd, and I
should saye   63
I set forth then vpon a lucky daie.   [*Exit.*
Hu. Oh thou confused man! thy pleasant
sins haue vndone thee, thy damnation has
beggerd thee! That heauen should say we
must not sin, and yet made women! giues
our sences waie to finde pleasure, which
being found confounds vs. Why shold we
know those things so much misuse vs?—oh,
would vertue had been forbidden! wee should
then haue prooued all vertuous, for tis our
bloude to loue what were forbidden. Had
not drunkennes byn forbidden, what man
wold haue been foole to a beast, and Zany to
a swine, to show tricks in the mire? what is
there in three dice to make a man draw thrice
three thousand acres into the compasse of
a round little table, & with the gentlemans

---

98 palsied *M*   99 the] this *conj. Percy*   102
Thus] This *con:. M*   Exit *add. M*   Scene IV. *etc.*
add. M   17 Umph, umph, umph ! *M*   23 and
might *Q 2, etc.*   24 now] is now *M*   34 thoughts
F 2, etc.   sleep *F 2, etc.*

46 mighty, mighty, mighty, mighty, *Ff, etc.*   S. D.
sermiugman *Q 1*   48 Sir (*rom.*) Hu. (*ital.*) Fil (*rom.*)
Q 1 : Sir *om. Q 2, etc.*   50 *Ends* mortall *Q 1 : corr.*
Q 2   57–61 *Prose all add.*   68 give *M*   74 were
Q 1 : we are *Q 2, etc.*   80 little round *Q 2, etc.*

palsy in the hand shake out his posteritie
thieues or beggars? Tis done! I ha dont,
yfaith: terrible, horrible misery.——How well
was I left! very well, very wel. My Lands
shewed like a full moone about mee, but
nowe the moon's ith last quarter, wayning,
waining: And I am mad to think that moone
was mine; Mine and my fathers, and my
forefathers—generations, generations: downe
goes the howse of vs, down, downe it sincks.
Now is the name a beggar, begs in me! that
name, which hundreds of yeeres has made
this shiere famous, in me, and my posterity,
runs out.   94
    In my seede fiue are made miserable
besides my selfe: my ryot is now my brothers
iaylor, my wiues sighing, my three boyes
penurie, and mine own confusion.
                  [Teares his haire.
Why sit my haires vpon my cursed head?
Will not this poyson scatter them? oh my
    brother's   100
In execution among deuells that
Stretch him & make him giue. And I in
    want,
Not able for to lyue, nor to redeeme him.
Divines and dying men may talke of hell,
But in my heart her seuerall torments dwell.
Slauery and mysery! Who in this case 106
Would not take vp mony vpon his soule,
Pawn his saluation, liue at interest?
I, that did euer in abundance dwell,   109
For me to want, exceeds the throwes of hel.

    Enters his little sonne with a top and
              a scourge.

Son. What, aile you father? are you not
well? I cannot scourge my top as long as you
stand so: you take vp all the roome with your
wide legs. Puh, you cannot make mee
afeard with this; I feare no vizards, nor bug-
beares.   116
Husb. takes vp the childe by the skirts of his
    long coate in one hand and drawes his
    dagger with th' other.
Hu. Vp, sir, for heer thou hast no inheritance left.
Sonne. Oh, what will you do, father? I am
your white boie.   120
    Hu. Thou shalt be my red boie: take that.
                    [strikes him.
    Son. Oh, you hurt me, father.
    Hu. My eldest beggar! thou shalt not liue

to aske an vsurer bread, to crie at a great
mans gate, or followe, good your honour,
by a Couch; no, nor your brother; tis charity
to braine you.   127
    Son. How shall I learne now my heads
broke?
    Hu. Bleed, bleed rather then beg, beg!
                    [stabs him.
Be not thy names disgrace: 131
Spurne thou thy fortunes first if they be base:
Come view thy second brother.—Fates,
My childrens bloud
Shall spin into your faces, you shall see
How Confidently we scorne beggery!   136
              [Exit with his Sonne.

    (SCENE V. *A bed-room in the same.*)

Enter a maide with a child in her armes, the
      mother by her a sleepe.

M⟨aide⟩. Sleep, sweet babe; sorrow makes
    thy mother sleep:
It boades small good when heauines falls so
    deepe.
Hush, prettie boy, thy hopes might haue been
    better.
Tis lost at Dice what ancient honour won:
Hard when the father plaies awaie the Sonne!
No thing but misery serues in this house. 6
Ruine and desolation, oh!

    Enter husband with the boie bleeding.

    Hu. Whore, giue me that boy.
          [Striues with her for the child.
    M⟨aide⟩. Oh help, help! out alas, murder
murder!
    Hus. Are you gossiping, prating, sturdy
    queane?   10
Ile breake your clamor with your neck: down
    staires!
Tumble, tumble, headlong! [*Throws her down.*]
    So!
The surest waie to charme a womans tongue
Is break hir neck: a pollitician did it.
    Son. Mother, mother; I am kild, mother.
    W⟨ife⟩ wakes. Ha, whose that cride? oh
me, my children!   16
Both, both, both; bloudy, bloudy.
            [catches vp the yongest.
    Hu. Strumpet, let go the boy, let go the
beggar.
    Wi. Oh my sweet husband!   20

101-2 *Lines end* make, lyue *Q 1*: stretch him, want
Q 2, Ff   103 for to lyue] to relieve *S*   106-7
End mysery, vpon his *Q 1: corr. Q 2*   111 Whataile
Qq, etc.   115 afraid *Q 2, etc.*   123-7 *Verse M, div.*
after beggar, bread, follow, brother

126 coach *Q 2, etc.*   130 *Ends* bleed *M* beg *once M*
133 brother's *M*   133-5 *Div. after* fates, faces, see *Qq*
133-4 *One line M* Scene V. *add. M* A . . same *add.*
pr. ed. 6 serues] survives *conj. S* 10 you prating
M Ends Ile *Q 1* 11 *Ends* neck *Q 2, Ff* 12 *Ends*
headlong *Qq*   S. *D.* W. wakes *after* 16 *Q 1*

Hus. Filth, harlot.

Wi. Oh what will you doe, deare husband?

Hus. Giue me the bastard.

Wi. Your owne sweet boy!

Hu. There are too many beggars.   25

Wi. Good my hus-band—

Hu. Doest thou preuent me still?

Wi. Oh god!

Hus. Haue at his hart!   29

    [*Stabs at the child in hir armes.*

Wi. Oh my deare boy! [*gets it from hir.*

Hu. Brat, thou shalt not liue to shame thy howse!

Wi. Oh heauen!

    [*shee's hurt and sinks downe.*

Hu. And perish! now begon:

Thers whores enow, and want wold make thee one.   35

Enter a lusty seruant.

Ser. Oh Sir, what deeds are these?

Hus. Base slaue, my vassail:

Comst thou between my fury to question me?

Ser. Were you the Deuil, I would hold you, sir.   40

Hu. Hould me? presumption! Ile vndoe thee for't.

Ser. Sbloud, you haue vndone vs all, sir.

Hu. Tug at thy master!

Ser. Tug at a Monster.   45

Hus. Haue I no power? shall my slaue fetter me?

Ser. Nay, then, the Deuil wrastles, I am thowne.

Hu. Oh, villane, now Ile tug thee, [*ouercomes him*] now Ile teare thee;   51

Set quick spurres to my vassaile, bruize him, trample him.

So! I think thou wilt not folow me in hast.

My horse stands reddy sadled. Away, away;

Now to my brat at nursse, my sucking begger.

Fates, Ile not leaue you one to trample on. 56

⟨SCENE VI.   *Court before the house.*⟩

The Master meets him.

Ma. How ist with you, sir? me thinks you looke

Of a distracted colour.

Hu. Who? I, sir? tis but your fancie.

Please you walke in, Sir, and Ile soone resolue you:

I want one small parte to make vp the som,   5

And then my brother shall rest satisfied.

Mr. I shall be glad to see it: sir, Ile attend you.   [*Exeu⟨nt⟩.*

⟨SCENE VII.   *The same as Scene V.*⟩

Ser. Oh I am scarce able to heaue vp my selfe:

Ha's so bruizd me with his diuelish waight,

And torne my flesh with his bloud-hasty spurre.

A man before of easie constitution

Till now hells power supplied, to his soules wrong.   5

Oh, how damnation can make weake men strong.

Enter Master, and two seruants.

Ser. Oh, the most pitteous deed, sir, since you came.

Mr. A deadly greeting! has he somde vp theis

To satisfie his brother? heer's an other: 9

And by the bleeding infants, the dead mother.

Wi. Oh, oh.

Mr. Surgeons, Surgeons! she recouers life.

One of his men al faint and bloudied!

1 Seru. Follow, our murderous master has took horse   14

To kill his child at nurse: oh, follow quickly.

Mr. I am the readiest, it shal be my charge

To raise the towne vpon him.

    [*Exit Mr. and seruants.*

1 Ser. Good sir, do follow him.

Wi. Oh my children.

1 Ser. How is it with my most afflicted Mistris?   20

Wi. Why do I now recouer? why half liue?

To see my children bleede before mine eies?

A sight able to kill a mothers brest

Without an executioner! what, art thou Mangled too?   25

1 Ser. I, thinking to preuent what his quicke mischiefes

Had so soone acted, came and rusht vpon him.

We strugled, but a fowler strength then his

Ore threw me with his armes; then did he bruize me

And rent my flesh, and robd me of my haire,

Like a man mad in execution;   31

Made me vnfit to rise and follow him.

Wi. What is it has beguild him of all grace

And stole awaie humanity from his brest?

To slaie his children, purpose to kill his wife,

And spoile his saruants.   36

---

35 enough *M*   52-3 *Prose Qq*   56 trample one
Qq   Scene VI. *etc. add. M S. D.* Enter Husband;
to him the Master of the College *M*   1-2 *Prose Qq,*
Ff: dir. after sir *M*

Scene VII. *add. M* The same, *etc. pr. ed.*   5
Hell *M*   8 hath *Q 2, etc.*   23 *Ends* without *M*
24-5 *One line Qq*   26-7 *Prose Qq*   35 purpose *M* :
purpos'd *Qq, Ff*

Enters two seruants.

Ambo Sir, please you leaue this most
    accursed place,
A surgeon waites within.

Wi. Willing to leaue it!
Tis guiltie of sweete bloud, innocent bloud: 40
Murder has tooke this chamber with ful hands,
And wil nere out as long as the house stands.
                        [Exeunt.

⟨SCENE VIII.   *A high road.*⟩
Enter Husband as being thrown off his horse,
        And falls.

Hu. Oh stumbling Iade, the spauin ouer-
    take thee,
The fiftie diseases stop thee!
Oh, I am sorely bruisde; plague founder thee:
Thou runst at ease and pleasure. Hart of
    chance!
To Throw me now within a flight oth Towne,
In such plaine euen ground, sfot, a man   6
May dice vp on't, and throw awaie the
    Medowes.
Filthy beast.
    Crie within. Follow, follow, follow.
Hus. Ha! I hear sounds of men, like hew
    and crie: 10
Vp, vp, and struggle to thy horse, make on;
Dispatch that little begger and all's done.
Kni. Heere, this waie, this waye!
Hus. At my backe? oh,
What fate haue I? my limbes deny mee go, 15
My will is bated: beggery claimes a parte.
Oh, could I here reach to the infants heart.

Enter M. of the Colledge, 3. Gentlemen, and
    others with Holberds.
                    [Finde him.
All. Heere, heere: yonder, yonder.
Mr. Vnnaturall, flintie, more then bar-
    barous:
The Scithians or the marble hearted fates 20
Could not haue acted more remorselesse deeds
In their relentlesse natures, then these of
    thine:
Was this the answear I long waited on,
The satisfaction for thy prisoned brother?
Hus. Why, he can haue no more on's then
    our skins,   25
And some of em want but fleaing.

S. D. Enter a Servant *M*   37 Ambo sir *(ital.) Q 1* :
Ambo *Q 2* : Both *Ff* : Serv. *M*   you *Qq, Ff* : you to *M*
Scene VIII. *etc. add. M*   4 hart, of *Q 1*   13 Kni.
Q 1 : Cry Within *Q 2, etc.*   Here, here *M*   16
bated] barred *conj. St.*   20 or the *conj. St.* : in their
Qq, Ff : even the *M*   fates] feats *conj. Percy*   25
Why *om. Q 2, Ff*   on's *Q 1* : of vs *Q 2, etc.*

1. Gen. Great sinnes haue made him im-
    pudent.
Mr. H'as shed so much bloud that he
    cannot blush.
2. Ge. Away with him, bear him a long to
    the Iustices;
A gentleman of woorship dwels at hand;   30
There shall his deeds be blazd.
Hus. Why, all the better.
My glory tis to haue my action knowne:
I grieue for nothing, but I mist of one.   34
Mr. Ther's little of a father in that griefe:
Beare him away.   *[Exeunt.*

⟨SCENE IX.   *A room in the house of a Magis-*
        trate.⟩

Enters a knight with two or three Gentle-
        men.

Knig. Endangered so his wife? murdered
his children?
1 Gen. So the Cry comes.
Kni. I am sorry I ere knew him,
That euer he took life and naturall being   5
From such an honoured stock, and fair
    discent;
Til this black minut without staine or blemish.
1 Gent. Here come the men.

Enter the master of the colledge and the rest,
    with the prisoner.

Kni. The serpent of his house! Ime sorry
For this time that I am in place of iustice. 10
Mr. Please you, Sir.
Kni. Doe not repeate it twice I know too
    muche,
Would it had nere byn thought on:
Sir, I bleede for you.
1 Gent. Your fathers sorrows are aliue in
    me: 15
What made you shew such monstrous crueltie?
Hu. In a worde, Sir, I haue consumd all,
plaid awaie long acre, and I thought it the
charitablest deed I could doe to cussen beggery
and knock my house oth head.   20
Kni. Oh, in a cooler bloud you will repent
    it.
Hus. I repent now, that ones left vnkild,
My brat at nurse. Oh, I would ful fain haue
    weand him.
Knigh. Well, I doe not think but in to
    morrowes iudgement
The terror will sit closer to your soule,   25

29 a long *om. Q 2, etc.*   Scene IX. *etc. add. M*
3 *Prefix* 1. Gent. *Q 2, etc.* : 4 Gen. *Q 1*   comes *Q 1* :
goes *Q 2, etc.*   8, 15 *Prefix* 4 Gent. *Q 1*   9, 10
Prose Qq : *corr. M*   17–20 Verse *Qq, Ff*

When the dread thought of death remembers
you;
To further which, take this sad voice from me:
Neuer was act plaid more vnnaturally.
Hus. I thank you, Sir.
Kni. Goe, leade him to the Iayle: 30
Where iustice claimes all, there must pitty
faile.
Hus. Come, come, awaie with me.
                              [*Exit prisoner.*
Mr. Sir, you deserue the worship of your
place.
Would all did so: in you the law is grace.
Kni. It is my wish it should be so.—
Ruinous man,   35
The desolation of his howse, the blot
Vpon his predecessors honord name!
That man is neerest shame that is past shame.
                                    [*Exit.*

⟨SCENE X.   *Before Calverly Hall.*⟩
*Enter Husband with the officers, The Maister
and gentlemen, as going by his house.*
Hu. I am right against my howse, seat of
my Ancestors: I heare my wif's aliue; but
much endangered. Let me intreat to speak
with her, before the prison gripe me.

Enter his wife, brought in a chaire.
Gent. See heer she comes of her selfe.   5
Wi. Oh my sweete Hus-band, my deere
distressed husband,
Now in the hands of vnrelenting lawes!
My greatest sorrow, my extremest bleeding,
Now my soule bleeds.   9
Hu. How now? kind to me? did I not
wound thee, left thee for dead?
Wife. Tut, farre greater wounds did my
brest feele:
Vnkindnes strikes a deeper wound then steele;
You haue been still vnkinde to mee.
Hus. Faith, and so I thinke I haue: 15
I did my murthers roughly, out of hand,
Desperate and suddaine, but thou hast deuiz'd
A fine way now to kill me, thou hast giuen
mine eies
Seauen woonds a peece; now glides the deuill
from mee,   19
Departes at euery ioynt, heaues vp my nailes.
Oh catch him new torments, that were near
inuented,
Binde him one thousand more, you blessed
Angells,
In that pit bottomlesse; let him not rise

To make men act vnnaturall tragedies,
To spred into a father, and in furie,   25
Make him his childrens executioners:
Murder his wife, his seruants, and who not?
For that man's darke, where heauen is quite
forgot.
Wi. Oh my repentant husband.
Hus. My deere soull, whom I too much
haue wrongd,   30
For death I die, and for this haue I longd.
Wi. Thou sholdst not (be assurde) for
these faults die,
If the law cold forgiue as soone as I.
Hus. What sight is yonder?
                        [*Children laid out.*
Wi. Oh, our two bleeding boyes   35
Laid forth vpon the thresholde.
Hu. Heer's weight enough to make a
heart-string crack.
Oh, were it lawfull that your prettie soules
Might looke from heauen into your fathers
eyes,   39
Then should you see the penitent glasses melt,
And both your murthers shoote vpon my
cheekes;
But you are playing in the Angells lappes,
And will not looke on me,
Who void of grace, kild you in beggery.
Oh that I might my wishes now attaine,   45
I should then wish you liuing were againe,
Though I did begge with you, which thing
I feard:
Oh, twas the enemy my eyes so bleard.
Oh, would you could pray heauen me to
forgiue,
That will vnto my end repentant liue.   50
Wi. It makes me eene forget all other
sorrowes
And liue aparte with this.
⟨*Officer*⟩. Come will you goe?
Hus. Ile kisse the bloud I spilt and then I goe:
My soull is bloudied, well may my lippes be so.
Farewell, deere wife, now thou and I must
parte,   56
I of thy wrongs repent me with my harte.
Wi. Oh staye, thou shalt not goe.
Hus. That's but in vaine, you see it must
be so.
Farewell, ye bloudie ashes of my boyes! 60
My punishments are their eternall ioyes.
Let euery father looke into my deedes,
And then their heirs may prosper, while mine
bleeds.

Scene X. etc. add. M   1-4 Verse M, div. after ancestors, endanger'd, before   6-7 Prose Qq, Ff   21 new
om. M, etc.

26 executioners Qq, Ff: executioner M, etc.   30
O my M   35 Ends vpon Q 1: corr. Q 2   43 Ends
grace M   52 live apart St.: leaue parte Qq, Ff
53 Prefix Officer add. Q 2

Wi. More wretched am I now in this
  distresse,
      [*Exeunt Husband with holberds.*
Then former sorrows made me.   65
  Mr. Oh kinde wife,
Be comforted. One ioy is yet vnmurdered:
You haue a boy at nursse; your ioy's in him.
  Wi. Dearer then all is my poore husbands
      life:
Heauen giue my body strength, which yet is
    faint   70
With much expence of bloud, and I will kneele,

Sue for his life, nomber vp all my friends,
To plead for pardon ⟨for⟩ my deare husbands life.
  Mr. Was it in man to woond so kinde a
    creature?
Ile euer praise a woman for thy sake.   75
I must returne with griefe; my answer's set:
I shall bring newes weies heauier then the
    debt.—
Two brothers: one in bond lies ouerthrowne,
This on a deadlier execution.

FINIS.

66 *Ends* comforted *Qq, Ff*   70 is yet *Ff, etc*   73 for *add. Q 2*

THE
PVRITAINE

Or

THE VVIDDOVV
of Watling-ftreete.

Acted by the Children of Paules.

Written by W. S.

Imprinted at London by G. E ld.
1607.

```
Q      = Quarto of 1607
F 1    = (Third) Folio Shakespeare, 1664
F 2    = (Fourth)  „          „      1685
R      = Rowe, 1709
Pope   = Supplement to Pope's Shakespeare, 1728
M      = Malone, 1780
St.    = Steevens, ibid.
Th.    = Theobald, ibid.
S      = Simms, 1848
T      = Tyrrell, 1851
Haz.   = Hazlitt, 1852
pr. ed. = present editor
```

THE PVRITAINE WIDDOW

(THE
ACTORS
NAMES
In the *Play* Intituled
The PURITAN WIDOW.

The Scene *London.*

Lady Plus, a Citizens Widow.
Frances } *her two Daughters.*
Moll
Sir Godfrey, Brother-in-Law to the Widow
Plus.
Master Edmond, Son to the Widow Plus.
George Pye-boord, a Schollar and a Citizen.
Peter Skirmish, an old Soldier.

Captain Idle, a Highway-man.
Corporall Oath, a vain-glorious Fellow.
Nicholas St. Antlings }
Simon St. Mary Overies } *Serving-men to*
Frailty } *the Lady Plus.*
Sir Oliver Muck-hill, a Suiter to the Lady Plus.
Sir Iohn Penny-Dub, a Suiter to Moll.
Sir Andrew Tipstaffe, a Suiter to Frances.
The Sheriffe of London.
Puttock }
Ravenshaw } *Two of the Sheriffs Serjeants.*
Dogson, a Yeoman.
A Noble-man.
A Gentleman Citizen.
Officers.) [1]

ACTVS PRIMVS.

(SCENE I. *A Garden behind the widow's house.*)

Enter the Lady Widdow-Plus, *her two Daughters* Franke *and* Moll, *her husbands Brother an old Knight* Sir Godfrey, *with her Sonne and heyre* Maister Edmond, *all in moorning apparell;* Edmond *in a Cypresse Hatte. The Widdow wringing her hands, and bursting out into passion, as newly come from the Buriall of her husband.*

Widow. Oh, that euer I was borne, that euer I was borne!

Sir Godfrey. Nay, good Sister, deare sister, sweete sister, bee of good comfort; shew your selfe a woman, now or neuer. 5

Wid. Oh, I haue lost the deerest man, I haue buried the sweetest husband that euer lay by woman.

Sir God. Nay, giue him his due, hee was indeed an honest, vertuous, discreet, wise man, —hee was my Brother, as right as right. 11

Wid. O, I shall neuer forget him, neuer forget him; hee was a man so well giuen to a woman—oh! 14

Sir Godf. Nay, but, kinde Sister, I could weepe as much as any woman, but, alas, our teares cannot call him againe: me thinkes you are well read, Sister, and know that death is as common as *Homo,* a common name to all men:—a man shall bee taken when hee's making water.—Nay, did not the learned Parson, Maister *Pigman,* tell vs een now, that all Flesh is fraile, wee are borne to dye, Man ha's but a time: with such like deepe and pro-

found perswasions, as hee is a rare fellow, you know, and an excellent Reader: and for example, (as there are examples aboundance,) did not Sir *Humfrey Bubble* dye tother day? There's a lustie Widdow; why, shee cryed not aboue halfe an houre—for sha:ne, for shame! then followed him old Maister *Fulsome,* the Vsurer: there's a wise Widdow; why, shee cryed nere a whitte at all. 33

Wid. O, rancke not mee with those wicked women: I had a Husband out-shinde 'em all.

Syr Godf. I, that he did, Ifaith: he out-shind 'em all. 37

Widd. Doost thou stand there and see vs all weepe, and not once shed a teare for thy fathers death? oh, thou vngratious sonne and heyre, thou! 41

Edm. Troth, Mother, I should not weepe, I'me sure; I am past a childe, I hope, to make all my old Schoole fellowes laughe at me; I should bee mockt, so I should. Pray, let one of my Sisters weepe for mee. Ile laughe as much for her another time. 47

Widd. Oh, thou past-Grace, thou! out of my sight, thou gracelesse impe, thou grieuest mee more then the death of thy Father! oh, thou stubborne onely sonne! hadst thou such an honest man to thy Father—that would deceaue all the world to get riches for thee—and canst thou not afforde a little salt water? he that so wisely did quite ouer-throw the right heyre of those lands, which now you respect not: vp euery morning betwixt foure and fiue; so duely at Westminster Hall euery Tearme-Time, with all his Cardes and writings, for thee, thou wicked *Absolon*—oh, deare husband! 61

---

¹ *Dram. Pers. add. F1* Scene I. *etc. add. M* 10
wise-man *Q*

59 Cardes] charts *conj. M*

135

Edm. Weep, quotha? I protest I am glad hee's Churched; for now hee's gone, I shall spend in quiet.

Fran. Deere mother, pray cease; halfe your Teares suffize.   65
Tis time for you to take truce with youre eyes;
Let me weepe now.

Widd. Oh, such a deere knight! such a sweete husband haue I lost, haue I lost!—If Blessed bee the coarse the raine raynes vpon, he had it powring downe.   71

Syr Godf. Sister, be of good cheere, wee are all mortall our selues. I come vppon you freshly. I neare speake without comfort, heere me what I shall say:—my brother ha's left you wellthy, y'are rich.   76

Widd. Oh!

Syr Godf. I say y'ar rich: you are also faire.

Widd. Oh !   79

Sir Godf. Goe too, y'are faire, you cannot smother it; beauty will come to light; nor are your yeares so farre enter'd with you, but that you will bee sought after, and may very well answere another husband; the world is full of fine Gallants, choyse enow, Sister,—for what should wee doe with all our Knights, I pray, but to marry riche widdowes, wealthy Cittizens widdowes, lusty faire-browd Ladies? go too, bee of good comfort, I say: leaue snobbing and weeping—Yet my Brother was a kinde hearted man—I would not haue the Elfe see mee now! —Come, pluck vp a womans heart—here stands your Daughters, who be well estated, and at maturity will also bee enquir'd after with good husbands, so all these teares shall bee soone dryed vp and a better world then euer— What, Woman? you must not weepe still; hee's dead, hee's buried—yet I cannot chuse but weepe for him!

Wid. Marry againe! no! let me be buried quick then!   100
And that same part of Quire whereon I tread
To such intent, O may it be my graue;
And that the Priest may turne his wedding praiers,
E'en with a breath, to funerall dust and ashes!
Oh, out of a million of millions, I should neuer finde such a husband; hee was vnmatchable,— vnmatchable! nothing was to hot, nor to deere for mee, I could not speake of that one thing, that I had not: beside I had keyes of all, kept all, receiu'd all, had money in my purse, spent what I would, went abroad when I would, came home when I would, and did all what I would.

Oh, my sweete husband! I shall neuer haue the like.   114

Sir Godf. Sister, nere say so; hee was an honest brother of mine, and so, and you may light vpon one as honest againe, or one as honest againe may light vpon you: that's the properer phrase, indeed.   119

Wid. Neuer! oh, if you loue me, vrge it not.
                                   ⟨*Kneels.*⟩
Oh may I be the by-word of the world,
The common talke at Table in the mouth
Of euery Groome and Wayter, if e're more
I entertaine the carnall suite of Man!   124

Mol. I must kneele downe for fashion too.

Franck. And I, whom neuer man as yet hath scalde,
Ee'n in this depth of generall sorrow, vowe
Neuer to marry, to sustaine such losse   128
As a deere husband seemes to be, once dead.

Mol. I lou'd my father well, too; but to say, Nay, vow, I would not marry for his death— Sure, I should speake false Lattin, should I not? Ide as soone vow neuer to come in Bed.   133
Tut! Women must liue by th' quick, and not by th' dead.

Wid. Deare Copie of my husband, oh let me kisse thee.   135
How like him is this Modell this briefe Picture
[*Drawing out her husbands Picture.*
Quickens my teares: my sorrowes are renew'd
At this fresh sight.

Sir Godf. Sister—

Wid. Away,   140
All honesty with him is turn'd to clay.
Oh my sweete husband, oh——

Franck. My deere father!
[*Exeunt mother and daughters.*

Mol. Heres a puling, indeede! I thinke my Mother weepes for all the women that euer buried husbands; for if from time to time all the Widdowers teares in England had beene bottled vp, I do not thinke all would haue fild a three-halfe-penny Bottle. Alasse, a small matter bucks a hand-kercher,—and som-times the spittle stands to nie Saint *Thomas* a Watrings. Well, I can mourne in good sober sort as well as another; but where I spend one teare for a dead Father, I could giue twenty kisses for a quick husband.   [*Exit Moll.*   155

Sir Godf. Well, go thy waies, old *Sir God-frey*, and thou maist be proud on't, thou hast a kinde louing sister-in-lawe; how constant! how passionate! how full of Aprill the poore

75 has *Ff, etc.*   101 o' the choir *M*   107 too hot *M* : so hot *Q, Ff* : too good *conj. S*

S. D. Kneels *add. R after* 124   131 vow .. his *Ff, etc.* : now .. her *Q*   136 this .. this *M* : their .. their *Q, Ff*   138 this *M* : their *Q, Ff*   147 widows' *conj. St.*

136

soules eyes are! Well, I would my Brother knew on't, he should then know what a kinde wife hee had left behinde him: truth, and twere not for shame that the Neighbours at th' next garden should heare me, betweene ioye and griefe I should e'en cry out-right!   165
                              [*Exit Sir Godfrey.*
Edmond. So, a faire riddance! My fathers layde in dust; his Coffin and he is like a whole-meate-pye, and the wormes will cut him vp shortlie. Farewell, old Dad, farewell. Ile be curb'd in no more. I perceiue a sonne and heire may quickly be made a foole, and he will be one, but Ile take another order.—Now she would haue me weepe for him, for-sooth, and why? because he cozn'd the right heire, beeing a foole, and bestow'd those Lands vpon me his eldest Son; and therefore I must weepe for him, ha, ha. Why, al the world knowes, as long as twas his pleasure to get me, twas his duety to get for me: I know the law in that point; no Atturney can gull me. Well, my Vncle is an olde Asse, and an Admirable Cockscombe. Ile rule the Roast my selfe. Ile be kept vnder no more; I know what I may do well inough by my Fathers Copy: the Lawe's in mine owne hands now: nay, now I know my strength, Ile be strong inough for my Mother, I warrant you.   [*Exit.* 187

(SCENE II. *A street.*)

Enter George Py-bord, *a scholler and a Citti-zen, and vnto him an old souldier,* Peter Skirmish.

Pye. What's to be done now, old Lad of War? thou that wert wont to be as hot as a turn-spit, as nimble as a fencer, & as lowzy as a schoole-maister; now thou art put to silence like a Sectarie.—War sitts now like a Iustice of peace, and does nothing. Where be your Muskets, Caleiuers and Hotshots? in *Long-lane,* at Pawne, at Pawne.—Now keies are your onely Guns, Key-guns, Key-guns, & Bawdes the Gunners, who are your centinells in peace, and stand ready charg'd to giue warning, with hems, hums, & pockey-coffs; only your Chambers are licenc'st to play vpon you, and Drabs enow to giue fire to 'em.   14
Skir. Well, I cannot tell, but I am sure it goes wrong with me, for since the cessure of the wars, I haue spent aboue a hundred crownes out a purse. I haue beene a souldier any time this forty yeares, and now I perceiue an olde souldier and an olde Courtier haue both

one destinie, and in the end turne both into hob-nayles.
Pie. Prety mistery for a begger, for indeed a hob-naile is the true embleme of a beggers shoo-soale.   25
Skir. I will not say but that warre is a bloud-sucker, and so; but, in my conscience, (as there is no souldier but has a peice of one, tho it bee full of holes like a shot Antient; no matter, twill serue to sweare by) in my conscience, I thinke some kinde of Peace has more hidden oppressions, and violent heady sinnes, (tho looking of a gentle nature) then a profest warre.   34
Pye. Troth, and for mine owne part, I am a poore Gentleman, & a Scholler: I haue beene matriculated in the Vniuersitie, wore out sixe Gownes there, seene some fooles, and some Schollers, some of the Citty, and some of the Countrie, kept order, went bare-headed ouer the Quadrangle, eate my Commons with a good stomacke, and Battled with Discretion; at last, hauing done many slights and trickes to maintaine my witte in vse (as my braine would neuer endure mee to bee idle,) I was expeld the Vniuersitie, onely for stealing a Cheese out of *Iesus* Colledge.
Skir. Ist possible?   48
Pye. Oh! there was one *Welshman* (God forgiue him) pursued it hard; and neuer left, till I turnde my staffe toward *London,* where when I came, all my friends were pitt-hold, gone to *Graues,* (as indeed there was but a few left before.) Then was I turnde to my wittes, to shift in the world, to towre among Sonnes and Heyres, and Fooles, and Gulls, and Ladyes eldest Sonnes, to worke vpon nothing, to feede out of Flint, and euer since has my belly beene much beholding to my braine. But, now, to returne to you, old *Skirmish:* I say as you say, and for my part wish a Turbulency in the world, for I haue nothing to loose but my wittes, and I thinke they are as mad as they will be: and to strengthen my Argument the more, I say an honest warre is better then a bawdy peace, as touching my profession. The multiplicitie of Schollers, hatcht and nourisht in the idle Calmes of peace, makes 'em like Fishes one deuoure another; and the communitie of Learning has so plaide vpon affections, and thereby almost Religion is come about to Phantasie, and discredited by being too much spoken off—in so many & meane mouths, I my selfe, being a Scholler and a Graduate, haue no other comfort by

164 betwixt *Ff*   Scene II. *etc. add. M*   18 of
purse *F ?*

31 ha's *Q*   62 nothing in the world but *Ff*   70
ha's *Q*   71 that thereby *M*

137

my learning, but the Affection of my words, to know how Scholler-like to name what I want, & can call my selfe a Begger both in Greeke and Lattin: and therfore, not to cogg with Peace, Ile not be afraide to say, 'tis a great Breeder, but a barren Nourisher: a great getter of Children, which must either be Theeues or Rich-men, Knaues or Beggers.   83

Skirmish. Well, would I had beene borne a Knaue then, when I was borne a Begger; for if the truth were knowne, I thinke I was begot when my Father had neuer a penny in his purse.   88

Pye. Puh, faint not, old *Skirmish*; let this warrant thee, *Facilis Descensus Auerni,* 'tis an easie iourney to a Knaue; thou maist bee a Knaüe when thou wilt; and Peace is a good Madam to all other professions, and an arrant Drabbe to vs, let vs handle her accordingly, and by our wittes thriue in despight of her; for since the lawe liues by quarrells, the Courtier by smooth God-morrowes; and euery profession makes it selfe greater by imperfections, why not wee then by shiftes, wiles, and forgeries? and seeing our braines are our onely Patrimonies, let's spend with iudgment, not like a desperate sonne and heire, but like a sober and discreete Templer,—one that will neuer marche beyond the bounds of his allowance. And for our thriuing meanes, thus: I my selfe will put on the Deceit of a Fortune-teller.   107

Skirm. A Fortune-teller? Very proper.

Pye. And you of a figure-caster, or a Con-iurer.

Skir. A Coniurer?   111

Pye. Let me alone; Ile instruct you, and teach you to deceiue all eyes, but the Diuels.

Skir. Oh I, for I would not deceiue him, and I could choose, of all others.   115

Pye. Feare not, I warrant you; and so by those meanes wee shall helpe one another to Patients, as the condition of the age affoords creatures enow for cunning to worke vpon.

Skir. Oh wondrous! new fooles and fresh Asses.   121

Pye. Oh, fit, fit! excellent.

Skir. What, in the name of Coniuring?

Pye-boord. My memorie greetes mee happily with an admirable subiect to graze vpon: The Lady-Widdow, who of late I sawe weeping in her Garden for the death of her Husband; sure she 'as but a watrish soule, and halfe on't

by this time is dropt out of her Eyes: deuice well managde may doe good vppon her: it stands firme, my first practise shall bee there.

Skir. You haue my voyce, *George.*   132

Pye-boord. Sh'as a gray Gull to her Brother, a foole to her onely sonne, and an Ape to her yongest Daughter.—I ouerheard 'em seuerally, and from their words Ile deriue my deuice; and thou, old *Peter Skirmish,* shall be my second in all slights.

Skir. Nere doubt mee, *George Pye-boord,*— onely you must teach me to coniure.   140

Enter Captaine Idle, *pinioned, & with a guarde of Officers passeth ouer the Stage.*

Pye. Puh, Ile perfect thee, *Peter.*—How now? what's hee?

Skir. Oh *George!* this sight kils me. Tis my sworne Brother, Captaine *Idle.*

Pye. Captaine *Idle!*   145

Skir. Apprehended for some fellonious act or other. Hee has started out, h'as made a Night on't, lackt siluer. I cannot but commend his resolution; he would not pawne his Buffe-Ierkin. I would eyther some of vs were employde, or might pitch our Tents at Vsurers doores, to kill the slaues as they peepe out at the Wicket.   153

Pye. Indeed, those are our ancient Enimies; they keepe our money in their hands, and make vs to bee hangd for robbing of 'em. But, come, letts follow after to the Prison, and know the Nature of his offence; and what we can steed him in, hee shall be sure of; and Ile vphold it still, that a charitable Knaue is better then a soothing Puritaine.   [*Exeunt.* 161

⟨Scene III. *A street.*⟩

Enter at one doore Corporall Oth, *a Vaine-glorious fellow; and at the other, three of the Widdow Puritaines Seruingmen,* Nicholas Saint-Tantlings, Simon Saint-Mary-Oueries, *and* Frailtie, *in black scuruie mourning coates, and Bookes at their Girdles, as comming from Church. They meete.*

Nich. What, Corporall *Oth?* I am sorry we haue met with you, next our hearts; you are the man that we are forbidden to keepe company withall. Wee must not sweare I can tell you, and you haue the name for swearing.   5

Sim. I, Corporall *Oth,* I would you would do so much as forsake vs, sir; we cannot abide you, wee must not be seene in your company.

76 Affliction *Q*   94 us. Let *M*   100 the onely *Ff* 108 A Fortune-teller *add. to line* 107 *Q, Ff: corr. M* 109 of *om. Ff, etc.*   117 those] these *Ff*   128 she'as] she's *Ff*: she has *M*   on't] of't *M*

136 drive *Ff*   Scene III. *etc. add. M*

138

Frail. There is none of vs, I can tell you, but shall be soundly whipt for swearing. 10

Corp. Why, how now, we three? Puritanicall Scrape-shoes, Flesh a good Fridayes! a hand.

All. Oh!

Corp. Why, *Nicholas Saint-Tantlings, Simon Saint Mary Oueries,* ha's the De'ele possest you, that you sweare no better? you halfe-Christned *Katomites,* you vngod-motherd Varlets, do's the first lesson teach you to bee proud, and the second to bee Cocks-combes? proud Cocks-combes! not once to doe dutie to a man of Marke! 21

Frail. A man of Marke, quatha! I doe not thinke he can shew a Beggers Noble.

Corpo. A Corporall, a Commander, one of spirit, that is able to blowe you vp all drye with your Bookes at your Girdles. 26

Simon. Wee are not taught to beleeue that, sir, for we know the breath of man is weake. [*Corporall breaths vpon* Frailtie.

Frail. Foh, you lie, *Nicholas*; for here's one strong inough. Blowe vs vp, quatha: hee may well blow me aboue twelue-score off an him. I warrant, if the winde stood right, a man might smell him from the top of Newgate, to the Leades of Ludgate. 34

Corp. Sirrah, thou Hollow-Booke of Waxe-candle—

Nicho. I, you may say what you will, so you sweare not.

Corp. I sweare by the—— 39

Nicho. Hold, hold, good Corporall *Oth*; for if you sweare once, wee shall all fall downe in a sowne presently.

Corp. I must and will sweare: you quiuering Cocks-combes, my Captaine is imprisoned, and by *Vulcans* Lether Cod-piece point——

Nich. O *Simon,* what an oth was there. 46

Frail. If hee should chance to breake it, the poore mans Breeches would fall downe about his heeles, for *Venus* allowes him but one point to his hose. 50

Corpor. With these my Bullye-Feete I will thumpe ope the Prison doores, and braine the Keeper with the begging Boxe, but Ile see my honest sweete Captaine *Idle* at libertie.

Nich. How, Captaine *Ydle*? my olde Aunts sonne, my deere Kinsman, in Capadochio? 56

Cor. I, thou Church-peeling, thou Holy-paring, religious outside, thou! if thou hadst any grace in thee, thou would'st visit him, releiue him, sweare to get him out. 60

Nicho. Assure you, Corporall, indeed-la, tis the first time I heard on't.

25 drye] three *M*   42 swoon *F2, etc.*   51
-Feete] -Fleet *F2*

Cor. Why do't now, then, *Marmaset*: bring forth thy yearly-wages, let not a Commander perish! 65

Simon. But, if hee bee one of the wicked, hee shall perish.

Nich. Well, Corporall, Ile e'en along with you, to visit my Kinsman: if I can do him any good, I will,—but I haue nothing for him. *Simon* Saint *Mary Oueris* and *Fraylty,* pray make a lie for me to the Knight my Maister, old *Sir Godfrey.*

Cor. A lie? may you lie then? 74

Fray. O, I, we may lie, but we must not sweare.

Sim. True, wee may lie with our Neighbors wife, but wee must not sweare we did so.

Cor. Oh, an excellent Tag of religion! 79

Nic. Oh *Simon,* I haue thought vpon a sound excuse; it will go currant: say that I am gon to a Fast.

Sim. To a Fast? very good.

Nic. I, to a Fast, say, with Maister *Ful-bellie* the Minister. 85

Sim. Maister *Ful-bellie*? an honest man: he feedes the flock well, for he's an excellent feeder.   [*Exit Corporal, Nicholas.*

Fray. O, I, I haue seene him eate vp a whole Pigge, and afterward falle to the pettitoes. 90
[*Exit Simon and Fraylty.*

⟨SCENE IV.⟩

The Prison, Marshalsea.

Enter Captaine Ydle *at one dore, and* ⟨later
Pyeboard and⟩ old souldier at the other.
George Py-boord, *speaking within.*

Pye. Pray turne the key.

Sker. Turne the key, I pray.

Cap. Who should those be? I almost know their voyces.— 4
O my friends!   [*Entring.*
Ya're welcome to a smelling Roome here.
You newly tooke leaue of the ayre; ist not a strange sauour?

Pie. As all prisons haue: smells of sundry wretches,
Who, tho departed, leaue their sents behind 'em. 10
By Gold, Captaine, I am sincerely sory for thee.

Cap. By my troth, *George,* I thanke thee; but pish,—what must be, must bee.

Skir. Captaine, what doe you lie in for? ist great? what's your offence? 15

Cap. Faith, my offence is ordinarie,—com-

75 me must *Q*   89 vp *om. F2, etc.*   90 falls *Q*:
fall *Ff, etc.*   Scene IV. *add. M*   7 ist] has it *M*

139

mon: A Hie-waye; and I feare mee my penaltie will be ordinarie and common too: a halter.

Pie. Nay, prophecy not so ill; it shall go heard,
But Ile shift for thy life.   20

Cap. Whether I liue or die, thou'art an honest *George.* Ile tell you—siluer flou'd not with mee, as it had done, (for now the tide runnes to Bawdes and flatterers.) I had a start out, and by chaunce set vpon a fat steward, thinking his purse had beene as pursey as his bodie; and the slaue had about him but the poore purchase of tenne groates: notwithstanding, beeing descryed, pursued, and taken, I know the Law is so grim, in respect of many desprate, vnsetled souldiours, that I feare mee I shall daunce after their pipe for't.   33

Skir. I am twice sory for you, *Captaine:* first that your purchase was so small, and now that your danger is so great.

Cap. Push, the worst is but death,—ha you a pipe of Tobacco about you?   38

Skir. I thinke I haue there abouts about me.
                              [*Cap. blowes a pipe.*

Cap. Her's a cleane Gentleman too, to receiue.

Pie. Well, I must cast about some happy slight.

Worke braine, that euer didst thy Maister right!

Cor. Keeper! let the key be turn'd!   44
                    [*Corporall and Nicholas within.*

Nic. I, I pray, Maister keeper, giues a cast of your office.

Cap. How now? more Visitants?—what, Corporal *Oth*?

Pie. Skir. Corporal?   49

Cor. In prison, honest Captaine? this must not be.

Nic. How do you, Captaine Kinsman?

Cap. Good Cocks-combe! what makes that pure, starch'd foole here?   54

Nic. You see, Kinsman, I am som-what bould to call in, and see how you do. I heard you were safe inough, and I was very glad on't that it was no worse.

Cap. This is a double torture now,—this foole by'th booke   59
Do's vexe me more then my imprisonment.
What meant you, Corporall, to hooke him hither?

Cor. Who, he? he shall releiue thee, and supply thee;
Ile make him doo't.   63

37 Pish *M*   59-61 *Prose Ff, etc.*   60 Do's] doth
Ff, etc.

Cap. ⟨*aside, to Oath*⟩ Fie, what vaine breath you spend! hee supply? Ile sooner expect mercy from a Vsurer when my bonds forfetted, sooner kindnesse from a Lawier when my mony's spent: nay, sooner charity from the deuill, then good from a Puritaine! Ile looke for releife from him, when Lucifer is restor'd to his bloud, and in Heauen againe!   71

Nic. I warrant, my Kinsman's talking of me, for my left eare burnes most tyrannically.

Pie. Captaine *Ydle,* what's he there? hee lookes like a Monkey vpward, and a Crane downe-ward.   76

Cap. Pshaw, a foolish Cozen of mine; I must thanke God for him.

Pie. Why, the better subiect to worke a scape vpon; thou shalt e'en change clothes with him, and leaue him here, and so—   81

Cap. Push, I publish't him e'en now to my Corporall: hee will be damn'd, ere hee do mee so much good; why, I know a more proper, a more handsome deuice then that, if the slaue would be sociable. Now, goodman *Fleere-face?*   87

Nic. Oh, my Cozen begins to speake to me now: I shall bee acquainted with him againe, I hope.

Skirmish. Looke what ridiculous Raptures take hold of his wrinckles.   92

Pye. Then, what say you to this deuice? a happy one, Captaine?

Capt. Speake lowe, *George*; Prison Rattes haue wider eares then those in Malt-lofts. 96

Nic. Cozen, if it lay in my power, as they say—to—do—

Cap. Twould do me an exceeding pleasure, indeed, that, but nere talke forder on't: the foole will be hang'd, ere he do't.   101
                              ⟨*To the Corporal.*⟩

Cor. Pax, Ile thump 'im to't.

Pie. Why, doe but trie the Fopster, and breake it to him bluntly.   104

Cap. And so my disgrace will dwell in his Iawes, and the slaue slauer out our purpose to his Maister, for would I were but as sure on't as I am sure he will deny to do't.

Nic. I would bee heartily glad, Cozen, if any of my friendships, as they say, might—stand—ah—   111

Pie. Why, you see he offers his friend-ship foolishly to you alreadie.

Captain. I, that's the hell on't, I would hee would offer it wisely.

Nich. Verily, and indeed la, Couzen— 116

Cap. I haue tooke note of thy fleeres a good while: if thou art minded to do mee good—as

100 but *om. Ff*   101 *S. D. add. M*   102 'im] 'em *Q*

thou gapst vpon me comfortably, and giu'st
me charitable faces, which indeede is but
a fashion in you all that are Puritaines—wilt
soone at night steale me thy Maisters chaine?
Nich. Oh, I shall sowne!
Pie. Corporal, he starts already.   124
Cap. I know it to be worth three hundred
Crownes, & with the halfe of that I can buy
my life at a Brokers, at second hand, which
now lies in pawne to th' Lawe: if this thou
refuse to do, being easie and nothing dangerous, in that thou art held in good opinion
of thy Maister, why tis a palpable Argument
thou holdst my life at no price, and these thy
broken & vnioynted offers are but only created
in thy lip, now borne, and now buried, foolish
breath onlie. What, woult do't? shall I looke
for happinesse in thy answere?   136
Nic. Steale my Maisters chaine, quo'the?
no, it shal nere bee sayd, that *Nicholas* Saint
Tantlings committed Bird-lime!
Cap. Nay, I told you as much; did I not?
tho he be a Puritaine, yet he will be a true
man.
Nich. Why, Couzen, you know tis written,
thou shalt not steale.   144
Cap. Why, and foole, *thou shalt loue thy
Neighbour,* and helpe him in extremities.
Nich. Masse, I thinke it bee, indeede: in
what Chapter's that, Couzen?
Cap. Why, in the first of Charity, the 2.
verse.   150
Nich. The first of Charity, quatha! that's
a good iest; there's no such Chapter in my
booke!
Cap. No, I knew twas torne out of thy
Booke, & that makes so little in thy heart. 155
Pie. Come, let me tell you, ya're too
vnkinde a Kinsman, yfaith; the Captaine louing you so deerely, I, like the Pomwater of
his eye, and you to be so vncomfortable: fie,
fie.   160
Nic. Pray, do not wish me to bee hangd:
any thing else that I can do, had it beene to
rob, I would ha don't; but I must not steale:
that's the word, the literall, *thou shalt not
steale;* and would you wish me to steale, then?
Pie. No, faith, that were to much, to speake
truth: why, woult thou nim it from him? 167
Nich. That I will!
Pie. Why, ynough, bullie; hee shall bee
content with that, or he shall ha none; let mee
alone with him now! Captaine, I ha dealt
with your Kins-man in a Corner; a good,
kinde-naturde fellow, mee thinkes: goe too,

you shall not haue all your owne asking, you
shall bate somewhat on't: he is not contented
absolutely, as you would say, to steale the
chaine from him,—but to do you a pleasure,
he will nim it from him.   178
Nich. I, that I will, Couzen.
Cap. Well, seeing he will doe no more, as
far as I see, I must bee contented with that.
Cor. Here's no notable gullery!   182
Pie. Nay, Ile come neerer to you, Gentleman: because weele haue onely but a helpe
and a mirth on't, the knight shall not loose
his chaine neither, but ⟨it shall⟩ be only laide
out of the way some one or two daies.
Nich. I, that would be good indeed,
Kinsman.   189
Pie. For I haue a farder reach to profit vs
better by the missing on't onelie, then if wee
had it out-right, as my discourse shall make
it knowne too you.—When thou hast the
chaine, do but conuay it out at back-dore into
the Garden, and there hang it close in the
Rosemary banck but for a small season; and
by that harmlesse deuise, I know how to
winde Captaine *Ydle* out of prison: the Knight
thy Maister shall get his pardon and release
him, & he satisfie thy Maister with his own
chaine, & wondrous thankes on both hands.
Nich. That were rare indeed, la: pray, let
me know how.   203
Pie. Nay, tis very necessary thou shouldst
know, because thou must be imploide as an
Actor.
Nich. An Actor? O no, that's a Plaier;
and our Parson railes againe Plaiers mightily,
I can tell you, because they brought him
drunck vpp'oth Stage once,—as hee will bee
horribly druncke.   211
Cor. Masse, I cannot blame him then,
poore Church-spout.
Pie. Why, as an Intermedler, then?
Nich. I, that, that.   215
Pie. Giue me Audience, then: when the
old Knight thy Maister has ragde his fill for
the losse of the chaine, tell him thou hast
a Kinsman in prison, of such exquisit Art,
that the diuill himselfe is french Lackey to
him, and runnes bare-headed by his horse-
bellie (when hee has one) whome hee will
cause with most *Yrish* Dexterity to fetch his
chaine, tho twere hid vnder a mine of sea-cole,
and nere make Spade or Pickaxe his instruments: tell him but this, with farder instruc-

154 know *Ff*   155 makes it so *R, etc.*   169 shall]
will *Ff, etc.*

186 it shall *add. M*   191 on't] of't *M*   194
at] at a *Ff, etc.*   208 against *Ff, etc.*   210 upo'th'
Ff   217 radge *Q*: rag'd *Ff*

141

tions thou shalt receiue from mee, and thou
shoust thy selfe a Kinsman indeed.

Cor. A dainty Bullie.

Skir. An honest Booke-keeper.   230

Cap. And my three times thrice hunnie
Couzen.

Nich. Nay, grace of God, Ile robbe him on't
suddainlie, and hang it in the Rosemary banck;
but I beare that minde, Couzen, I would not
steale any thing, mee thinkes, for mine owne
Father.   237

Skir. He beares a good minde in that,
Captaine!

Pie. Why, well sayde; he begins to be an
honest fellow, faith.

Cor. In troth, he does.   242

Nich. You see, Couzen, I am willing to do
you any kindnesse, alwaies sauing my selfe
harmelesse.   [*Exit Nicholas.*

Captaine. Why, I thanke thee; fare thee
well, I shall requite it.

Cor. Twill bee good for thee, Captaine, that
thou hast such an egregious Asse to thy
Coozen.   250

Cap. I, is hee not a fine foole, Corporall?
But, *George,* thou talkst of Art and Coniuring;
How shall that bee?

Pib. Puh, bee't not in your care:
Leaue that to me and my directions.   255
Well, Captaine, doubt not thy deliuerie now,
E'en with the vantage, man, to gaine by
prison,
As my thoughts prompt me: hold on, braine
and plot!
I ayme at many cunning far euents,
All which I doubt not but to hit at length. 260
Ile to the Widdow with a quaint assault.
Captaine, be merry.

Capt. Who, I? Kerrie, merry, Buffe-
Ierkin.

Pye. Oh, I am happy in more slights, and
one will knit strong in another.—Corporall
Oth.   266

Corp. Hoh, Bully?

Pye. And thou, old *Peter Skirmish;* I haue
a necessary taske for you both.

Skir. Lay't vpon, *George Pye-boord.* 270

Corp. What ere it bee, weele manage it.

Pye. I would haue you two maintaine a
quarrell before the Lady Widdowes doore, and
drawe your swords i'th edge of the Euening;
clash a little, clash, clash.   275

Corp. Fuh!
Let vs alone to make our Blades ring noone,
Tho it be after Supper.

247 *S. D.* Exit Nich. *repeated Q*   254 *Prefix* Peb *Q*
270 it upon us *M*

Pye. ⟨I⟩ Know you can. And out of that
false fire, I doubt not but to raise strange
beleefe—And, Captaine, to countenance my
deuice the better, and grace my words to the
Widdow, I haue a good plaine Sattin sute,
that I had of a yong Reueller t'other night:
for words passe not regarded now a dayes,
vnlesse they come from a good suite of
cloaths, which the Fates and my wittes haue
bestowed vpon me. Well, Captaine *Idle,* if
I did not highly loue thee, I would nere bee
seene within twelue score of a prison, for I
protest at this instant, I walke in great danger
of small debts; I owe money to seuerall
Hostisses, and you know such Iills will quickly
be vpon a mans Iack.

Capt. True, *George.*   295

Pye. Fare thee well, Captaine. Come, Corporall and Ancient! thou shalt heare more
newes next time we greete thee.

Corp. More newes! I, by yon Beare at
Bridge-Foote in heauen shalt thou.   300
[*Exeunt ⟨Pyeboard, Skirmish, and Oath.⟩*

Capt. Inough: my friends, farewell.
This prison shewes as if Ghosts did part in Hell.

⟨ACT II.⟩

⟨SCENE I. *A room in the widow's house.*⟩

Enter Moll *yongest Daughter to the Widdow:*
alone.

Moll. Not *Marry*? forsweare Marriage?
why, all women know 'tis as honorable a thing
as to lye with a man; and I to spight my Sisters
vowe the more, haue entertainde a suter
already, a fine gallant Knight of the last
Fether: hee sayes he will Coach mee too, and
well appoint mee, allow mee money to Dice
with-all, and many such pleasing protestations
hee sticks vpon my lips; indeed, his short-
winded Father ith' Countrie is wondrous
wealthy, a most abhominable Farmer, and
therefore hee may doote in time: troth, Ile
venture vpon him. Women are not without
wayes enow to helpe them-selues: if he proue
wise and good as his word, why, I shall loue
him, and vse him kindly: and if hee prooue an
Asse, why, in a quarter of an houres warning
I can transforme him into an Oxe;—there
comes in my Reliefe agen.   19

Enter Frailtie.

Frail. O, Mistresse *Moll,* Mistresse *Moll.*

Moll. How now? what's the newes?

279 I *add.* F1   300 in heauen] in the even *conj.*
M   302 if *om. M*   Act II. *add. R*   Scene I. *etc.*
add. M   12 doote] dote *Ff* : do it *M*

Frail. The Knight your suter, sir *Iohn*
 Penny-Dub—
Moll. Sir *Iohn Penny-Dub?* where? where?
Frail. Hee's walking in the Gallerie.
Moll. Has my Mother seene him yet? 25
Frail. O no, shee's—spitting in the Kitchin.
Moll. Direct him hether softly, good
 Frailtie,——
Ile meete him halfe way.
Frail. That's iust like running a Tilt; but
I hope heele breake nothing this time. ⟨*Exit.*⟩

      Enter Sir Iohn Penny-Dub.

Moll. 'Tis happinesse my Mother saw him
 not: 31
O welcome, good Sir *Iohn.*
Penny-dub. I thanke you, faith.—Nay, you
must stand mee, till I kisse you: 'tis the fashion
euery where, I-faith, and I came from Court
enow.   36
Moll. Nay, the Fates forfend that I should
anger the fashion!
Penny. Then, not forgetting the sweete of
new ceremonies, I first fall back, then recouer-
ing my selfe, make my honour to your lip thus:
and then accost it.   42
Moll. Trust me, very pritty, and mouing;
y'are worthy on't, sir.
Kissing: Enter Widdow and Sir Godfr.
O, my Mother, my Mother! now shee's here,
weele steale into the Gallery.   [*Exeunt.* 46
Sir Godf. Nay, Sister, let Reason rule you,
doe not play the foole; stand not in your owne
light. You haue wealthy offers, large tendrings;
doe not with-stand your good fortune: who
comes a wooing to you, I pray? no small foole;
a rich Knight ath Citty, Sir *Oliuer Muck-hill*—
no small foole I can tell you: and furthermore,
as I heard late by your Maide-seruants, (as
your Maide-seruants will say to mee any
thing, I thanke 'em) both your Daughters are
not without Suters, I, and worthy ones too!
one a Briske Courtier, Sir *Andrew Tip-staffe,*
suter a farre off to your eldest Daughter, and
the third a huge-welthie Farmers sonne, a
fine young Countrie Knight, they call him Sir
Iohn Penny-Dub: a good name, marry; hee
may haue it coynde when hee lackes money.
What blessings are these, Sister!   64
Wid. Tempt me not, Satan.
Sir Godf. Satan? doe I looke like Satan?
I hope the Deuill's not so old as I, I tro.
Wid. You wound my sences, Brother, when
 you name

A suter to me:—oh, I cannot abide it,
I take in poison, when I heare one nam'd. 70

      Enter Simon.

How now, *Simon?* where's my sonne *Edmund?*
Sim. Verily Madame, hee is at vaine
Exercise, dripping in the Tennis-court.
Wid. At Tennis-court? oh, now his father's
gon, I shall haue no rule with him; oh, wicked
Edmond, I might well compare this with the
Prophecie in the Chronicle, tho farre inferior:
as *Harry* of *Monmouth* woone all, and *Harry*
of *Windsor* lost all; so *Edmund* of *Bristow,*
that was the Father, got all, and *Edmond* of
London, that's his sonne now, will spend all.
Sir Godf. Peace, Sister, weele haue him
reformd, there's hope on him yet, tho it be but
a little.   84

      Enter Frailtie.

Frail. Forsooth, Madam, there are two or
three Archers at doore would very gladly
speake with your Ladyship.
Wid. Archers?
Sir Godf. Your husbands Fletcher, I
warrant.   90
Wid. Oh!
Let them come neere, they bring home things
 of his.
Troth, I should ha forgot 'em. How now,
 Villaine?
Which be those Archers?   94

Enter the suters Sir Andrew Tipstaffe, *Sir*
 Oliuer Muck-hill, *and* Penny-dub.

Frail. Why, do you not see 'em before you?
are not these Archers? what do you call 'em?
Shooters: Shooters and Archers are all one,
I hope.
Wid. Out, ignorant slaue.
Muck. Nay, pray be patient, Lady,   100
We come in way of honorable loue.
Tipst. Penny. Wee doe.
Muck. To you.
Tipst. Penny. And to your Daughters. 104
Widdow. O, why will you offer mee this
Gentlemen? indeed I will not looke vppon you
—when the Teares are scarce out of mine Eyes,
not yet washt off from my Cheekes, and my
deere husbands body scarce so colde as the
Coffin, what reason haue you to offer it?
I am not like some of your Widdowes that will
burie one in the Euening, and bee sure to
another ere morning. Pray, away; pray,
take your answeres, good Knights, and you

---

25 Ha's *Q*   *S. D.* Exit *add. M*   36 e'now *F2 :*
even now *M*   39 of] in *conj. St.*   44 on't] of it *M*
62 Penny-Dab·*Q*

82 him] hem *Q*   83 on] of *M*   93 *Ends* now *Q,*
Ff : corr. M   112 sure to have *M*

143

bee sweete Knights. I haue vow'd neuer to marry;—and so haue my daughters too! 116

Penny. I, two of you haue, but the thirds a good wench!

Muck. Lady, a shrewde answere, marry; the best is, tis but the first, and hee's a blunt wooer, that will leaue for one sharpe answere.

Tip. Where bee your daughters, Lady? I hope theile giue vs better encouragements. 123

Wid. Indeed, theyle answere you so; tak't a my word, theile giue you the very same answere *Verbatim,* truely la.

Penny. Mum: *Moll's* a good wench still, I know what shee'le doo.

Muck. Well, Lady, for this time weele take our leaues, hoping for better comfort.   130

Wid. O neuer, neuer! and I liue these thousand yeares! and you bee good Knights, doe not hope; twill bee all Vaine, Vayne,—looke you, put off all your suites, and you come to me againe.   135

⟨*Exeunt Sir John and Sir Andrew.*⟩

Fray. Put off all their suites, quatha? I, that's the best wooing of a Widdow, indeed, when a man's Nonsuted; that is, when he's a bed with her. [*Going out, Muckhill and sir Godfrey.*

Muck. Sir *Godfrey,* here's twenty Angells more: worke hard for me; there's life int yet.
[*Exit Muckhill.*

Sir Godf. Feare not, Sir *Oliuer Muckhill,* Ile stick close for you; leaue all with me. 143

Enter George Py-boord, *the scholler.*

Pye. By your leaue, Ladie Widdow.

Wid. What, another suiter now?

Py. A suiter! no, I protest, Ladie, if you'de giue me your selfe, Ide not be troubled with you.

Wid. Say you so, Sir? then you're the better welcome, sir.   150

Pie. Nay, Heauen blesse mee from a Widdow, vnlesse I were sure to bury her speedily!

Wid. Good bluntnesse: well, your businesse, sir?

Pie. Very needfull; if you were in priuate once.

Wid. Needfull? brother, pray leaue vs; and you, sir.   158

Fray. I should laugh now, if this blunt fellow should put 'em all by side the stirrop, and vault into the saddle himselfe. I haue seene as mad a trick.   [*Exit Frailtie.*

Enter Daughters.

Wid. Now Sir?—here's none but we—Daughters, forbeare.   164

134 your] yours *Q*   135 *S. D. add. M*

Pyb. O no, pray, let 'em stay, for what I haue to speake importeth equally to them as to you.

Wid. Then you may stay.

Pyb. I pray bestow on me a serious eare, For what I speake is full of weight and feare.

Wid. Feare?   171

Pyb. I, ift passe vnregarded, and vneffected; Else peace and ioy:—I pray, Attention. Widdowe, I haue beene a meere stranger for these parts that you liue in, nor did I euer know the Husband of you, and Father of them, but I truly know by certaine spirituall Intelligence, that he is in Purgatorie.   178

Wid. Purgatorie? tuh; that word deserues to bee spit vpon. I wonder that a man of sober toung, as you seeme to be, should haue the folly to beleeue there's such a place.   182

Pyb. Well, Lady, in cold bloud I speake it; I assure you that there is a Purgatory, in which place I know your husband to recide, and wherein he is like to remaine, till the dissolution of the world, till the last generall Bon-fire, when all the earth shall melt into nothing and the Seas scalde their finnie labourers: so long is his abidance, vnlesse you alter the propertie of your purpose, together with each of your Daughters theirs; that is, the purpose of single life in your selfe and your eldest Daughter, and the speedie determination of marriage in your youngest.   195

Moll. How knowes hee that? what, has some Deuill told him?

Wid. Strange he should know our thoughts:——Why, but, Daughter, haue you purposde speedy Marriage?   200

Pyb. You see she tels you I, for shee sayes nothing. Nay, giue me credit as you please. I am a stranger to you, and yet you see I know your determinations, which must come to mee Metaphisically, and by a super-naturall intelligence.   206

Wid. This puts Amazement on me.

Franck. Know our seacrets!

Mol. Ide thought to steale a marriage: would his tongue Had dropt out when he blabt it!   210

Wid. But, sir, my husband was too honest a dealing man to be now in any purgatories—

Pie. O, Do not loade your conscience with vntruths; Tis but meere folly now to guild him ore, 214 That has past but for Copper. Praises here Cannot vnbinde him there: confesse but truth.

166-7 as you *Ff*   196 ha's *Q*   201 for *om. Ff*
203 and and *Q*   209-10 *Prose M*   214 him *M* :
hem *Q* : 'em *Ff*

I know he got his wealth with a hard gripe:
Oh hardly, hardly.
Wid.   This is most strange of all: how
knowes he that?
Pie.   He would eate fooles and ignorant
heires cleane vp;   220
And had his drinck from many a poore mans
browe,
E'en as their labour brewde it.
He would scrape ritches to him most vn-
iustly;
The very durt betweene his nailes was Il-got,
And not his owne,—oh, I groane to speake
on't,   225
The thought makes me shudder—shudder!
Wid.   It quakes me too, now I thinke on't.
—Sir, I am much grieu'd, that you, a stranger,
should so deeply wrong my dead husband!
Pie.   Oh!   230
Wid.   A man that would keepe Church so
duly; rise early, before his seruants, and e'en
for Religious hast, go vngarterd, vnbuttend,
nay, sir Reuerence, vntrust, to Morning Prayer.
Pie.   Oh, vff.   235
Wid.   Dine quickly vpon hie-dayes, and
when I had great guests, would e'en shame
me and rize from the Table, to get a good
seate at an after-noone Sermon.   239
Pie.   There's the diuill, there's the diuill!
true, hee thought it Sanctity ynough, if he
had kild a man, so tad beene done in a Pue, or
vndon his Neigh(b)our, so ta'd beene nere
ynough to'th Preacher. Oh,—a Sermon's a
fine short cloake of an houre long, and wil
hide the vpper-part of a dissembler.—Church!
I, he seem'd al Church, & his conscience was
as hard as the Pulpit!
Pie.   Nor I, widdow, endure to flatter. 250
Wid.   Is this all your businesse with me?
Pie.   No, Lady, tis but the induction too'te.
You may beleiue my straines, I strike all true,
And if your conscience would leap vp to your
tongue, your selfe would affirme it: and that
you shall perceiue I knowe of things to come
as well as I doe of what is present, a Brother
of your husbands shall shortly haue a losse.
Wid.   A losse; marry, heauen for-fend!
Sir Godfrey, my brother?   260
Pie.   Nay, keepe in your wonders, till I haue
told you the fortunes of you all; which are
more fearefull, if not happily preuented:—for
your part & your daughters, if there be not
once this day some bloud-shed before your

dore, wheerof the humaine creature dies, two
of you—the elder—shall run mad.   267
Mother and Franck.   Oh!
Mol.   That's not I yet!
Pie.   And with most impudent prostitution
show your naked bodies to the veiw of all
beholders.
Wid.   Our naked bodies? fie, for shame!
Pie.   Attend mee: and your yonger daughter
bee strocken dumbe.   275
Mol.   Dumbe? out, alasse: tis the worst
paine of all for a Woman. Ide rather bee
madde, or runne naked, or any thing: dumbe?
Pie.   Giue eare: ere the euening fall vpon
Hill, Bogge, and Meadow, this my speech shal
haue past probation, and then shal I be
belieued accordingly.   282
Widdow.   If this bee true, wee are all
sham'de, all vndon.
Mol.   Dumbe? Ile speake as much as euer
I can possible before euening!   286
Pie.   But if it so come to passe (as for your
faire sakes I wish it may) that this presage of
your strange fortunes be preuented by that
accident of death and bloud-shedding which
I before told you off: take heed vpon your liues
that two of you, which haue vow'd neuer to
marry, seeke you out husbands with all present
speede, and you, the third, that haue such a
desire to out-strip chastitie, looke you meddle
not with a husband.   296
Moll.   A double torment.
Pyb.   The breach of this keepes your father
in Purgatorie, and the punishments that shall
follow you in this world would with horror
kill the Eare should heare 'em related.   301
Wid.   Marry? why I vowd neuer to marry.
Franke.   And so did I.
Moll.   And I vowde neuer to be such an
Asse, and to marry: what a crosse Fortune's
this!   306
Pyb.   Ladies, tho I bee a Fortune-teller,
I cannot better Fortunes; you haue 'em from
me as they are reueald to me: I would they
were to your tempers, and fellowes with your
blouds, that's all the bitternesse I would you.
Widdow.   Oh, 'tis a iust vengeance for my
husbands hard purchases.   313
Pyb.   I wish you to be-thinke your selues,
and leaue 'em.
Wid.   Ile to Sir *Godfrey,* my Brother, and
acquaint him with these fearefull presages.
Franck.   For, Mother, they portend losses
to him.
Wid.   Oh, I, they doe, they doe.   320

222-6 *End* scrape, dirt, own, me, shudder *M*   225
Ends oh, *Q, Ff*   237 guests *F 2* : guesse *Q, F 1*
242 tad] it had *M*

266-7 of you two the elder *Ff*   eldest *R*   286
possibly *M*   293 you *om. Ff, etc.*   315 leaue m *Q*

If any happy issue crowne thy words,
I will reward thy cunning.

Pyb. 'Tis enough Lady; I wish no higher.
                    [*Exit* ⟨Wid. *and* Fran.⟩

Mol. Dumbel and not marry, worse!   324
Neither to speake, nor kisse, a double curse.
                                            [*Exit.*

Pyb. So all this comes well about yet. I
play the Fortune-teller as well as if I had
had a Witch to my Grannam: for by good
happinesse, being in my Hostisses Garden,
which neighbours the Orchard of the Widdow,
I laid the hole of mine eare to a hole in the
wall, and heard 'em make these vowes, &
speake those words vpon which I wrought
these aduantages; and to encourage my forgerie the more, I may now perceiue in 'em
a naturall simplicitie which will easily swallow
an abuse, if any couering be ouer it: and to
confirme my former presage to the Widdow,
I haue aduizde old *Peter Skirmish,* the Souldier, to hurt Corporall *Oth* vpon the Leg; and
in that hurry Ile rush amongst 'em, and in
stead of giuing the Corporal some Cordiall to
comfort him, Ile power into his mouth a potion of a sleepy Nature, to make him seeme as
dead; for the which the old souldier beeing
apprehended, and ready to bee borne to execution, Ile step in, & take vpon me the cure of
the dead man, vpon paine of dying the con-
demneds death: the Corporall will wake at his
minute, when the sleepy force has wrought it
selfe, and so shall I get my selfe into a most
admired opinion, and vnder the pretext of that
cunning, beguile as I see occasion: and if that
foolish *Nicholas* Saint *Tantlings* keepe true
time with the chaine, my plot will be sound,
the Captaine deliuered, and my wits applauded
among schollers and souldiers for euer.   357
                                    [*Exit Py·boord.*

⟨SCENE II. *A Garden.*⟩

*Enter Nicholas Saint Tantlings with the
chaine.*

Nic. Oh, I haue found an excellent aduantage to take away the chaine: my Maister put
it off e'en now to say on a new Doublet, and
I sneak't it away by little & little most Puritanically. Wee shal haue good sport anon
when ha's mist it about my Cozen the Coniurer. The world shall see I'me an honest
man of my word, for now I'me going to hang
it betweene Heauen & Earth among the Rosemary branches.   [*Exit Nich.*

Actus 3.

⟨SCENE I. *The street before the Widow's house.*⟩

*Enter Simon Saint Mary-Oueries and
Frailty.*

Frai. Sirrah *Simon Saint Mary-Oueries,*my
Mistris sends away all her suiters and puts
fleas in their eares.

Sim. Frailty, she dos like an honest, chast,
and vertuous woman; for widdowes ought not
to wallow in the puddle of iniquity.   6

Fra. Yet, *Simon,* many widdowes wil do't,
what so comes do't.

Sim. True, *Frailtie,* their filthy flesh desires
a Coniunction Copulatiue. What strangers are
within, *Frailty?*   11

Frai. Ther's none, *Simon,* but Maister
Pilfer the Tailer: he's aboue with *Sir Godfreie*
praysing of a Doublet: and I must trudge anon
to fetch Maister Suds, the Barber.   15

Simon. Maister Suds,—a good man; he
washes the sinns of the Beard cleane.

Enter old Skirmish the souldier.

Skir. How now, creatures? whats a clock?

Frai. Why, do you take vs to be Iacke
ath' Clock-house?   20

Skir. I say agen to you what's a clocke?

Sim. Truly la, wee goe by the clocke of
our conscience: all worldly Clockes, we know,
goe false, and are set by drunken Sextons.   24

Skir. Then what's a clock in your conscience?—oh, I must breake off, here comes
the corporall—hum, hum!—what's a clock?

Enter Corporall.

Corp. A clock? why, past seuenteene.

Frai. Past seuenteene? nay, ha's met with
his match now, Corporall *Oth* will fit him.   30

Skir. Thou doost not bawke or baffle me,
doost thou? I am a Souldier —past seuenteene!

Corp. I, thou art not angry with the figures,
art thou? I will prooue it vnto thee: 12. and 1.
is thirteene, I hope, 2. foureteene, 3. fifteene,
4. sixteene, and 5. seauenteene; then past
seauenteene: I will take the Dyals part in a
iust cause.

Skir. I say 'tis but past fiue, then.   40

Corp. Ile sweare 'tis past seauenteene, then:
doost thou know numbers? canst thou not
cast?

---

323 *S. D.* Wid. *etc. add. R*   357 amongst *F 2, etc.*
Scene II. *etc. add. M*   6 ha's *Q* : has *F 1* : he has
F 2, etc.

Scene I. *etc. add. M*   16 Sud's a *Ff*   *S. D.*
follows 18 *Q, Ff*   soulders *Q* : corr. *F 2*   19-20 at
'h *Q* : at th' *Ff*   Jacks o' the *M*   21, 25, 27 what
is't o'clock *M*

Skir. Cast? dost thou speake of my casting
ith' street?   [*Draw.*
Corp. I, and in the Market place.   46
Sim, Clubs, clubs, clubs!
                                    [*Simon runs in.*
Frail. I, I knew by their shuffling, Clubs
would be Trumpe; masse, here's the Knaue,
and hee can doe any good vppon 'em: Clubs,
clubs, clubs!   51

            Enter Py-boord.

Corp. O villaine, thou hast opend a vaine
in my leg.
Pyb. How now! for shame, for shame; put
vp, put vp.   55
Corp. By yon blew Welkin, 'twas out of
my part, *George,* to bee hurt on the leg.

            Enter Officers.

Pyb. Oh peace now—I haue a Cordiall here
to comfort thee.
Offi. Downe with 'em, downe with em; lay
hands vpon the villaine.   61
Skir. Lay hands on me?
Pyb. Ile not be seene among em now.
                        ⟨*Exit Pyeboard.*⟩
Corp. Ime hurt, and had more need haue
Surgeons
Lay hands vpon me then rough Officers.
Offi. Goe, carry him to be drest then.   66
⟨*Exeunt some of the Sheriffs Officers
                        with Corporal Oath.*⟩
This mutinous Souldier shall along with me to
prison.
Skir. To prison? where's *George?*
Offi. Away with him. [*Exeunt with* Skir.

            ⟨*Re-enter* Pyeboard.⟩

Pyb. So.   71
All lights as I would wish. The amazd
widdow
Will plant me strongly now in her beleefe,
And wonder at the vertue of my words:
For the euent turnes those presages from
em   75
Of being mad and dumbe, and begets
ioy
Mingled with admiration. These emptie crea-
tures,
Souldier and Corporall, were but ordaind
As instruments for me to worke vpon.
Now to my patient; here's his potion.   80
                            [*Exit* Pyboord.

52, 56, 64 *Prefix* Cap. *Q, Ff*   63 *S. D. add. M*
66 *S. D. add. M* after 68   70 hem *Q*   *S. D.*
Scene II. The same. Re-enter Pyeboard *M*   75
em] them *M*

⟨SCENE II.   *An apartment in the Widow's
                            house.*⟩
        *Enter the Widdow with her two
                    Daughters.*

Wid. O wondrous happinesse, beyond our
    thoughts:
O luckie faire euent! I thinke our fortunes,
Were blest een in our Cradles: we are quitted
Of all those shamefull violent presages
By this rash bleeding chance. Goe, *Frailtie,*
    run, and know,   5
Whether he be yet liuing, or yet dead,
That here before my doore receiu'd his hurt.
Frail. Madam, hee was carryed to the
superiour, but if he had no money when hee
came there, I warrant hee's dead by this time.
                            [*Exit* Frailtie.
Franck. Sure, that man is a rare fortune-
teller; neuer lookt vpon our hands, nor vpon
any marke about vs: a wondrous fellow, surelie,
Moll. I am glad, I haue the vse of my
tongue yet: tho of nothing else. I shall finde
the way to marry too, I hope, shortly.   16
Wid. O where's my Brother, sir *Godfrey?*
I would hee were here, that I might relate to
him how prophetically the cunning Gentleman
spoke in all things.   20

        Enter Sir Godfrey *in a rage.*

Sir Godf. O my Chaine, my Chaine! I haue
lost my Chaine. Where be these Villains,
Varlets?
Wid. Oh! has lost his Chaine.
Sir Godf. My Chaine, my chaine!   25
Widdow. Brother, bee patient, heare mee
speake: you know I told you that a cunning
man told me that you should haue a losse, and
he has prophicied so true.   29
Sir Godf. Out, he's a villaine, to prophecy
of the losse of my chaine: twas worth aboue
three hundred Crownes,—besides, twas my
Fathers, my fathers fathers, my Grand-fathers
huge grand-fathers. I had as lieue ha lost my
Neck, as the chaine that hung about it. O, my
chaine, my chaine!   36
Wid. Oh, brother, who can be against a
misfortune! tis happy twas no more.
Sir Godf. No, more! O goodly godly sister,
would you had me lost more? my best gowne,
too, with the cloth of gold-lace? my holiday
Gascoines, and my Ierkin set with pearle? no
more!   43
Wid. Oh, Brother! you can reade—

Scene II. *etc.*] Scene III. *etc M*   9 superiour]
surgeon *conj. St.*   24 has *Q* : h'as *Ff* : he has *M*
34 lieue *Ff* : liue *Q*   40 had] (?) have had

Sir Godf. But I cannot reade where my
chaine is.—What strangers haue beene here?
you let in strangers, Theeues, and Catch-poles;
how comes it gonne? there was none aboue
with mee but my Taylor; and my Taylor will
not—steale, I hope?   50
Mol. No, he's afrayde of a chaine!

Enter Fraylty.

Wid. How now, sirrah? the newes?
Fray. O Mistres, he may well be cald a
Corporall now, for his corpes are as dead as
a cold Capons.   55
Wid. More happinesse.
Sir Godf. Sirrah, what's this to my chaine?
where's my chaine, knaue?
Fray. Your chaine, sir?
Sir Godf. My chaine is lost, villaine.   60
Fray. I would hee were hang'd in chaines
that has it then for me. Alasse, sir, I saw none
of your chaine, since you were hung with it
your selfe.
Sir Godf. Out, varlet! it had full three
thousand Lincks.   65
I haue oft told it ouer at my praiers:
Ouer and ouer, full three thousand Lincks.
Frayl. Had it so, sir: sure, it cannot be lost
then; Ile put you in that comfort.
Sir Godf. Why, why?   70
Frayl. Why, if your chaine had so many
Lincks, it cannot chuse but come to light.

Enter Nicholas.

Sir Godf. Delusion! now, long *Nicholas*,
wheres my chaine?
Nich. Why, about your Neck, ist not, sir?
Sir Godf. About my neck, Varlet! My chaine
is lost.   75
Tis stole away, Ime robd.
Wid. Nay, Brother, show your selfe a man.
Nic. I, if it be lost or stole, if he would be
patient, Mistres, I could bring him to a Cunning Kinsman of mine that would fetcht againe
with a Sesarara.   81
Sir Godf. Canst thou? I will be patient: say,
where dwells he?
Nic. Marry, he dwels now, Sir, where he
would not dwell, and he could choose: in the
Marshalsea, sir; but hee's an exlent fellow if
he were out; has trauyld all the world ore, he,
and beene in the seauen and twenty Prouinces:
why, he would make it be fetcht, Sir, if twere
rid a thousand mile out of towne.   90
Sir Godf. An admirable fellow: what lies
he for?
Nic. Why, hee did but rob a Steward of ten

groats tother Night, as any man would ha
done, and there he lies fort.   95
Sir Godf. Ile make his peace: a Trifle! Ile
get his pardon,
Beside a bountifull reward. Ile about it.
But see the Clearkes, the Iustice will doe much.
I will about it straight: good sister, pardon me.
All will be well, I hope, and turne to good,   100
The name of Coniurer has laid my blood.
                                              [*Exeunt.*

(SCENE III. *A street.*)

Enter two seriants ⟨with Yeoman Dogson⟩ to
arrest the Scholer, George Pyeboord.

Put. His Hostesse where he lies will trust
him no longer: she has feed me to arest him;
and if you will accompany me, because I know
not of what Nature the Scholler is, whether
desperate or swift, you shall share with me,
Seriant *Rauen-shaw.* I haue the good Angell
to arrest him.   7
Rauen. Troth, Ile take part with thee, then,
Sariant, not for the sake of the mony so much,
as for the hate I beare to a Scholler: why,
Seriant, tis Naturall in vs, you know, to hate
Scholers, naturall: besides, they will publish
our imperfections, Knaueryes, and Conuayances vpon Scaffolds and Stages.   14
Put. I, and spightfully, to; troth, I haue
woundered how the slaues could see into our
brests so much, when our doublets are but-
tond with Pewter.   18
Rauen. I, and so close without yeelding;
oh, their parlous fellows, they will search more
with their wits then a Cunstable with all his
officers.
Put. Whist, whist, whist! Yeoman *Dogson!*
Yeoman *Dogson.*
Dog. Ha, what saies Sariant?   25
Put. Is he in the Pothecaryes shop stil?
Dog. I, I.
Put. Haue an eye, ⟨haue an⟩ eye.
Rauen. The best is, Sariant, if he be a true
Scholler, he weares no weapon, I thinke.   30
Put. No, no, he weares no weapon.
Rauen. Masse, I am right glad of that:
'tas put me in better heart. Nay, if I clutch
him once, let me alone to drage him if he be
stiff-necked. I haue beene one of the sixe my
selfe, that has dragd as tall men of their hands,
when their weapons haue bin gone, as euer
bastinadoed a Sariant—I haue done, I can tel
you.   39

97 Besides *Ff, etc.*   Scene III. *etc.*] Scene IV.
etc. M   *S. D.* with, *etc. add. Ff*   3 and *om. Ff*
12 besides] because *conj. M*   17 doublers *Q*   28
haue an *add. F1*

54 arc] is *M*   87 has] ha's *Ff*

Dog. Sariant *Puttocke*, Sariant *Puttocke*.
Put. Hoh.
Dog. Hees comming out single.
Put. Peace, peace, bee not to greedy; let
him play a little, let him play a litle: weele
ierke him vp of a sudaine. I ha fisht in my
time. 46
Rauen. I, and caught many a foole, Seriant.

Enter Pyeboord.

Pye. I parted now from *Nicholas*: the
chaynes coucht,
And the old Knight has spent his rage vpont;
The widdowe holds me in great Admiration
For cunning Art: mongst ioyes I am 'een lost,
For my deuice can no way now be crost. 52
And now I must to prison to the captaine,
And there—
Put. I arrest you, sir. 55
Pye. Oh—I spoke truer then I was a ware,
I must to prison indeed.
Put. They say your a scholler: nay, sir—
Yeoman *Dogson*, haue care to his armes—
youle rayle againe Sariants, and stage 'em!
you tickle their vices! 61
Pye. Nay, vse me like a Gentleman, I'me
little lesse.
Put. You a Gentleman? thats a good Iest,
ifaith; can a Scholler be a Gentleman,—when
a Gentleman will not be a Scholler? looke vpon
your welthy Citizenes sonnes, whether they
be Scholers or no, that are Gentlemen by their
fathers trades: a Scholler a Gentleman! 69
Pye. Nay, let Fortune driue all her stings
into me, she cannot hurt that in me: a Gentleman is *Accidens Inseperabile* in my bloud.
Rauen. A rablement, nay, you shall haue
a bloudy rablement vpon you, I warrant you.
Put. Goe, Yeoman *Dogson*, before, and
Enter the Action 'ith Counter. 76
Pie. Pray do nit hand me Cruelly, Ile
goe, [*Exet* Dogson.
Whether you please to haue me.
Put. Oh, hees tame; let him loose, seriant.
Pie. Pray, at whose sute is this? 80
Put. Why at your Hostisses suite where
you lie, Mistres *Cunnyburrow*, for bed and
boord, the somme foure pound fiue shillings
and fiue pence.
Pie. I know the somme to true, yet I pre-
sumde 85
Vpon a farder daie; well, tis my starres
And I must beare it now, tho neuer harder.
I sweare now, my deuice is crost indeed.

Captaine must lie bite: this is Deceytes seed.
Put. Come, come away. 90
Pye. Pray, giue me so much time as to knit
my garter, and Ile a way with you.
Put. Well, we must be paid for this waiting
vpon you, this is no paynes to attend thus. 94
[⟨Pyboard⟩ *Making to tie his garter.*
Pye. I am now wretched, and miserable.
I shall nere recouer of this disease: hot Yron
gnaw their fists! they haue strucke a Feuer
into my shoulder, which I shall nere shake
out agen, I feare me, till with a true *Habeas
Corpus* the Sexton remooue me. Oh, if I take
prison once, I shall bee prest to death with
Actions, but not so happy as speedilie; perhaps
I may bee forty yeare a pressing, till I be a thin
old man; that, looking through the grates, men
may looke through me. All my meanes is
confounded: what shall I doe? has my wits
serued me so long, and now giue me the slippe
(like a Traynd seruant) when I haue most
need of 'em? no deuice to keepe my poore
carcase fro these Puttocks?—yes, happines!
haue I a paper about me now? yes, too! Ile
trie it, it may hit: *Extremity is Touch-stone
vnto wit.* I, I. 113
Put. Sfoot, how many yards are in thy
Garters, that thou art so long a tying on
them? come away, sir.
Pyb. Troth, Seriant, I protest, you could
neuer ha tooke me at a worse time; for now
at this instant I haue no lawfull picture about
me. 120
Put. Slid, how shall we come by our fees
then?
Rau. We must haue fees, Sirra.
Pib. I could ha wisht, ifaith, that you had
tooke me halfe an hower hence for your owne
sake; for I protest, if you had not crost me, I
was going in great ioy to receiue fiue pound
of a Gentleman, for the Déuice of a Maske
here, drawne in this paper. But now, come, I
must be contented: tis but so much lost, and
answerable to the rest of my fortunes. 131
Put. Why, how far hence dwells that Gentleman?
Rau. I, well said, seriant, tis good to cast
about for mony. 135
Put. Speake; if it be not far—
Pyb. We are but a little past it, the next
street behind vs. 138
Put. Slid, we haue waited vpon you
grieuously already: if youle say youle be liberall
when you hate, giue vs double fees, and spend

53 *Ends* there *Q, Ff*   61 you'll *M*   72 is *om.*
Ff   77-8 *Prose M*   82 Misters *Q*   88 sweare]
fear *conj. M*
89 bite] by't *Ff, etc.*   106 have *M*   wit *Q, Ff*
110 fro] from *Ff, etc.*   112 the touchstone *M*   121
we] me *Q*   141 hate] ha't *Ff*; have it *M*

149

vpon's, why weele show you that kindnes, and
goe along with you to the Gentleman.
Rau. I, well said still, seriant, vrge that. 144
Pyb. Troth, if it will suffice, it shall be all
among you; for my part ile not pocket a penny:
my hostisse shall haue her foure pound fiue
shillings, and bate me the fiue pence, and the
other fifteene shillings Ile spend vpon you. 149
Rauinsh. Why, now thou art a good
Scholler.
Put. An excellent Scholler, Ifaith; has proceeded very well alate; come, weele along with
you.   154
    [*Exeunt with him: passing in they
    knock at the doore with a Knocker
    withinside.*

⟨SCENE IV. *A gallery in a gentleman's house.*
        Enter a Servant.⟩
Ser. Who knocks? whose at doore? we had
need of a Porter.
Pyb. A few friends here:—pray, is the
Gentleman your maister within?
Ser. Yes, is your businesse to him?   5
Pyb. I, he knows it, when he see's me: I
pray you, haue you forgot mee?
Ser. I, by my troth, sir. Pray come neere;
Ile in and tell him of you: please you to walke
here in the Gallery till he comes.   10
Pyb. Wee will attend his worship.—Worship, I thinke, for so much the Posts at his
doore should signifie, and the faire comming
in, and the wicket; else I neither knew him
nor his worship, but 'tis happinesse he is
within doores, what so ere he bee: if he be not
too much a formall Citizen, hee may doe me
good.—Seriant and Yeoman, how doe you like
this house? ist not most wholsomly plotted?
Rauen. Troth, prisoner, an exceeding fine
house.   21
Pyb. Yet I wonder how hee should forget
me,—for hee nere knew mee.—No matter, what
is forgot in you will bee remembred in your
Maister. A pritty comfortable roome this, me
thinkes: You haue no such roomes in prison
now?
Put. Oh, dog-holes toote.   28
Pyb. Dog-holes, indeed. I can tell you, I
haue great hope to haue my Chamber here
shortly, nay, and dyet too, for hee's the most
free-hartedst Gentleman where he takes: you
would little thinke it! and what a fine Gallery
were here for mee to walke and study, and
make verses.   35

Scene IV. *etc.*] Scene V. *etc.* M   24 you .. your]
him .. his *conj.* M

Put. O, it stands very pleasantly for a
Scholler.
        Enter Gentleman.
Pyb. Looke what maps, and pictures, and
deuices, and things: neatly, delicately—masse,
here he comes: he should be a Gentleman;
I like his Beard well.—All happinesse to your
worship.   42
Gentle. You're kindly welcome, sir.
Put. A simple salutation.
Rauen. Masse, it seemes the Gentleman
makes great account of him.
Pyb. I haue the thing here for you, sir. 47
Pyb. I beseech you conceale me, sir, Ime
vndone else,—I haue the Maske here for you,
sir, Looke you, sir.—I beseech your worship
first to pardon my rudenesse, for my extreames
makes mee boulder then I would bee. I am
a poore Gentleman and a Scholler, and now
most vnfortunately falne into the Fangs of
vnmercifull officers, arrested for debt, which
tho small, I am not able to compasse, by reason
Ime destitute of lands, money, and friends; so
that if I fall into the hungrie swallow of the
prison, I am like vtterly to perish, and with
fees and extortions bee pincht cleane to the
bone. Now, if euer pitty had interest in the
bloud of a Gentleman, I beseech you vouchsafe but to fauour that meanes of my escape,
which I haue already thought vpon.
Gent. Goe forward.   65
Put. I warrant he likes it rarely.
Pyb. In the plundge of my extremities,
being giddy, and doubtfull what to doe, at last
it was put into my labouring thoughts, to make
happy vse of this paper; and to bleare their
vnlettered eyes, I told them there was a Deuice
for a Maske drawne int', and that (but for
their interception,) I was going to a Gentleman
to receiue my reward for't: they, greedy at
this word, and hoping to make purchase of
me, offered their attendance, to goe along with
mee. My hap was to make bolde with your
doore, Sir, which my thoughts showde mee
the most fairest and comfortablest entrance,
and I hope I haue happened right vpon vnder-
standing and pitty: may it please your good
Worship, then, but to vphold my Deuice,
which is to let one of your men put me out
at back-doore, and I shall bee bound to your
worship for euer.   85
Gent. By my troth, an excellent deuice.
Puttock. An excellent deuice, hee sayes;
hee likes it wonderfully.

47 *Prefix* Gent. Ff   54 Fangs *Q*: hands Ff   69-
70 make a happy Ff, *etc.*   84 at] at a Ff, *etc.*

Gent. A my faith, I neuer heard a better.

Rauenshaw. Harke, hee sweares hee neuer heard a better, Serieant.   91

Put. O, there's no talke on't, hees an excellent Scholler, and especially for a Maske.

Gent. Giue me your Paper, your Deuice; I was neuer better pleasde in all my life: good witte, braue witte, finely rought! come in, sir, and receiue your money, sir.   97

Pyb. Ile follow your good Worship.— You heard how he likte it now?

Put. Puh, we know hee could not choose but like it: goe thy wayes; thou art a witty fine fellow, ifaith, thou shalt discourse it to vs at Tauerne anon, wilt thou?   103

Pyb. I, I, that I will. Looke, Seriants, here are Maps, and prittie toyes: be dooing in the meane time. I shall quickly haue told out the money, you know.   107

Put. Goe, goe, little villaine, fetch thy chinck. I begin to loue thee; Ile be drunke to night in thy company.

Pyb. ⟨*Aside*⟩ This Gentleman I may well call a part

Of my saluation, in these earthly euils,   112
For hee has sau'd mee from three hungrie Deuils.   [*Exit George.*

Puttock. Sirrah Seriant, these Mappes are prittie painted things, but I could nere fancie 'em yet: mee thinkes they're too busie, and full of Circles and Coniurations; they say all the world's in one of them, but I could nere finde the Counter in the Poultrie.   119

Rauen. I thinke so: how could you finde it? for you know it stands behind the houses.

Dogson. Masse, thats true; then we must looke ath' back-side fort. Sfoote, here's nothing, all's bare.

Rauen. I warrant thee, that stands for the Counter, for you know theres a company of bare fellowes there.   127

Put. Faith, like enough, Seriant; I neuer markt so much before. Sirrah Seriant, and Yeoman, I should loue these Maps out a crye now, if wee could see men peepe out of doore in em: oh, wee might haue em in a morning to our Breake-fast so finely, and nere knocke our heeles to the ground a whole day for em.

Rauen. I, marry, sir, Ide buye one then my selfe. But this talke is by the way: where shall's sup to night? Fiue pound receiu'd! let's talke of that. I haue a trick worth all: you two shall beare him to 'th Tauerne, whilst I goe close with his Hostisse, and worke out of her. I know shee would bee glad of the

summe to finger money, because shee knowes tis but a desperat debt, and full of hazard. What will you say, if I bring it to passe that the Hostisse shall bee contented with one halfe for all; and wee to share tother fifty-shillings, bullies?   147

Put. Why, I would call thee King of *Seriants*, and thou shouldst be Chronicled in the Counter booke for euer.

Ra. Well, put it to me, weele make a Night on't, yfaith.

Dog. Sfoote, I thinke he receiues more money, he staies so long.   154

Put. Hee tarries long, indeed: may be, I can tell you, vpon the good liking ont the Gentleman may proue more bountifull.

Ra. That would be rare; weele search him.

Put. Nay, be sure of it, weele search him! and make him light ynough.   160

Enter the Gentleman.

Ra. Oh, here comes the Gentleman. By your leaue, sir.

Gen. God you god den, sirs,—would you speake with me?   164

Put. No, not with your worship, sir; only wee are bould to stay for a friend of ours that went in with your worship.

Gen. Who? not the scholler?

Put. Yes, e'en he, and it please your worship.   170

Gen. Did he make you stay for him? hee did you wrong, then: why, I can assure you hees gon aboue an houre agoe.

Ra. How, sir?

Gent. I payd him his money, and my man told me he went óut at back-dore.   176

Put. Back-dore?

Gen. Why, whats the matter?

Put. He was our prisoner, sir; we did arrest him.   180

Gen. What! he was not! you the Sheriffes Officers! You were to blame then. Why did you not make knowne to me as much? I could haue kept him for you: I protest he receiued all of me in *Brittaine* Gold of the last coyning.   186

Ra. Vengeance dog him with't!

Put. Sfoote, has he guld vs so?

Dog. Where shall wee sup now Serieants?

Put. Sup, *Simon*, now! eate Porridge for a month. Well, wee cannot impute it to any lacke of good-will in your Worship,—you did but as another would haue done: twas our hard fortunes to misse the purchase, but if

ere wee clutch him againe, the Counter shall
charme him.   196
Rauen. The hole shall rotte him.
Dog. Amen.   [*Exeunt.*
Gent. So,
Vex out your Lungs without doores. I am
   proud,   200
It was my hap to helpe him; it fell fit.
He went not emptie neither for his wit.
Alasse, poore wretch, I could not blame his
   braine
To labour his deliuerie, to be free
From their vnpittying fangs—Ime glad it
   stood   205
Within my power to doe a Scholler good. [*Exit.*

⟨SCENE V. *A room in the Marshalsea
prison.*⟩

Enter in the Prison, meeting, George *and Captaine,* George *comming in muffled.*

Cap. How now, whose that? what are you?
Pyb. The same that I should be, Captaine.
Capt. George Pye-boord, honest *George?*
why camst thou in halfe fac'd, muffled so?   4
Pyb. Oh, Captaine, I thought we should
nere ha laught agen, neuer spent frolick houre
agen.
Capt. Why? why?
Pyb. I comming to prepare thee, and with
newes
As happy as thy quick deliuerie,   10
Was trac'd out by the sent, arrested, Captaine.
Capt. Arrested, *George!*
Pyb. Arrested: gesse, gesse; how many
Dogges doe you thinke Ide vpon me?
Capt. Dogs? I say? I know not.   15
Pyb. Almost as many as *George Stone* the
Beare:
Three at once, three at once.
Capt. How didst thou shake 'em of, then?
Pyb. The time is busie, and calls vpon our
witts.
Let it suffice,   20
Here I stand safe, and scapt by miracle.
Some other houre shall tell thee, when weele
steepe
Our eyes in laughter. Captaine, my deuice
Leanes to thy happinesse, for ere the day
Be spent toth' Girdle, thou shalt be set free. 25
The Corporal's in his first sleepe, the Chaine
is mist,
Thy Kinsman has exprest thee, and the old
Knight

With Palsey-hams now labours thy release:
What rests is all in thee, to Coniure, Captaine.
Capt. Coniure! sfoote, *George,* you know
the deuill a coniuring I can coniure.   31
Pib. The Deuill of coniuring? nay, by my
fay, Ide not haue thee do so much, Captaine,
as the Deuill a coniuring: looke here, I ha
brought thee a circle ready characterd and all.
Capt. Sfoote, *George,* art in thy right wittes?
doost know what thou saist? why doost talke
to a Captaine a coniuring? didst thou euer
heare of a Captaine coniure in thy life? doost
cal't a Circle? tis too wide a thing, me thinkes:
had it beene a lesser Circle, then I knew what
to haue done.   42
Pib. Why, euery foole knowes that, Captaine: nay, then, Ile not cogge with you,
Captaine; if youle stay and hang the next
Sessions, you may.
Capt. No, by my faith, *George:* come, come,
lets to coniuring, lets to coniuring.   48
Pib. But if you looke to be releasd—as my
wittes haue tooke paine to worke it, and all
meanes wrought to farther it—besides to put
crownes in your purse, to make you a man of
better hopes, and whereas before you were
a Captaine or poore Souldier, to make you now
a Commander of rich fooles, (which is truly
the onely best purchase peace can allow you)
safer then High-wayes, Heath, or Cunny-
groues, and yet a farre better bootie; for your
greatest theeues are neuer hangd, neuer
hangd, for, why, they're wise, and cheate
within doores: and wee geld fooles of more
money in one night, then your false tailde
Gelding will purchase in a twelue-moneths running; which confirmes the olde Beldamssaying,
hee's wisest, that keepes himselfe warmest;
that is, hee that robs by a good fire—   66
Capt. Well opened, yfaith, *George;* thou
hast puld that saying out of the huske.
Pib. Captaine *Idle,* tis no time now to
delude or delay: the old Knight will be here
suddenly. Ile perfect you, direct you, tell you
the trick on't: tis nothing.   72
Capt. Sfoote, *George,* I know not what to
say toot: coniure? I shall be hangd ere I
coniure.   75
Pyb. Nay, tell not me of that, Captaine;
youle nere coniure after your hangd, I warrant
you. Looke you, sir, a parlous matter, sure!
first, to spred your circle vpon the ground,
then, with a little coniuring ceremonie, as Ile

32 of] a *M*   38 captain of *M*   40 me] my *Q*
47-8 let's to conjuring *once Ff, etc.*   54 of poor
soldiers *conj. M*   57 Hig-wayes *Q*   60 for why?
Ff, etc.   63 a *om. M*   71 tell] till *Q*

152

haue an Hackney-mans wand siluerd ore
a purpose for you,—then arriuing in the circle,
with a huge word, and a great trample, as for
instance:—haue you neuer seene a stalking-
stamping Player, that will raise a tempest with
his toung, and thunder with his heeles?   86
Cap. O yes, yes, yes: often, often.
Pyb. Why, be like such a one, for any
thing will bleare the old Knights eyes: for you
must note that heele nere dare to venture into
the roome, onely perhaps peepe fearefully
through the Key hole, to see how the Play
goes forward.   93
Capt. Well, I may goe about it when I will,
but marke the end ont: I shall but shame my
selfe, ifaith, *George.* Speake big words, and
stampe and stare, and he looke in at Key-hole!
why, the very thought of that would make me
laugh out-right, and spoile all: nay, Ile tell
thee, *George,* when I apprehend a thing once,
I am of such a laxatiue laughter, that if the
Deuill him-selfe stood by, I should laugh in
his face.   103
Pyb. Puh, thats but the babe of a man,
and may easily bee husht; as to thinke vpon
some disaster, some sad misfortune, as the
death of thy Father ithe Country!
Cap. Sfoote, that would be the more to
driue me into such an extasie, that I should
nere lin laughing.   110
Pib. Why, then, thinke vpon going to hanging else.
Cap. Masse, that's well remembred; now
ile do well, I warrant thee, nere feare me now:
but how shall I do, *George,* for boysterous
words, and horrible names?   116
Pyb. Puh, any fustian inuocations, Captaine, will serue as well as the best, so you
rant them out well; or you may goe to a
Pothecaries shop, and take all the words from
the Boxes.   121
Cap. Troth, and you say true, *George*;
there's strange words enow to raise a hundred
Quack-saluers, tho they be nere so poore when
they begin. But here lyes the feare on't, how
(if) in this false coniuration, a true Deuill
should pop vp indeed?   127
Pyb. A true Deuill, Captaine? why there
was nere such a one:·nay, faith, hee that has
this place is as false a Knaue as our last
Church-warden.   131
Capt. Then hees false inough a conscience,
ifaith, *George.*

The Crie at Marshalsea.

Crie prisoners. Good Gentlemen ouer the

112 else *om. F2, etc.*   126 if *add. F2*

way, send your reliefe. Good Gentlemen ouer
the way,—Good sir *Godfrey!*   136
Pyb. Hees come, hees come.
Nich. Maister, thats my Kinsman yonder
in the Buff-Ierkin—Kinsman, thats my Mais-
ter yonder ith' Taffetie Hatt—pray salute him
intirely! [*They salute: and* Py-boord *salutes*
Maister Edmond.
Sir God. Now, my friend.
Pib. May I pertake your name, sir?
Edm. My name is Maister *Edmund.*
Pyb. Maister *Edmond?*—are you not a
Welchman, sir?   146
Edm. A Welshman? why?
Pyb. Because Maister is your Christen
name, and *Edmond* your sir name.
Edm. O no; I haue more names at home:
Maister *Edmund Plus* is my full name at
length.   152
Pyb. O, crie you mercy, sir. (*Whispering.*)
Cap. I vnderstand that you are my Kins-
mans good Maister, and in regard of that, the
best of my skill is at your seruice: but had
you fortunde a meere stranger, and made no
meanes to me by acquaintance, I should haue
vtterly denyed to haue beene the man; both
by reason of the Act past in Parliament
against Coniurers and Witches, as also, because I would not haue my Arte vulgar, trite,
and common.   163
Sir Godf. I much commend your care
therein, good Captaine Coniurer, and that I
will be sure to haue it priuate enough, you
shall doote in my Sisters house,—mine owne
house, I may call it, for both our charges
therein are proportiond.
Capt. Very good, sir—what may I call your
losse, sir?   171
Sir Godf. O you may call't· a great losse,
sir, a grieuous losse, sir; as goodly a Chaine of
gold, tho I say it, that wore it:·how saiest thou,
Nicholas?   175
Nich. O 'twas as delicious a Chaine a Gold!
Kinsman, you know,—
Sir God. You know? did you know't, Captaine?   179
Capt. Trust a foole with secrets!—Sir, hee
may say I know: his meaning is, because my
Arte is such, that by it I may gather a know-
ledge of all things.
Sir Godf. I, very true.   184
Capt. A pax of all fooles—the excuse stucke
vpon my toung like Ship-pitch vpon a Mari-
ners gowne, not to come off in hast—Ber-lady,

160 past in *Q*: of *Ff, etc.*   165 there *Ff, etc·*
173 sir *om. Ff, etc.*   176 of Gold *F2, etc*

Knight, to loose such a faire Chaine a gold were a foule losse. Well, I can put you in this good comfort on't: if it bee betweene Heauen and Earth, Knight, Ile ha't for you.

Sir God. A wonderfull Coniurer!—O, I, tis betweene heauen and earth, I warrant you; it cannot goe out of the realme.—I know tis some-where aboue the earth. 195

Capt. I, nigher the earth then thou wotst on.

Sir Godf. For, first, my Chaine was rich, and no rich thing shall enter into heauen, you know. 200

Nich. And as for the Deuill, Maister, he has no need on't, for you know he ha's a great chaine of his owne.

Sir Godf. Thou saiest true, *Nicholas,* but hee has put off that now; that lyes by him. 205

Capt. Faith, Knight, in few wordes, I presume so much vpon the power of my Art; that I could warrant your Chaine againe.

Sir Godf. O daintie Captaine! 209

Capt. Marry, it will cost me much sweate; I were better goe to sixteene whot-houses.

Sir Godf. I, good man, I warrant thee.

Capt. Beside great vexation of Kidney and Liuer. 214

Nich. O, twill tickle you here-abouts, Coozen, because you haue not beene vsde toot.

Sir Godf. No? haue you not beene vsd too't, Captaine? 218

Capt. Plague of all fooles still!—Indeed, Knight, I haue not vsde it a good while, and therefore twill straine me so much the more, you know.

Sir Godf. Oh, it will, it will. 223

Cap. What plunges hee puts me to! were not this Knight a foole, I had beene twice spoyld now; that Captaynes worse then accurst that has an asse to his Kinsman. Sfoote, I feare hee will driuell't out before I come toote. —Now, sir—to come to the poynt in deede— you see I sticke here in the iawe of the Marshalsea, and cannot doo't. 231

Sir Godf. Tut, tut, I (k)now thy meaning; thou wouldst say thou'rt a prisoner. I tell thee thou'rt none.

Cap. How none? why, is not this the Marshialsea? 236

Sir Godf. Woult heare me speake? I hard of thy rare cuniuring;
My chayne was lost; I sweate for thy release,
As thou shalt doe the like at home for me.
Keeper.   [*Enter Keeper.*
Keep. Sir. 241
Sir Godf. Speake, is not this man free?

188 of Gold *F 2, etc.*   195 aboue] about *Ff*

Keep. Yes, at his pleasure, sir, the fees dischargd.

Sir Godf. Goe, goe, Ile discharge them I. 244

Keep. I thanke your worship. [*Exet Keeper.*

Cap. Now, trust me, yar a deere Knight. Kindnes vnexpected! oh theirs nothing to a free Gentle man.—I will cuniure for you, sir, till Froath come through my Buffe-ierkin! 249

Sir Godf. Nay, then thou shalt not passe with so little a bounty, for at the first sight of my chaine agen, Forty fine Angells shall appeare vnto thee. 253

Cap. Twil be a glorious showe, ifaith, Knight, a very fine show; but are all these of your owne house? are you sure of that, sir?

Sir Godf. I, I—no, no, whats he younder, talking with my wild Nephew? pray heauen, he giue him good counsell.

Cap. Who, he? hee's a rare friend of mine, an admirable fellow, Knight, the finest fortune-teller. 262

Sir Godf. Oh, tis he indeed that came to my Lady sister, & foretold the losse of my chaine. I am not angry with him now, for I see twas my fortune to loose it.—By your leaue, M⟨aister⟩ Fortune-teller, I had a glimps on you at home at my Sisters the Widdowes, there you prouisied of the losse of a chaine:— simply tho I stand here, I was he that lost it.

Pie. Was it you, sir? 271

Edm. A my troth, Nunckle, hee's the rarest fellow: has told me my fortune so right; I find it so right to my nature.

Sir Godf. What ist? God send it a good one!

Edm. O, tis a passing good one, Nuncle: for he sayes I shall proue such an excelent gamster in my time, that I shall spend al faster then my father got it.

Sir Godf. There's a fortune, in deed! 280

Edm. Nay, it hits my humour so pat.

Sir Godf. I, that will be the end ont: will the Curse of the beggar preuaile so much, that the sonne shall consume that foolishlie, which the father got craftilie? I, I, I; twill, twill, twill. 286

Pie. Stay, stay, stay.
[*Pyeboord with an Almanack and the Captaine.*
Cap. Turne ouer, *George.*
Pie. Iune—Iulie: here, *Iulie;* thats this month. Sunday thirteene, yester day forteene, to day fifteene. 291
Cap. Looke quickly for the fifteene day:— if within the compasse of these two dayes there would be some Boystrous storme or other, it would be the best, Ide defer him off till then: some tempest, and it be thy will. 296

243 fee's *Q*   252 forty fiue *Ff*   292 fifteenth *M, etc.*

Pie. Heres the fifteene day—hot and fayre.

Cap. Puh, would t'ad beene hot and foule.

Pie. The sixteene day; thats to morrow: the morning for the most part faire and pleasant—   301

Cap. No lucke.

Pie. But about hye-none, lighning and thunder.

Cap. Lighning and thunder! admirable, best of all: Ile coniure to morrow iust at hie none, *George.*   307

Pye. Happen but true to morrow, Almanack, and ile giue thee leaue to lie all the yeare after.

Cap. Sir, I must craue your patience, to bestowe this day vpon me, that I may furnish my selfe strongly. I sent a spirit into Lanckishire tother day, to fetch backe a knaue Drouer, and I looke for his returne this euening. To morrow morning my friend here and I will come and breake-fast with you.   316

Sir Godf. Oh, you shall be both most welcome.

Cap. And about Noone, without fayle, I purpose to coniure.   320

Sir Godf. Mid noone will be a fine time for you.

Edm. Coniuring! do you meane to coniure at our house to morrow, sir?   324

Cap. Marry, do I, sir: tis my intent, yong Gentleman.

Edm. By my troth, Ile loue you while I liue fort. O rare, *Nicholas,* we shall haue coniuring to morrowe.   329

Nic. Puh! I, I could ha tould you of that.

Cap. Law, hee could ha told him of that! foole, cockscombe, could yee?

Edm. Do you heare me, sir? I desire more acquaintance on you: you shall earne some money of me, now I knowe you can coniure; but can you fetch any that is lost?   336

Capt. Oh, any thing thats lost.

Edm. Why, looke you, sir, I tel't you as a frend and a Coniurer, I should marry a Poticaries daughter, and twas told me she lost her maidenhead at Stonie-stratford; now if youle do but so much as coniure fort, and make all whole agen—

Cap. That I will, sir.

Edm. By my troth, I thanke you, la.   345

Cap. A litle merry with your sisters sonne, sir.

Sir Godf. Oh, a simple yong man, very simple: come, Captaine, and you, sir, weele een part with a gallon of wine till to morrow breake-fast.   351

Pie. Cap. Troth, agreed, sir.

352 *Prefix* Tip. Cap. *Q*

Nic. Kinsman—Scholler?

Pye. Why, now thou art a good Knaue, worth a hundred Brownists.   355

Nic. Am I indeed, la? I thanke you truely, la.   [*Exeunt.*

Actus. 4.

⟨SCENE I. *An apartment in the Widow's house.*⟩

Enter Moll, *and Sir* Iohn Penny-dub.

Penne. But I hope you will not serue a Knight so, Gentlewoman, will you? to casheere him, and cast him off at your pleasure? what, do you thinke I was dubd for nothing? no, by my faith, Ladies daughter.   5

Moll. Pray, Sir *Iohn Pennydub,* let it be deferd awhile. I haue as bigge a heart to marry as you can haue; but as the Fortune-teler told me—   9

Penny. Pax a'th Fortune-teller! would Derecke had beene his fortune seauen yeare agoe, to crosse my loue thus! did hee know what case I was in? why, this is able to make a man drowne himselfe in's Fathers fish-pond.

Moll. And then hee told mee more-ouer, Sir *Iohn,* that the breach of it kept my Father in Purgatorie.   17

Penny. In Purgatorie? why let him purge out his heart there, what haue we to do with that? there's Phisitions enow there to cast his water: is that any matter to vs? how can hee hinder our loue? why, let him bee hangd now hee's dead!—Well, haue I rid poste day and night, to bring you merry newes of my fathers death, and now—   25

Moll. Thy Fathers death? is the old Farmer dead?

Penny. As dead as his Barne doore, *Moll.*

Moll. And you'le keepe your word with mee now, Sir *Iohn,* that I shall haue my Coach and my Coach-man?   31

Penny. I, faith.

Moll. And two white Horses with black Fethers to draw it?

Penny. Too.   35

Moll. A guarded Lackey to run befor't, and pyed liueries to come trashing after't.

Penny. Thou shalt, *Moll.*

Moll. And to let me haue money in my purse to go whether I will.   40

Penny. All this.

Moll. Then come what so ere comes on't, weele bee made sure together before the Maides a' the Kitchin.   [*Exeunt*

356 truely *Q* : heartily *Ff, etc.*   Scene I. *etc.* add. M   7 as bigge *om.* Ff   44 i' the *M*

(SCENE II. *A room in the Widow's house, with
a door at the side, leading to another
apartment.*)

*Enter Widow, with her eldest Daughter
Franck and* Frailtie.

Wid. How now? where's my Brother, Sir
Godfrey? went hee forth this morning?
Frail. O no, Madame, hee's aboue at
breake-fast, with, sir reuerence, a Coniurer.
Wid. A Coniurer? what manner a fellow is
he?   6
Frail. Oh, a wondrous rare fellow, Mistris,
very strongly made vpward, for he goes in a
Buff-ierkin: he sayes hee will fetch Sir *God-
freys* Chaine agen, if it hang betweene heauen
and earth.   11
Wid. What, he will not? then hee's an
exlent fellow, I warrant. How happy were that
woman to be blest with such a Husband! a
man a cunning! how do's hee looke, *Frailtie*?
very swartlie, I warrant, with black beard,
scorcht cheekes, and smokie eyebrowes.   17
Frail. Fooh, hee's neither smoake-dryed,
nor scorcht, nor black, nor nothing. I tell you,
Madame, hee lookes as faire to see to, as one
of vs; I do not thinke but if you saw him once,
youde take him to be a Christian.   22
Frank. So faire, and yet so cunning: that's
to bee wonderd at, Mother.

Enter Sir Oliuer Muck-hill, *and Sir*
Andrew Tip-staffe.

Muck. Blesse you, sweete Lady.   25
Tip. And you, faire Mistrisse.
                                    [*Exit* Frailtie.
Wid. Coades? what doe you meane, Gen-
tlemen? fie, did I not giue you your answeres?
Muck. Sweete Lady.
Wid. Well, I will not stick with you now
for a kisse.   30
Daughter, kisse the Gentleman for once.
Frank. Yes, forsooth.
Tip. Ime proud of such a fauour.
Wid. Truly la, sir *Oliuer*, y'are much to
blame to come agen, when you know my
minde, so well deliuerd as a Widdow could
deliuer a thing.
Muck. But I expect a farther comfort,
Lady.   39
Wid. Why la you now, did I not desire you
to put off your sute quite & cleane, when
you came to me againe? how say you? did I
not?

Scene II. *etc. add.* M   15 a man cunning *Ff* : a
cunning man *M*   S. D. Sir Andrew Muck-hill *Ff*
30 now *om. Ff, etc.*

Muc. But the sincere loue which my heart
beares you—   45
Wid. Go to, ile cut you off: & Sir *Oliuer*, to
put you in comfort a farre off, my fortune is
read me: I must marry againe.
Muck. O blest fortune!
Wid. But not as long as I can choose;—
nay, Ile hold out well.   51
Muc. Yet are my hopes now fairer.

Enter Frailtie.

Frail. O Madam, Madam.
Wid. How now, what's the hast?
                                    [*In her eare.*
Tipst. Faith, Mistrisse *Francis*, Ile main-
taine you gallantly. Ile bring you to Court,
weane you among the faire society of ladies,
poore Kinswomen of mine, in cloth of siluer :
beside, you shal haue your Monckie, your
Parrat, your Muskat, & your pisse, pisse, pisse.
Frank. It will do very well.   61
Wid. What, dos he meane to coniure here
then? how shal I do to bee rid of these Knights?
—Please you, Gentlemen, to walke a while ith
Garden: go gather a pinck, or a Lilly-flower.
Both. With all our hearts, Lady, and count
vs fauourd.   [*Exit. Within Sir Go.*
Si. Go. Step in, *Nicholas*; looke, is the
coast cleare.
Nic. Oh, as cleare as a Cattes eye, sir.   70
Sir Go. Then enter, Captaine Coniurer:—
now—how like you your Roome, sir?

Enter Sir Godf. Capt. Pyb. Edm. Nick.

Cap. O, wonderfull conuenient.
Edm. I can tell you, Captaine, simplie tho
it lies here, tis the fayrest Roome in my
Mothers house: as dainty a Roome to Coniure
in, mee thinkes—why, you may bidde, I cannot tell how many diuills welcome in't; my
Father has had twentie here at once!
Pie. What, diuills?   80
Edm. Diuills? no, Deputies, & the welthiest
men he could get.
Sir God. Nay, put by your chattes now,
fall to your businesse roundly: the feskewe of
the Diall is vpon the Chrisse-crosse of Noone,
but oh, heare mee, Captaine, a qualme comes
ore my stomack.
Cap. Why, what's the matter, sir?
Sir Godf. Oh, how if the diuill should proue
a knaue, and teare the hangings?   90
Cap. Fuh, I warrant you, Sir Godfrey.
Edm. I, Nuncle, or spit fire vpp'oth seeling!
Sir Godf. Very true, too, for tis but thin

45 bears to you *Ff*   52 *om. Ff*   65 go *Q* : to *Ff*,
etc.   70 Cattes *Q* : Carter's *Ff*   72 your] our
Ff   79 here *Q* : in't *Ff, etc.*

playsterd, and twill quickly take hold a the laths, and if hee chance to spit downeward too, he will burne all the boords.   96

Cap. My life for yours, Sir Godfrey.

Sir Godf. My Sister is very curious & dainty ore this Roome, I can tell, and therefore if he must needes spit, I pray desire him to spit ith Chimney.   101

Pie. Why, assure you, Sir Godfrey, he shall not be brought vp with so little manners to spit and spaule a'th flower.   104

Sir Godf. Why, I thanke you, good Captaine; pray haue a care. I, fall to your Circle; weele not trouble you, I warrant you: come, weele in to the next Roome, & be cause weele be sure to keepe him out there, weele bar vp the dore with some of the Godlies zealous workes.

Edm. That will bee a fine deuice, Nuncle, and because the ground shall be as holy as the doore, Ile teare two or three rosaries in peices, and strew the leaues about the Chamber.   114
                                              [*Thunders.*
Oh, the deuill already.   [*runs in.*

Py. Sfoote, Captaine, speake somwhat for shame; it lightens & thunders before thou wilt begin: why, when?

Cap. Pray, peace, *George,*—thou'lt make mee laugh anon and spoile all.   120

Pie. Oh, now it begins agen: now, now, now, Captaine.

Cap. Rumbos—ragdayon, pur, pur, colucundrion, Hois-Plois.

Sir Godf. Oh admirable Coniurer! has fetcht Thunder already: 126
            [*Sir Godfrey through the
               keyhole; within.*

Pie. Harke, harke! agen, Captaine!

Cap. Beniamino,—gaspois—kay—gosgothoteron—vmbrois.   129

Sir Godf. Oh, I would the deuill would come away quicklie, he has no conscience to put a man to such paine.

Pie. Agen!

Cap. Flowste — Kakopumpos — dragone—Leloomenos—hodge—podge.   135

Pie. Well sayd, Captaine.

Sir Godf. So long a comming? oh, would I had nere begun't now, for I feare mee these roaring tempest will destroy all the fruites of the earth, and tread vpon my corne—oh!—ith Country.   141

Cap. Gog de gog, hobgoblin, huncks, hounslow, hockley te coome parke.

Wid. ⟨*at the door*⟩. O brother, brother, what

a tempests ith Garden: sure there's some coniuration abroad.   146

Sir Godf. Tis at home, sister!

Pie. By and by, Ile step in, Captaine.

Cap. Nunck—Nunck—Rip —Gascoynes, Ipis, Drip—Dropite.   150

Sir God. Hee drippes and droppes, poore man! alasse, alasse.

Pie. Now I come.

Cap. O Sulphure Sooteface—

Pie. Arch-coniurer, what wouldst thou with me?   156

Sir Godf. O the diuill, sister, ith dyning Chamber! sing, Sister, I warrant you that will keepe him out: quickly, quickly, quickly.
                                          [*goes in.*

Pie. So, so, so, Ile release thee : ynough, Captaine, ynough; allowe vs some time to laughe a little: they're shuddering and shaking by this time, as if an Earth-quake were in their kidneyes.   164

Cap. Sirrah *George,* how wast, how wast? did I do't well ynough?

Pie. Woult beleeue mee, Captaine? better then any Coniurer, for here was no harme in this, and yet their horrible expectation satisfied well. You were much beholding to thunder & lightning at this time: it gracst you well I can tell you.   172

Cap. I must needes say so, *George.* Sirrah, if wee could ha conuoide hether cleanly a cracker or a fire-wheele t'ad beene admirable.   176

Pie. Blurt, blurt! theirs nothing remaines to put thee to paine now, Captaine.

Cap. Paine? I protest, *George,* my heeles are sorer, then a Whitson Morris-dancer. 180

Pie. All's past now,—onely to reueale that the chaines ith Garden where thou knowst it has laine these two daies.

Cap. But I feare that fox *Nicholas* has reueald it already.   185

Pie. Feare not, Captaine, you must put it to'th venture now. Nay, tis time: call vpon e'm, take pitty on e'm, for I beleeue some off 'em are in a pittifull case by this time.

Cap. Sir Godfrey? Nicholas, Kinsman—Sfoot, they'r fast at it still, *George.* Sir *Godfrey!*

Sir Godf. Oh, is that the diuils voyce? how comes he to know my name?   193

Cap. Feare not, Sir *Godfrey,* all's quieted.

Sir Godf. What, is he layd?

Cap. Layde; and has newly dropt your chaine ith Garden.   197

99 ore] of *M*   tell] tell you *Ff, etc.*   104 flower] floor *Qq, etc.*   114 leaues] pieces *M*   *S. D.* runs in *part of Edmond's speech Q*   144 at . . door *add. M*

174 convey'd *M*   180 dancer's *Ff, etc.*   194-5 *S. D.* Enter Sir Godfrey, The Widow, Frances, and Nicholas *M*

Sir Godf. Ith Garden! in our Garden?
Cap. Your Garden.
Sir Godf. O sweete Coniurer! where abouts
there?   201
Cap. Looke well about à banck of Rose-
mary.
Sir Godf. Sister, the Rosemary banck!
come, come, ther's my chaine, he saies.
Wid. Oh happinesse! run, run.   206
                              [*supposed to goe.*
Edm. Captaine Coniurer?
                              [*Edm. at keyhoole.*
Cap. Who? Maister *Edmond?*
Edm. I, Maister *Edmond*: may I come in
safely, without danger, thinke you?   210
Cap. Fuh, long agoe: tis all as twas at first.
Feare nothing, pray come neere—how now,
man?
Edm. Oh this Roomes mightily hot, ifaith:
slid, my shirt sticks to my Belly already. What
a steame the Rogue has left behind him! foh,
this roome must be ayrd, Gentlemen; it
smells horribly of Brimstoone—lets open the
windowes.
Pye. Faith, maister *Edmond,* tis but your
conceite.   220
Edm. I would you could make me beleeue
that, ifaith. Why, do you thinke I cannot
smell his sauour from another? yet I take it
kindly from you, because you would not put
me in a feare, ifaith; a my troth, I shal loue
you for this the longest day of my life. 226
Cap. Puh, tis nothing, sir: loue me when
you see more.
Edm. Masse, now I remember, Ile looke
whether he has singed the hangings or no.
Pye. Captaine, to entertaine a litle sport
till they come, make him beleeue youle charme
him inuisible: hes apt to admire any thing,
you see. Let me alone to giue force too'te.
Cap. Goe, retire to yonder end then. 235
Edm. I protest you are a rare fellowe, are
you not?
Cap. O maister *Edmond,* you know but the
least part of me yet: why, now at this instant
I could but florish my wand thrice ore your
head, and charme you inuisible.   241
Edm. What, you could not? make me
walke inuisible, man! I should laugh at that,
ifaith; troth, ile requite your kindnes and
youle doo't, good Captaine coniurer.   245
Cap. Nay, I should hardly deny you such
a small kindnesse, Master *Edmond Plus*: why,
looke you, sir, tis no more but this and thus
and agen, and now yar inuisible!   249
Edm. Am I, ifaith? who would thinke it?

212-13 *S. D.* Enter Edmond *M*   248-9 thus agen *Ff*

Cap. You see the fortune-teller yonder at
farder end ath chamber: goe toward him, do
what you will with him; he shall nere finde
you.   254
Edm. Say you so? ile trie that, ifaith,——
                              [*Iustles him.*
Pie. How now? Captaine, whose that
iustled me?
Cap. Iustled you? I saw no body.   258
Edm. Ha, ha, ha!——say twas a spirit.
Cap. Shall I?—may be some spirit that
haunts the circle.
                  [⟨*Edmond*⟩ *Puls him by the Nose.*
Pye. O my nose agen! pray coniure then,
Captaine.   263
Edm. Troth, this is exlent; I may do any
knauery now and neuer be seene,—and now
I remember mee, Sir *Godfrey* my Vncle abusde
me tother day, & told tales of me to my Mother
—Troth, now Ime inuisible, ile hit him a sound
wherrit ath' eare, when he comes out ath'
garden.—I may be reuengd on him now
finely.   271

Enter Sir Godfrey, Widdow, Franck, Nicholas
            with the Chaine.

Sir God. I haue my Chaine againe, my
Chaine's found againe. O sweete Captaine,
O admirable Coniurer. [*Edm. strikes him.*
Oh! what meane you by that, Nephew?
Edm. Nephew? I hope you do not know
mee, Vncle?   277
Wid. Why did you strike your Vncle, sir?
Edm. Why, Captaine, am I not inuisible?
Capt. A good iest, *George!*—not now you
are not, Sir.
Why, did you not see me when I did vncharme
you?   281
Edm. Not I by my troth, Captaine. Then
pray you pardon mee, Vncle; I thought Ide
beene inuisible when I struck you.
Sir Godf. So, you would doo't? go,—y'are
a foolish Boy,   285
And were I not ore-come with greater ioy,
Ide make you taste correction.
Edm. Correction, push!—no, neither you
nor my Mother shall thinke to whip me as
you haue done.   290
Sir Godf. Captaine, my ioy is such, I know
not how to thanke you: let me embrace you,
hug you. O my sweete Chaine! Gladnesse
'een makes me giddy. Rare man! twas as
iust ith' Rosemarie banck, as if one should ha
laide it there—oh cunning, cunning!   296
Wid. Well, seeing my fortune tels mee

256 How] Hoe *Ff*   261 *S. D.* Puls . . Nose *after*
263 Q   293 hug you *om. Ff, etc.*

158

I must marry, let me marry a man of witte,
a man of parts. Here's a worthy Captaine,
and 'tis a fine Title truely la to bee a Captaines
Wife. A Captaines Wife, it goes very finely;
beside all the world knows that a worthy
Captaine is a fitte Companion to any Lord,
then why not a sweete bed-fellow for any Lady,
—Ile haue it so——   305

Enter Frailtie.

Frail. O Mistris, Gentlemen, there's the
brauest sight comming along this way.
Wid. What braue sight?
Frai. Oh, one going to burying, & another
going to hanging.   310
Wid. A ruefull sight.
Pyb. Sfoot, Captaine, Ile pawne my life the
Corporals coffind, and old *Skirmish* the souldier going to execution, & 'tis now full about
the time of his waking; hold out a little longer,
sleepie potion, and we shall haue exlent admiration; for Ile take vpon me the cure of him.

(SCENE III. *The street before the
Widow's house.*)

*Enter the Coffin of the Corporall, the souldier
bound, and lead by Officers, the Sheriffe
there. (From the house, Sir Godfrey, the
Widow, Idle, Pyeboard, Edmond, Frailty,
and Nicholas.)*

Frail. Oh here they come, here they come!
Pyb. Now must I close secretly with the
Souldier, preuent his impatience, or else all's
discouered.   4
Wid. O lamentable seeing! these were
those Brothers, that fought and bled before
our doore.
Sir Godf. What, they were not, Sister?
Skirm. George, looke toote, Ile peach at
Tyburne else.   10
Pyb. Mum,—Gentles all, vouchsafe mee
audience, and you especially, Maister Shiriffe:
Yon man is bound to execution,
Because he wounded this that now lyes coffind?
Shir. True, true; he shall haue the law,—
and I know the law.   16
Pyb. But vnder fauour, Maister Sheriffe, if
this man had beene cured and safe agen, he
should haue beene releasde then?
Shir. Why make you question of that, Sir?
Pyb. Then I release him freely, and will
take vpon mee the death that he should dye,
if within a little season, I do not cure him to
his proper health agen.

Shir. How Sir? recouer a dead man?   25
That were most strange of all.
                    [Franke *comes to him.*
Frank. Sweete Sir, I loue you deerely, and
could wish my best part yours,—oh do not
vndertake such an impossible venture.
Pyb. Loue you me? then for your sweet
    sake Ile doo't: 30
Let me entreate the corps to be set downe.
Shir. Bearers, set downe the Coffin.—This
were wonderfull, and worthy *Stoes* Chronicle.
Pyb. I pray bestow the freedome of the
ayre vpon our wholsome Arte.—Masse, his
cheekes begin to receiue naturall warmth: nay,
good Corporall, wake betime, or I shall haue
a longer sleepe then you.—Sfoote, if he should
proue dead indeed now, he were fully reuengd
vpon me for making a property on him, yet I
had rather run vpon the Ropes, then haue the
Rope like a Tetter run vpon mee. Oh—he
stirs—hee stirs agen—looke, Gentlemen, he
recouers, he starts, he rises.
Shir. Oh, oh, defend vs!—out, alasse. 45
Pyb. Nay, pray be still; youle make him
more giddy else:—he knowes no body yet.
Corp. Zounes: where am I? couerd with
Snow? I maruaile.   49
Pyb. Nay, I knew hee would sweare the
first thing hee did, as soone as euer he came
to his life agen.
Corp. Sfoote, Hostesse, some hotte Por-
ridge,—oh, oh, lay on a dozen of Fagots the
Moone parler, there.   55
Pyb. Lady, you must needs take a little
pitty of him, yfaith, and send him in to your
Kitchin fire.
Wid. Oh, with all my heart, sir. *Nicholas*
and *Frailtie,* helpe to beare him in.   60
Nich. Beare him in, quatha? pray call out
the Maides, I shall nere haue the heart to doo't,
indeed la.
Frai. Nor I neither, I cannot abide to
handle a Ghost of all men.   65
Cor. Sbloud, let me see: where was I drunke
last night, heh—
Wid. Oh, shall I bid you once agen take
him away?
Frai. Why, we're as fearefull as you, I
warrant you—oh—   71
Wid. Away, villaines; bid the Maides make
him a Cawdle presently to settle his braine,—
or a Posset of Sack; quickly, quickly.
        [*Exeunt* (Frailty and Nicholas) *pushing in
                                    the corpes.*

314 full *om. Ff, etc.*   315 waking *Ff, etc.*: walking *Q*   Scene III. *etc. add. M.   No change of scene
intended by author   S. D. From.. Nicholas add. M*

33 were] is *Ff*   40 on] of *M*   48 where *Ff, etc.*:
who *Q*   51, 52 euer, his *om. Ff*   74 *S. D.* Frailty,
etc. add. M

Shir. Sir, what so ere you are, I do more
then admire you.   76
Wid. O, I, if you knew all, Maister Shiriffe,
as you shall doe, you would say then, that
here were two of the rarest men within the
walls of Christendome.   80
Shir. Two of 'em? O wonderfull. Officers,
I discharge you, set him free, all's in tune.
Sir Godf. I, and a banquet ready by this
time, Maister Sheriffe, to which I most cheere-
fully enuite you, and your late prisoner there.
See you this goodly chaine, sir? mun, no more
words, twas lost, and is found againe; come,
my inestimable bullies, weele talke of your
noble Acts in sparkling Charnico, and in stead
of a Iester, weele ha the ghost ith white sheete
sit at vpper end a'th Table.   91
Sheriff. Exlent merry, man, yfaith.
                    (*Exeunt all but Frances.*)
Franck Well, seeing I am enioynd to loue
    and marry,
My foolish vow thus I casheere to Ayre
Which first begot it.—Now, loue, play thy part;
The scholler reades his lecture in my heart. 96
                                (*Exit.*)

Actus 5.

Scen. I. (*The street before the Widow's house.*)
Enter in hast Maister Edmund *and*
                Frayltie.

Ed. This is the marriage morning for my
mother & my sister.
Frail. O me, Maister *Edmund*; we shall ha
rare doings.   4
Ed. Nay, go, *Frayltie*, runne to the Sexton;
you know my mother wilbe married at Saint
Antlings. Hie thee, tis past fiue; bid them open
the Church dore; my sister is almost ready.
Fra. What, al ready, Maister *Edmond?*   9
Ed. Nay, go, hie thee: first run to the
Sexton, and runne to the Clarke, and then run
to Maister *Pigman* the Parson, and then run
to the Millanor, and then run home agen.
Frail. Heer's run, run, run——
Ed. But harke, *Frailty*.   15
Fra. What, more yet?
Edm. Has the maides remembred to strew
the way to the Church.
Frail. Fagh, an houre ago; I helpt 'em my
selfe.   20
Ed. Away, away, away, away then.
Frail. Away, away, away then.
                        [*Exit* Frailty.

75 *Prefix* Skir. *Q*   91 at the upper *M*   *S. D.*
Exeunt.. Frances *M* : Exit *Q*   *S. D.* Exit *add. M*
S. D. The street .. house *add. M*   19 help *Q*   22
then *Q* : away then *Ff, etc.*

Edm. I shall haue a simple Father inlawe,
a braue Captaine able to beate all our streete:
Captaine *Idle.* Now my Ladie Mother wilbe
fitted for a delicate name: my Ladie *Idle*, my
Ladie *Idle*, the finest name that can be for
a woman; and then the Scholler, Maister *Pie-
boord*, for my sister *Francis*, that wilbe Mistris
Francis Pie-boord.—Mistris *Francis Pie-boord!*
theill keepe a good table I warrant you. Now
all the knights noses are put out of ioynt; they
may go to a bone setters now.   33

Enter Captaine and Pie-boord.

Harke, harke! oh who comes here with two
Torches before 'em? my sweete Captaine, and
my fine Scholler! oh, how brauely they are
shot vp in one night; they looke like fine
Brittaines now, me thinkes. Heres a gallant
chaunge, ifaith: slid, they haue hir'd men and
all by the clock.   40
Cap. Maister *Edmund*, kinde, honest,
dainty Maister *Edmond.*
Edm. Fogh, sweete Captaine Father inlaw,
a rare perfume, ifayth.   44
Pie. What, are the Brides stirring? may
wee steall vpon 'em, thinkst thou, Maister
Edmond?
Edm. Faw, there e'en vpon reddines, I can
assure you, for they were at there Torch e'en
now: by the same token I tumbled downe the
staires.   51
Pie. Alas, poore Maister *Edmond.*

Enter musitians.

Cap. O, the musitians! I pree the, Maister
Edmond, call 'em in and licquour 'em a little.
Ed. That I will, sweete Captaine father in
law, and make ech of them as drunck as a
common fiddeler.   [*Exeunt omnes.*

(Scene II. *The same.*)
Enter Sir Iohn Penidub, *and* Moll *aboue lacing
of her clothes.*

Pen. Whewh, Mistris Mol, Mistris Mol.
Mol. Who's there?
Pen. Tis I.
Mol. Who? Sir *Iohn Penidub?* O you'r an
early cocke, ifayth: who would haue thought
you to be so rare a stirrer?   6
Pen. Preethe, Mol, let me come vp.
Mol. No, by my faith, Sir Iohn, Ile keepe
you downe, for you Knights are very dangerous
if once you get aboue.   10
Pen. Ile not stay, ifaith.
Mol. Ifaith, you shall staie, for, Sir Iohn,

Scene II. *etc. add. M*

you must note the nature of the Climates: your
Northen wench in her owne Countrie may
well hold out till shee bee fifteene, but if she
touch the South once, and come vp to *London*,
here the Chimes go presently after twelue.

Pen. O th'art a mad wench, *Moll*, but I
pree thee make hast, for the Priest is gone
before.   20

Moll. Do you follow him, Ile not be long
after.   [*Exeunt.*

(SCENE III. *A room in Sir* Oliver
Muckhill's *house.*)

Enter Sir Oliuer Muck-hill, *Sir* Andrew Tip-
staffe, *and old* Skirmish *talking.*

Muck. O monstrous, vn-heard of forgerie.

Tip. Knight, I neuer heard of such villany
in our owne countrie in my life.

Muck. Why, 'tis impossible; dare you
maintaine your words?   5

Skir. Dare wee? een to their wezen pipes.
We know all their plots, they cannot squander
with vs; they haue knauishly abusd vs, made
onely properties on's to aduance their selues
vpon our shoulders, but they shall rue their
abuses. This morning they are to bee married.

Muck. Tis too true; yet if the Widdow bee
not too much besotted on slights and forgeries,
the reuelation of their villanies will make 'em
loathsome: and to that end, be it in priuate
to you, I sent late last night to an honourable
personage, to whom I am much indebted in
kindnesse, as he is to me, and therefore presume vpon the paiment of his tongue, and that
hee will lay out good words for me: and to
speake truth, for such needfull occasions, I
onely preserue him in bond, and some-times
he may doe mee more good here in the Cittie
by a free word of his mouth, then if hee had
paide one halfe in hand, and tooke Doomesday
for t'other.   26

Tip. In troth, Sir, without soothing bee it
spoken, you haue publisht much iudgement in
these few words.

Muck. For you know, what such a man
vtters will be thought effectuall and to waighty
purpose, and therefore into his mouth weel
put the approoued theame of their forgeries.

Skir. And Ile maintaine it, Knight, if
yeele be true.   35

Enter a seruant.

Muck. How now, fellow?

Seru. May it please you, Sir, my Lord is
newly lighted from his Coache.

Muc. Is my Lord come already? his hon-
nors earlly.

You see he loues me well: vp before
seauen!   40

Trust me, I haue found him night capt at
eleuen.

Ther's good hope yet; come, Ile relate all to
him.   [*Exeunt.*

(SCENE IV. *A street; a church appearing.*)

*Enter the two Bridegromes, Captaine and Schol-
ler; after them, Sir* Godfrey *and* Edmond,
Widdow *changde in apparell, mistris*
Francis *led betweene two Knights, Sir*
Iohn Penny-dub *and* Moll: *there meetes
them a Noble man, Sir* Oliuer Muckil, *and
Sir* Andrew Tip-staffe.

Nob. By your leaue, Lady.

Wid. My Lord, your honour is most chastly
welcome.

Nob. Madam, tho I came now from court,
I come not to flatter you: vpon whom can I
iustly cast this blot, but vpon your owne fore-
head, that know not inke from milke? such
is the blind besotting in the state of an
vnheaded woman thats a widdow. For it is
the property of all you that are widdowes
(a hand full excepted) to hate those that
honestly and carefully loue you, to the maintenance of credit, state, and posterity, and
strongly to doat on those, that only loue you
to vndo you: who regard you least are best
regarded, who hate you most are best beloued.
And if there be but one man amongst tenne
thousand millions of men that is accurst,
disastrous, and euilly planeted, whome Fortune beates most, whome God hates most,
and all Societies esteeme least, that man is
suere to be a husband.—Such is the peeuish
Moone that rules your bloods. An Impudent
fellow best woes you, a flattering lip best wins
you, or in a mirth who talkes roughliest is
most sweetest; nor can you distinguish truth
from forgeries, mistes from Simplisity: witnes
those two deceitfull monsters that you haue
entertaine for bride-groomes.   29

Wid. Deceitfull!

Pie. All will out.

Cap. Sfoote, who has blabd, *George*? that
foolish *Nicholas*?

Nob. For what they haue besotted your
easie blood withall weare nought but forgeries:
the fortune telling for husbands, the con-

40 seauen *Q*: heauen *Ff*   41 at a eleuen *Q*   42
Ile] Iee *Q*   Scene IV. *etc. add. M*   11 handfull
F1   23 you bloods *Q*   25 a *om. Ff*

iuring for the chaine *Sir Godfrey* heard the falshod of: al nothing but meere knauery, deceit, and coozenage.   39

Wid. O wonderfull! indeed I wondred that my husband with all his craft could not keepe himselfe out of purgatory.

Sir Godf. And I more wonder that my chaine should be gon and my Taylor had none of it.   45

Mol. And I wondred most of all that I should be tyed from marriage, hauing such a mind too't. Come, S⟨ir⟩ *Iohn Pennydub*, faire wether on our side; the moone has chaingd since yester night.   50

Pie. The Sting of euery euill is with-in mee.

Nob. And that you may perceaue I faine not with you, behould their fellow actor in those forgeries; who, full of Spleene and enuy at their so suddaine aduancements, reueled all there plot in anger.   56

Pie. Base Souldier, to reueall vs.

Wid. Ist possible wee should be blinded so, and our eys open?

Nob. Widdow, wil you now beleeue that false, which to soone you beleeued true?   61

Wid. O, to my shame I doe.

Sir Godf. But vnder fauour, my Lord, my chaine was truely lost and straingly found againe.   65

Nob. Resolue him of that, Souldier.

S⟨k⟩ir. In few words, Knight, then, thou wert the arch-gull of all.

Sir Godf. How, Sir?   69

Skir. Nay, ile proue it: for the chayne was but hid in the rosemary bancke all this while, and thou gotst him out of pryson to Coniure for it, who did it admirably fustianly; for indeed what neede any others when he knew where it was?   75

Sir Godf. O vilainy of vilanies! but how came my chaine there?

Skir. Wheres *truly la, in deed la*, he that will not sweare, but lie, he that will not steale, But rob: pure *Nicholas Saint Antlings?*   80

Sir Godf. O Villaine! one of our society, Deemd alwaies holy, pure, religious. A Puritan a theefe, when wast euer hard? Sooner wee'll kill a man then Steale, thou knowst.

Out, slaue! Ile rend my lyon from thy back 85

With mine owne hands.

Nich. Deare Maister, oh.

Nob. Nay, Knight, dwell in patience. And now, widdow, being so neere the Church, twer great pitty, nay vncharity, to send you home againe without a husband: drawe nerer you of true worship, state and credit, that should not stand so farre of from a widdow, and suffer forged shapes to come betweene you. Not that in these I blemish the true Title of a Captaine, or blot the faire margent of a Scholler; For I honnor worthy and deseruing parts in the one, and cherrish fruitfull Vertues in the other. Come Lady, and you, Virgin; bestowe your eys and your purest affections vpon men of estimation both in Court and Citty, that hath long woed you, and both with there hearts and wealth sincearly loue you. 103

Sir Godf. Good Sister, doe: Sweet little *Franke*, these are men of reputation; you shalbe welcome at Court: a great creddit for a Cittizen, sweet Sister.

Nob. Come, her scilence doos consent too't.

Wid. I know not with what face—   109

Nob. Pah, pah! why, with your owne face; they desire no other.

Wid. Pardon me, worthy Sirs; I and my daughter haue wrongd your loues.

Muck. Tis easily pardon'd, Lady, If you vouchsafe it now.   115

Wid. With all my soule.

Fran. And I with all my heart.

Moll. And I, Sir *Iohn*, with soule, heart, lights and all.

Sir Ioh. They are all mine, *Moll*.   120

Nob. Now, Lady, What honest Spirit but will applaud your choyce, And gladly furnish you with hand and voyce? A happy change which makes een heauen reioyce. Come, enter into your Ioyes, you shall not want   125 For fathers now; I doubt it not, beleeue me, But that you shall haue hands inough to giue (ye).   [*Exeunt omnes.*
Deus dedit his quoq⟨ue⟩ finem.

FINIS

37 heare *S*   43 wonder'd *M*   74 needed *Ff, etc.*
other *M*   76 vilanies] villains *Ff*

91 near *Ff*   102 hath *Q*: have *Ff, etc.*   120
Prefix Sir Godf. *Ff*   125 into] in *Ff*   127 give ye
R: giue *Q*: give me *Ff*   128 Deus, *etc. om. Ff, etc.*

162

NOTES

A YORKSHIRE TRAGEDY

i. This scene, which, as Steevens remarks, is not necessary to the plot, has given rise to much discussion. The circumstances to which the servants allude at the beginning are made clear by reference to *The Miseries of Enforced Marriage*, by George Wilkins. Mr. P. A. Daniel (*Athenaeum*, No. 2710, Oct. 4, 1879) first pointed out that the two plays treat of the same incidents, though the *Miseries* stops practically where our play begins. The *yong Mistresse* of line 1 is the Clare Harcop of Wilkins's drama. There is some difficulty as to the servants; they would appear to belong to the same household, and yet Ralph and Oliver seem to serve the *yong Mistresse*, while Sam is certainly in Calverley's employ. The truth probably is that the author of this hasty work had not imagined very consistently the details of Calverley's previous life.

32. *capcase*: cf. *Locrine*, I. ii. 106.

62, 63. Percy's emendations, quoted by Malone, are utterly unjustified.

74, 75. *potingsticks*: cf. Ford, *Love's Sacrifice*, IV. i. 15. The more usual spelling is *poking-stick*, as in Rowe and succeeding editors.

77, 82–3. A common proverb is alluded to. Steevens quotes from the *Stationers' Register*, 1566: 'a playe intituled Farre fetched and deare bowght ys good for ladies.'

78, 80. There is no sufficient reason for the alteration in the division of speeches introduced by Malone.

ii. 14. Some causal conjunction, such as *that* or *because*, is in Rowe understood before *His*. Cf. Abbott, *Sh. Gr.* § 311. Hazlitt's indefensible displacement of the line is due to failure to grasp the meaning of the passage. Steevens had already suggested that lines 14 and 13 be transposed.

101. *blood*: 'nature'; cf. iv. 74 and N.E.D.

120. God den: cf. *Puritan*, III. iv. 163 and note.

149. *country* is, of course, used adjectivally. Cf. Abbott, *Sh. Gr.* § 22.

iii. 75. The substitution of *pleasant* for *comely* is probably the result of mere carelessness on the compositor of Q 2, who unintentionally substituted for one adjective a more familiar one with the same meaning.

iv. 120. *white boie*: a term of endearment. Cf. Ford, '*Tis Pity*, I. iv (*Mermaid* ed., p. 114).

125, 126. The meaning is: follow a coach, crying 'Good your Honour!' to the occupant.

v. 13, 14. The reference is to Leicester and Amy Robsart. Steevens quotes an apposite passage from *Leicester's Commonwealth* (1584, &c.).

viii. 16. *bated*: the meaning is probably not *abated* or *barred*, as Malone and Steevens re-spectively explain it, but *tormented*, as in bear-baiting. Cf. N.E.D. s. v. *Bait* v.[1] 4.

x. 22. *one thousand more*: sc. years. The reference, as Percy points out, is to *Revelation* xx. 2.

52. Some emendation is obviously required. Steevens suggests, as an alternative to the reading adopted in the text, *leave* (i. e. cease), *to part*.

THE PURITAN

It will be noted that the title of this play is given on the title-page as *The Puritaine or the Widdow of Watling-streete*, whereas the heading of the first page of text gives the abbreviated title *The Puritaine Widdow*. The inconsistency is of no importance except as explaining references to the play both as *The Puritan* and as *The Puritan Widow*.

ACT I

i. 89. *snobbing*: 'weeping'; the primary meaning of the verb seems to be *hiccup*. Cf. Stratmann, *M. E. Dict.* s. v. *Snobben*, and Wright, *Dial. Dict.*

107. *to hot, nor to deere*: a proverbial expression = 'too difficult of attainment'. Cf. notes of Malone and Steevens. Simms proposes the unnecessary emendation *good* for *hot*.

132. *speake false Lattin*: 'lie'.

136–8. Malone conjectures plausibly that the thrice repeated *their* of Q for *this*, which is almost certainly correct, is due to the use of an abbreviation in the MS. How common such abbreviations of familiar words were in Elizabethan cheirography is well known.

147. *Widdowers*: it would be convenient to take this word, as Malone suggests, in the sense of *widows*', but I have found no authority for such a use.

ii. 4, 5. *put to silence like a Sectarie*: a reference apparently to the silencing of the Puritans under the primacy of Archbishop Bancroft, appointed 1603.

29. *Antient*: 'ensign'; cf. N.E.D. s. v. *Ancient* sb.[2] 2.

41, 42. *Quadrangle, Battled*: Dr. Farmer pointed out that these terms are peculiar to Oxford. Peele, the probable original of Pye-board, was educated at Broadgates Hall, Oxford, and the author of this play was most likely a member of the same university.

46–9. *a Cheese out of Iesus Colledge ... Welshman*: this is another indication that Pye-board is alluding to Oxford, for there is no connexion between Jesus College, Cambridge, and the Welsh.

92. *and Peace*: 'if Peace'; cf. Stratmann, *M. E. Dict.* s. v. *And* [2].

161 *soothing*: 'flattering', 'hypocritical'.

iii. 11. *we three*: Steevens refers to *Twelfth Night*, II. iii. 16, 17, 'How now, my hearts! Did you never see the picture of "we three"?' The picture represented two men in fools' coats, the spectator making the third.

25. *drye*: cf. *dry blows*, said of blows not drawing blood. N.E.D. s. v. *Dry* a. 12.

42. *sowne*: 'swoon'.

56. *Capadochio*: 'prison'. N.E.D. gives only this instance, but cf. Heywood, 1 *King Edward IV*, ed. 1874, p. 72: 'My son's in Dybell here, in *Caperdochy*, itha gaol.'

iv. 71. *bloud*: 'hereditary dignity'; cf. N.E.D. s. v. *Blood* 9.

158. *Pomwater*: 'apple'; cf. *Love's Labour's Lost*, IV. ii. 4.

159. *vncomfortable*: 'unconsoling'; cf. N.E.D. s. v. *Comfortable* 6.

299, 300. *Beare at Bridge-Foote*: a well-known inn by London Bridge; cf. Shirley, *Lady of Pleasure*, v. ii (*Mermaid* ed., p. 342); Middleton, *No Wit, no Help, etc.*, v. i. 267–8, and Bullen's note. There is no need of altering the words *in heauen*. The Corporal jocularly confuses in his oath the well-known tavern sign and the constellation of Ursa Major, calling the latter the Bear at Bridge-Foot of heaven.

ACT II

i. 36. *enow* seems to stand for *e'en now*.

97. Cf. note to *London Prodigal*, I. ii. 39.

112. *sure*: 'betrothed'. Cf. *As You Like It*, v. iv. 142.

201. *I*: 'Ay'.

234. *sir Reuerence*: 'save-reverence'; cf. Skeat, *Etymol. Dict.*, and IV. ii. 4.

237. The spelling *guesse* for *guests* is very common and doubtless represents the pronunciation.

357. Steevens has the following interesting note: 'Here is an odd agreement between a few circumstances in the present scene, and a few others in the last act of *Othello*. I shall only point them out, without any attempt to account for them. *Pyeboard* (Iago) advises *Skirmish* (Roderigo) to wound *Oath* (Cassio) In the confusion occasioned by this attempt, *Pyeboard* (Iago again) rushes among them, and instead of giving *Oath* (Cassio again) assistance, prepares somewhat to make him seem dead. Thus Iago wounds Cassio. The cut too is given on the *leg*; and *Pyeboard* takes on him the cure, as Iago comes out and proffers to bind up Cassio's wound. Query, which of these pieces was the elder?' The *Puritan* was entered on the Stationers' Register in 1607; there is no earlier reference to it, while *Othello* was acted before Lord Ellesmere and the Queen as early as 1602.

ii. 3. *say on*: as say or try on.

ACT III

i. 14. *praysing*: 'appraising'.

45. *casting*: 'vomiting'; cf. N.E.D. s. v. *Cast* v. 25.

ii. 9. *superiour*: Frailty must mean *surgeon*.

72. *Lincks*: a play, of course, on *link* = 'torch'.

81. *Sesarara*: according to Steevens, *Certiorari* is meant.

88. *seauen and twenty Prouinces*: this, Percy thinks, is a mistake for the seventeen provinces of the Low Countries.

iii. Steevens calls attention to the similarity of this scene to that in which Fang and Snare arrest Falstaff at the suit of his hostess. Cf. 2 *Henry IV*, II. i.

110. *Puttocks*: 'vultures'; cf. *Cymbeline*, I. i. 140; 2 *Henry VI*, III. ii. 191.

154. S. D. This stage direction is a good illustration of the simplicity of Elizabethan stage requirements. The author did not intend a change of scene.

iv. 12. *Posts*: symbols of civic authority.

116. *busie*: 'elaborate', 'intricate'; cf. N.E.D. s. v. *Busy* a. 8.

163. *god den*: 'good e'en'. Cf. *Love's Labour's Lost*, IV. i. 42; *Gammer Gurton's Needle*, IV. iii. 5; *Yorkshire Tragedy*, ii. 120; Tourneur, *Revenger's Tragedy*, IV. ii (*Mermaid* ed., p. 405).

190. *Sup, Simon, now*: an allusion, according to Steevens, to 'Simon of Southampton, alias Supbroth' in *Thomas of Reading, or the sixe worthie Yeomen of the West*, by Dekker.

197. *hole*: one of the worst rooms in the Woodstreet Counter; cf. *Eastward Hoe* (*Belles Lettres* ed., 1904), v. ii. 56.

v. 16, 17. *George Stone the Beare*: a famous bear at Paris Garden. Malone refers to *The Silent Woman* (III. i).

110. *lin*: cease; cf. N.E.D.

161, 162. *Act . . . Coniurers and Witches*: passed 1604.

271. *simply tho I stand here*: cf. IV. ii. 74, 75, and *Merry Wives*, I. i. 226.

ACT IV

i. 4. *dubd for nothing*: one of the innumerable references to King James's traffic in knighthoods. Cf. *Eastward Hoe* (*Belles Lettres* ed.), IV. i. 214.

11. *Derecke* was the hangman of the period. Steevens quotes several other contemporary references to him. Cf. Stat. Reg. (ed. Arber) ult. Mar. 1606.

36. *guarded Lackey*: one whose livery was adorned with guards or facings. Cf. N.E.D. s. v. *Guard* v. 7.

37. *trashing*: cf. *trace*, *Mucedorus*, IV. iii. 30, and *Cambises* (ed. Manly), 490.

iii. 41. *run vpon the Ropes*: take desperate risks; a metaphor from tight-rope walking.

90, 91. *ghost . . . Table*: an allusion, as Dr. Farmer pointed out, to Banquo's ghost at the banquet. Cf. *Macbeth*, III. iv.

ACT V

iii. 7. *squander*: cf. 'squandering glances', *As You Like It*, II. vii. 57.

iv. 27. *mistes*: 'deceits'; cf. N.E.D. s. v. *Mist* sb.[1] 2. b.

Bibliography

Armstrong, Edward A. *Shakespeare's Imagination*. Lincoln, University of Nebraska Press, 1963.

Baskerville, C. R., et al., editors. *Elizabethan and Stuart Plays*. New York, Holt, Rinehart and Winston, 1934.

Bowers, Fredson, general editor. *The Dramatic Works in the Beaumont and Fletcher Canon*, Vol. II. Cambridge, Cambridge University Press, 1970.

Evans, G. Blakemore, textual editor. *The Riverside Shakespeare*. Boston, Houghton Mifflin, 1974.

Foster, Donald W. "'Shall I Die' Post Mortem: Defining Shakespeare." *Shakespeare Quarter* 38 (1987), pp. 58-77.

Frost, David L. *The School of Shakespeare*. Cambridge, Cambridge University Press, 1968.

Halliday, F. E. *A Shakespeare Companion 1564-1964*. Baltimore, Penguin, 1964.

Honigmann, E. A. J. *Shakespeare's Impact on His Contemporaries*. Totowa, NJ, Barnes & Noble, 1982.

Hoy, Cyrus. "The Shares of Fletcher and his Collaborators in the Beaumont and Fletcher Canon" (I), in *Evidence for Authorship*, edited by David V. Erdman and Ephim G. Fogel. Ithaca, NY, Cornell University Press, 1966, pp. 204-23.

Lake, David J. *The Canon of Thomas Middleton's Plays*. Cambridge, Cambridge University Press, 1975.

Logan, Terence P., and Smith, Denzell S., editors. *The Popular School: A Survey of Recent Studies in English Renaissance Drama*. Lincoln, University of Nebraska Press, 1975.

Maxwell, Baldwin. *Studies in the Shakespeare Apocrypha*. New York, Greenwood Press, 1969.

Meagher, John C. "Hackwriting and the Huntingdon Plays," in *Elizabethan Theatre: Stratford-upon-Avon Studies 9*, edited by John Russell Brown and Bernard Harris. New York, St. Martin's Press, 1967, pp. 197-219.

Middleton, Thomas. *Michaelmas Term*. Ed. Richard Levin. Lincoln, University of Nebraska Press, 1966.

Muir, Kenneth. *Shakespeare as Collaborator*. New York, Barnes & Noble, 1960.

Parker, R. B. "Middleton's Experiments with Comedy and Judgement," in *Jacobean Theatre*, edited by John Russell Brown and Bernard Harris. New York, Capricorn, 1967, pp. 179-99.

Partridge, Edward B. "Ben Jonson: The Making of the Dramatist (1596-1602)," in *Elizabethan Theatre: Stratford-upon-Avon Studies 9*, edited by John Russell Brown and Bernard Harris. New York, St. Martin's Press, 1967, pp. 221-44.

Schoenbaum, Samuel. "*A Chaste Maid in Cheapside* and Middleton's City Comedy," in *Studies in the English Renaissance Drama*, edited by J. W. Bennett, et al. New York, New York University Press, 1959.

———. *Internal Evidence and Elizabethan Dramatic Authorship*. Evanston, IL, Northwestern University Press, 1966.

———. *Middleton's Tragedies*. New York, Columbia University Press, 1955.

Spurgeon, Caroline. *Shakespeare's Imagery and What It Tells Us*. Cambridge, Cambridge University Press, 1935.

Taylor, Gary. "Shakespeare's New Poem," *The New York Times Book Review*, Dec. 15, 1985.

Index